REASONED RATIONALES

REASONED RATIONALES: EXPLORING THE EDUCATIONAL VALUE OF DEBATE

Joseph P. Zompetti, editor

International Debate Education Association

New York, London & Amsterdam

Published by
International Debate Education Association
400 West 59th Street
New York, NY 10019

Library of Congress Cataloging-in-Publication Data
Reasoned rationales: exploring the educational value of debate/
Joseph P. Zompetti, editor.
   p. cm.
  ISBN 978-1-61770-023-1
  1. Debates and debating.   2. Communication in education.   3. Critical thinking—Study and teaching (Higher)   I. Zompetti, Joseph P., 1970–
  PN4192.S78R43 2011
  808.53—dc23   2011036890

Design by Kathleen Hayes
Composition by Brad Walrod/Kenoza Type, Inc.
Printed in the USA

 IDEBATE Press

Contents

Acknowledgments

A book of this type and size is not the work of just one person. I have been extremely fortunate to have been a part of the International Debate Education Association (IDEA) in a variety of capacities: researcher, trainer, committee member, exchange presenter, member of the board of directors, and finally the president of the board for IDEA Netherlands. In these different ways, I have had the pleasure of working with many fine people from all over the world who have provided friendship, guidance, and motivation. Their influence on me is unmeasurable and provides the impetus, at least in part, for my motivation to produce this book.

Two people in particular from the IDEA Network deserve special recognition. Marcin Zaleski, former executive director of IDEA-NL, has been a good friend and inspiration to me since I first met him in 2003. His passion and love for debate and international exchange is insightful. Another good friend of mine, Veronika Vlckova, is the director of the IDEA Youth Forum. She does many other things for IDEA as well, not the least of which is answering my mundane emails and helping me to retrieve information from my previous Exchange presentations. Marcin and Veronika alike have been vital for my growth in IDEA.

Some of the material in this book was originally presented at an academic exchange hosted by IDEA in Prague in 2006. My co-presenter was Chris Baron, debate coach at Towson University in Baltimore, who initially compiled most of the original research. As such, this book would not have been possible without his help. During the preparation of this volume, I was fortunate to have the aid of a student assistant, Ashley Wall, who provided crucial help in obtaining some of the more obscure source material.

Of course, a book like this would not be possible without the assistance of a hard-working and generous editorial group. Martin Greenwald, Kevin Thomas Duffy, and Eleanora von Dehsen have been instrumental to me and my work. In particular, Eleanora provided invaluable advice and reassurance during the production of the book. To all of them I am very grateful.

Finally, I would be remiss if I did not acknowledge and thank two "people" who are very near and dear to me: Midnight—my dog, who is more like my daughter—and my father, both of whom keep me balanced and believe in me. I owe them and many others a debt that I doubt I will ever be able to repay.

Introduction

The key to the pursuit of civility and the tolerance of incivility where we find it lies in the creation of a culture of argument and debate, through nuts-and-bolts techniques well known to many educators. It is through argument and critique that students and adults learn best. And it is through argument that citizens can most fruitfully interact to strengthen local democracy and national political discourse.

—Susan Herbst (2010)

OVERVIEW

Many have lamented the recent challenges to the functioning of participatory democracy. Growing vitriol, apathy, and feelings of inefficacy plague democracies throughout the world. While the problems are complex and varied, we know that political knowledge, skill-development, and experience are crucial for maintaining and sustaining democracy. As the quote above from Susan Herbst, in her book *Rude Democracy*, indicates, the pedagogy of debate is vital for citizenship and political dialogue. Debate teaches us skills for research, listening, dialogue, and advocacy (Herbst, 2010; Hess, 2009; Hillygus, 2005). These are all of the necessary ingredients for a functioning democracy.

And as Herbst intimates, argument and debate educators have known this for years. They have seen firsthand how debate enhances the lives of students. Students are more knowledgeable about political and current issues, better able to engage with their communities, and command the communication skills necessary to advocate important issues of the day. These educators maintain their passion for training others in debate, in part, because they know that debate has transformative potential. Debate not only impacts students' ability to participate more fully in a democracy, it also strengthens the ways they live their lives.

Thus, it is no wonder that academic debate engages millions of students on every continent except Antarctica. Competitive debate occurs as early as junior high school (middle school) and goes on through the collegiate level. Of course, for most students debate is fun. It provides them an opportunity to participate in a competition of winning and losing, allows their voices to be heard, gives them a chance to make friends with similar interests, and for some, it offers a chance for travel. But are there other benefits to debating?

In the United States, competitive debate has enjoyed a degree of support from high schools and universities not only financially but also by providing teaching and coaching positions focused on argumentation and debate. As a result, debate professionals have argued for decades about how academic debate yields a series of benefits for participants: research skills, critical thinking skills, listening skills, public speaking and advocacy skills, higher matriculation rates for high school debaters, better careers for college debaters, and more democratic engagement as an overall result of debate experience.

The numerous articles in this anthology on the benefits of debate demonstrate its pedagogical value. Many studies describe debate's value from the perspective of participants and alumni. Others use social scientific methodologies to ascertain correlative and causal relationships between debate and some of the beneficial skills it develops. Regardless of the approach, studies about the value of debate provide crucial insight into why students all over the world embrace debate. More than insight, however, these articles offer us key arguments to promote debate to administrators, parents, community leaders, donors, and others. Given that the studies have been conducted by professors and scholars, the arguments presented about the value of debate have a certain level of legitimacy. As a result, we have a pool of information supporting the need for teaching and engaging in debate.

We also know that different styles of debate are performed in different parts of the world. Some of the studies conducted on the value of debate concentrate on specific styles. Others, however, look at debate as a whole and discuss its educational value *in toto*. All debate styles have core elements in common: debate involves research, speaking, listening, arguments, and clash of ideas. The articles presented in this volume look at the value of debate in accordance with these common characteristics.

Theme and Purpose

The usefulness of debate, with its focus on learning and skill development, is obvious to some. By concentrating on learning information and the process of engaging in dialogue, debate fosters important skills. Furthermore, debate often provides for teamwork with one's partner(s), depending on the style of debate, and intercultural experiences with one's opponents. Although the significance of these experiences may be evident to many, access to social scientific research to buttress the claims of debate's significance can help convince those who are skeptical. Over the years, many researchers have explored debate's worth in educational terms, mostly to provide additional evidence to justify the time, money, and effort spent on this activity.

However, there are two main drawbacks to our articles about debate. First, many of the debate studies are difficult to locate and access. Almost all of them are published in debate or argument journals, newsletters, book chapters, or conference proceedings. And most of them are published solely in English, written by Americans. Second, most of the studies suffer from flaws in methodology. Some are anecdotal reports, which are not widely applicable and tend to be biased. The social scientific and quantitative studies also tend to rely on self-reporting and lack comparisons with control groups, and their reliability and validity are difficult to establish. In effect, virtually all debate studies preach to the proverbial choir. This does not make them bad or invaluable, but it does limit their usefulness, especially when more methodologically sound studies could be conducted.

This book is an attempt to address the first drawback. We have compiled some of the most valuable, interesting, and useful articles on the educational value of debate. We are acutely aware that most of these articles are extremely difficult to locate and access, especially for non-Americans. That being said, the volume is not an exhaustive compilation of articles on debate's value. Such a compendium would be too large to produce. Many other articles on the subject exist (Arbenz and Beltran 2001; Barfield 1989; Colbert 1994; Foster 2004; Goodwin 2003; Harrigan 2008; Prichard and McCroskey 1967; Semlak and Shields 1977; Warner and Bruschke 2001), including a recent master's thesis at Illinois State University, by Nathan Stewart, that utilizes social scientific methodologies to examine the impact of debate on civic and political engagement (2010). These articles either reflect the themes presented in this book or are tangentially related to the book's overarching theme. However, some studies were excluded because of difficulty securing copyright permission, and others were simply not useful enough for the intended readers of this book. Nevertheless, we think readers will agree that this book presents a wide selection of helpful and useable materials for anyone interested in the benefits of debate in general and the educational value of academic competitive debate in particular.

Little can be done about the second weakness of the studies. Some methodological concerns associated with debate studies exist, but the relative merits of such studies are still important. In fact, for most administrators, community leaders, and potential donors, the existing studies on debate's relative merits are more than sufficient to provide reasonable justification for its continued development. Of course, some will still be unconvinced, and we hope that with the production of this volume, the conversation will continue about the value of debate, and this will stimulate interest for future academic studies.

Another unexplored area is the educational value of debate in specific international contexts. We have included "The Benefits and Costs of Participating in Competitive Debate Activities," by Narahiko Inoue and Mika Nakano, which explores the comparative merits of debate in the U.S. and Japanese contexts. However, there is a paucity of academic study involving research on education and global debate. Despite the lack of academic studies, some discussions of global debate and education exist (e.g., Zompetti 2006), and we invite readers to examine other IDEBATE Press books on this subject.

Although the direct connections between educational utility and debate are far from being completely understood, we do have scholarly studies that address the issue, and the compilation of such studies is the reason for this book. It is a vital resource for anyone promoting the value of debate, for debaters who need to explain what they do, for debate trainers and teachers who find themselves defending the significance of their roles, and for program coordinators and directors who have to defend and promote debate. The educational value of debate is quite powerful, and *Reasoned Rationales* offers anyone interested in debate the tools to justify its impact on teaching and learning.

ORGANIZATION OF THE BOOK

Reasoned Rationales focuses on why debate matters for education. As such, this volume consists of five different parts: making the case for academic debate, skills learned through debate, debate teaching, debate and advocacy, and debate and career training. Each section presents influential studies by preeminent scholars in the debate, argumentation, and communication disciplines.

Part 1: Making the Case for Academic Debate is the executive section to the book, outlining the main arguments for why debate is important for education. Charles DeLancey and Halford Ryan's article, "Intercollegiate, Audience-style Debating: Quo Vadis," focuses on audience-style and parliamentary debate, while Timothy O'Donnell's "A Rationale for Intercollegiate Debate in the Twenty-first Century" centers on policy-style debate. Both articles present a persuasive case for the overall value of debate.

Part 2: Skills Learned through Debate is the largest section of the book because most of the studies conducted in this area involve the type of skills learned with debate. "A Meta-analysis of the Impact of Forensics and Communication Education on Critical Thinking," by Mike Allen et al., is an oft-cited piece on how debate fosters critical thinking. Similarly, Robert Greenstreet's "Academic Debate and Critical Thinking: A Look at the Evidence" discusses how debate cultivates critical thinking skills. Both "The Effects of Debate Participation on Argumentativeness and Verbal Aggression," by Kent R. Colbert, and "Argumentativeness, Verbal Aggressiveness, and Relational Satisfaction in the Parliamentary Debate Dyad," by Crystal Lane Swift and Christina Vourvoulias, relate to how debate training facilitates learning to minimize argumentative aggressiveness. Relatedly, Donald J. Bingle argues, in "Parliamentary Debate Is More Serious Than You Think: Forensics at the University of Chicago," that parliamentary debate has unique value particularly for university students. In "Measuring Refutation Skill: An Exploratory Study," Don Faules argues for the importance of refutation skills. Finally, "The Benefits and Costs of Participating in Competitive Debate Activities: Differences between Japanese and American College Students," by Narahiko Inoue and Mika Nakano, and "University Student Perceptions of the Efficacy of Debate Participation: An Empirical Investigation," by David E. Williams et al., report on the overall efficacy of skills learned in debate, including the costs and benefits of such training.

Part 3: Debate Teaching provides important articles on the

teaching of debate. These studies may be helpful for debate teachers and trainers as well as program leaders who need to defend the merits of debate to donors and community leaders. "A Research-based Justification for Debate Across the Curriculum," by Joe Bellon, discusses the importance of teaching debate in a wide variety of contexts. In "Competitive Forensics Experience as a Predictor of Teaching Effectiveness," Sheila L. Hughes argues that debate training and experience provide valuable skills for effective teaching. And in "An Assessment of University Administrators: Do They Value Competitive Debate and Individual Events Programs?" Robert S. Littlefield presents a study on the arguments that are compelling to administrators and donors who support debate initiatives.

Part 4: Debate and Advocacy concentrates on the relationship between debate training and the ability to support, defend, and persuade communities about important social issues. Gordon R. Mitchell's "Pedagogical Possibilities for Argumentative Agency in Academic Debate" demonstrates why debate training is vital for future advocates. Similarly, Joseph P. Zompetti's "The Role of Advocacy in Civil Society" argues that debate training is necessary for the maintenance of a vibrant civil society, anchored by the advocacy of citizens.

The final section of the book, Part 5: Debate and Career Training, offers insight into how debate training can prepare students for future careers. In "High School Student Perceptions of the Efficacy of Debate Participation," Robert S. Littlefield reports on students' perceptions about how debate prepares them for higher education and a variety of careers. "Graduate School, Professional, and Life Choices: An Outcome Assessment Confirmation Study Measuring Positive Student Outcomes beyond Student Experiences for Participants in Competitive Intercollegiate Forensics," by Jack E. Rogers, presents a study that measures the skills acquired through debate for career preparation. Finally, in "The Impact of Prior Experience in Intercollegiate Debate upon a Postsecondary Educator's Skill-set," Doyle Srader offers a study that asked professionals with debate experience to explain how debate supported them in their careers.

This book provides invaluable material for debate educators, students, and advocates. It is designed to supply some of the best academic studies on the subject for those involved in justifying the educational merits of academic debate. While many studies have examined the impact and value of debate, we believe this volume offers the most comprehensive collection of such work to date. Undoubtedly the "debate about debate" will continue, and we welcome the ongoing dialogue that views debate's contribution from different methodological perspectives. In the meantime, *Reasoned Rationales* serves as a single-volume treatise for the promotion of debate as an educational tool.

REFERENCES

Arbenz, C., and S. Beltran. *Empowering Latinas through Debate: An Analysis of Success at SCUDL Tournaments of Latina Debaters.* Paper presented at the Western States Communication Association annual convention. C'oeur D'Alene, Idaho, 2001, http://communications.fullerton.edu/forensics/documents/Silly%20and%20Jason%2002%20NCA%20Paper.pdf (accessed March 8, 2011).

Barfield, K. E. "A Study of the Relationship Between Active Participation in Interscholastic Debating and the Development of Critical Thinking Skills with Implications for School Administrators and Instructional Leaders." PhD diss., University of Alabama, 1989. Dissertation Abstracts International, 50-09: 2714.

Colbert, K. R. "Replicating the Effects of Debate Participation on Argumentativeness and Verbal Aggression." *Forensic of Pi Kappa Delta* 79 (1994): 1–13.

Foster, D. E. "In Defense of the Argument Culture: A Response to Recent Criticisms against the Use of Adversarial Debate as a Method of Societal Decision-Making." *Forensic of Pi Kappa Delta* 89 (Winter 2004): 13–29.

Goodwin, J. "Students' Perspectives on Debate Exercises in Content Area Classes." *Communication Education* 52 (2003): 157–163.

Harrigan, C. "Against Dogmatism: A Continued Defense of Switch Side Debate." *Contemporary Argumentation and Debate* 29 (2008): 37–66.

Herbst, S. *Rude Democracy: Civility and Incivility in American Politics.* Philadelphia: Temple University Press, 2010.

Hess, D. E. *Controversy in the Classroom: The Democratic Power of Discussion.* New York: Routledge, 2009.

Hillygus, G. S. "The Missing Link: Exploring the Relationship between Higher Education and Political Engagement." *Political Behavior* 27, no. 1 (2005): 25–47.

Prichard, S. V. O., and J. C. McCroskey. "An Empirical Look at an International Debate." *Journal of the American Forensic Association* 4, no. 1 (1967): 21–25.

Semlak, W., and D. Shields. "The Effects of Debate Training on Students' Participation in the Bicentennial Youth Debates." *Journal of the American Forensic Association* 13 (1977): 193–196.

Stewart, N. T. "Debating the Pedagogy of Political Engagement: Pursuing the Application of Competitive Academic Debate to Achieve the Political Engagement Project's Goals." Master's thesis, Illinois State University, 2010. Paper available from the editor.

Warner, E., and J. Bruschke J. "Gone on Debating: Competitive Academic Debate as a Tool of Empowerment." *Contemporary Argumentation and Debate* 22 (2001): 1–21.

Zompetti, J. P. "Listening and Intercultural Communication: Viewing International Debate as a Means of Improving Listening Effectiveness." *Controversia: An International Journal of Debate and Democratic Renewal* 5 (2006): 85–101.

PART 1

Making the Case for
Academic Debate

In this first section, we present two important articles regarding the overall case that debate has enormous educational value. Both present a generalized, holistic case for the benefits of debate. "Intercollegiate, Audience-style Debating: Quo Vadis," by Charles DeLancey and Halford Ryan, which concerns audience-style and parliamentary debate, posits that parliamentary-style debating provides significant educational experience for its participants. Timothy O'Donnell's "A Rationale for Intercollegiate Debate in the Twenty-first Century" centers on policy-style debate. O'Donnell articulates the many skills and benefits associated with debate. While these two articles are not social scientific studies themselves, they do report and reference other studies to support the overall persuasive argument that debate has profound educational impact.

Intercollegiate, Audience-style Debating: Quo Vadis

*by Charles DeLancey and Halford Ryan**

Audience-style debating has a distinguished history in intercollegiate forensics. Initiated by literary societies on American college campuses in the eighteenth century, audience-style debates provided students with opportunities for socializing and for stimulating discussions. From the Spy Club at Harvard in 1722 to the Young Ladies's Association, the first women's debating society, at Oberlin in 1835, the one common thread in literary societies was student interest in debating important issues. At first, the debates were intramural, limited to society members. By 1830, however, the Demosthenians met Phi Beta Kappa at the University of Georgia, and in 1881 literary societies at Illinois College and Knox College met in what may have been the first intercollegiate debate. From time to time, debates were held before interested students, faculty members, and occasionally, townsfolk. Although most literary societies died in the nineteenth century, the impetus to debate important issues remains on college campuses. Many students satisfy this desire by debating in tournaments, using National Debate Tournament (NDT), American Debate Association (ADA), Cross-Examination Debate Association (CEDA), or Lincoln-Douglas (LD) rules and formats. An alternative mode of intercollegiate debating is the audience-style debate.[1]

In form, intercollegiate, audience-style debating is closely related to the other kinds of college debating activities. Usually two teams of two-to-three members discuss an issue of mutual interest. The debate begins with a speech affirming the proposition. Subsequent constructive speeches attack or defend arguments supporting the proposition. Following the constructive speeches, there is a break for participation by members of the audience who direct questions

Reasoned Rationales: Exploring the Educational Value of Debate or comments to an individual debater or to one or both of the debating teams. Following the audience forum, rebuttal speeches from both teams close the debate; and then the audience may or may not vote to determine the outcome of the debate. The overall length of the debate usually lasts an hour to an hour and a half.

The fairly standard format for intercollegiate, audience-style debates accommodates considerable flexibility. With the consent of the debaters and their faculty advisors, the format can be adapted to meet existing expectations and conditions. Sometimes intercollegiate, audience-style debates include cross-examination of each debater by another. [. . .] Sometimes each debater delivers a rebuttal speech; other times the rebuttal period is limited to one speech per team. In this case, a third debater from each team can deliver the team's rebuttal speech thus increasing the number of students who participate in the debate. Sometimes an audience vote is not taken on the resolution.

Despite its close relationship with the other kinds of college debating, intercollegiate, audience-style debating is a forensic activity that offers unique opportunities and challenges for participants and administrators. The purpose of this essay is to delineate the rhetorical values of intercollegiate, audience-style debating and the value of this type of debating to forensic programs and to the institutions they represent. [. . .]

RHETORICAL VALUES

Intercollegiate, audience-style debate requires a set of forensic skills and a style of speaking that are consistent with the goals of classes in public speaking, persuasion, advocacy, argumentation, and debate. The successful student speaker must learn and apply the lessons of invention, organization, style, and delivery to the forensic situation. Intercollegiate, audience-style debates serve students as an out of class laboratory where they can test their ideas as advocates (Wenzel 258).

When confronted with an audience that participates in the debate through its questions and comments, students recognize that their ideas must be structured clearly, that their language must be understandable, and that their delivery must be dynamic and their speaking rate comprehensible. Audiences do react to the presentation of ideas in intercollegiate, audience-style debates. [...] The audience plays a crucial role in the outcome of the intercollegiate, audience-style debate. The reaction of the audience to the speaker's claims and proofs influences the perceived persuasiveness of the speaker's argument. An audience member's query during the open forum segment of the debate may bring the knowledgeability and effectiveness of a debater into question. A well-made probe from the audience also may raise an important issue for rebuttal speeches that follow the open forum.

Audiences sometimes see these intercollegiate competitions as settings where they can demonstrate the truth of their beliefs on issues. [...]

At its best, intercollegiate, audience-style debate promotes two-sided argumentation. That is, one set of speakers presents constructive speeches in which they provide reasons and evidence for supporting the proposition while another set of speakers presents constructive speeches in which they provide reasons and evidence for denying the proposition. [...]

The prospect of an audience facilitates clash in the debate. Audiences do discourage affirmative teams from offering obscure or "squirrel" interpretations of a proposition. When the affirmative case does not conform, in large part, to the expectations of the audience, the negative team can exploit this issue in the debate. Audience-style debating also obligates the negative team to build a case that clashes with some of the affirmative team's points while advancing claims in defense of prevailing sentiment or policy. Audiences are often unswayed by speeches that employ solely the strategy of direct refutation by members of the negative team. When audience members do not hear a clear choice of policies or values in the unfolding issues of the debate, they frequently ask negative speakers to clarify their positions. Variations on the theme "You have said what policy will be ineffective, what do you think we should do?" are inevitably articulated during forum periods when negative speakers fail to defend a clear position. Therefore, negative speakers, as well as affirmative speakers, must posit and support a set of ideas while attacking the ideas and evidence offered by the opposing team.

Audience-style debating thus enables students to test their understanding of principles of advocacy they have encountered in their speaking classes. Audience-style debating encourages students to construct and assess affirmative and negative ground, to develop skills of persuasion such as audience adaptation and deftness in delivery, and to appreciate how audience members may react to suasory discourse. By participating in audience-style debates, students often learn important lessons in rhetorical principles, lessons that are sometimes poorly learned or quickly forgotten in classroom exercises. Classroom audiences tend to be more forgiving of a speaker's foibles than are debate audiences who identify less closely with the speaker.

Intercollegiate, audience-style debating also offers benefits for students in the audience. Audience-style debates provide student listeners with accessible means to hear effective and not so effective exam-pies of advocacy. These debates can serve as effective tools to reinforce or to clarify principles that are introduced in public speaking and in argumentation classes. With the guidance of the instructor, students can recognize the importance of key concepts in debate, such as stock issues, refutation, and preemptive argumentation. Many students come to appreciate the conflicted nature of issues as they reflect on the evidence and reasons offered by both teams in the debate. Furthermore, through class discussions students can check their understandings of what was said in the debate as they listen to others retell the narrative of the debate. Class discussions dramatize for students an inherent feature of human interaction—the conflict of plausible perspectives of a situation.[4] Different students often recount very dissimilar versions of the content of the debate. Lively dialogue ensues as students attempt to defend their impressions.

[...]

VALUES TO DEBATING PROGRAMS

In addition to providing rhetorical instruction for student speakers and audiences, intercollegiate, audience-style debates help publicize the values and activities of a forensics program. Whether the size of the audience is twenty-five or nine hundred, intercollegiate, audience-style debating attracts students to participate in debating activities. These audience members often identify with the student speakers and envision their own participation in such debates as an opportunity to improve rhetorical skills that they have learned in public speaking or in composition classes. After each debate, a group of students invariably comes forward to congratulate the debaters and to discuss further the issues of the debate. "Thus," as Don Boileau noted, "forensic programs offer a segment of instruction that the classroom does not replicate. This curriculum segment gains its uniqueness by giving the student critiques by many different listeners" (92). Several students from these encounters ask questions concerning the debating society and attend subsequent meetings. "I never knew there was a debating society on our campus" is an all-too-frequent comment heard during these after-debate discussions. Students who are initially attracted to the debating society as a consequence of attending an intercollegiate, audience-style debate then may choose to participate in other forensics activities of the debating society such as attending debating or forensics tournaments, becoming involved in a student congress, or speaking in an intramural debate.

These public forums also provide administrators and faculty colleagues in other departments with insights into the valuable lessons of the discipline of speech communication: research, audience analysis, invention, reasoning, refutation, adaptation, and delivery. This is especially important for those who, like us, work in very small speech communication programs. Without audience-style debating, the only access many faculty members or administrators may have to the forensics program at their institution is the bothersome excused absence request or the often dusty trophy case. Given a more concrete understanding of the aims and methods of the discipline of speech communication, faculty colleagues are in a better position to advise their students to enroll in speech courses or to attend debating society meetings.

[...]

At Furman University, for example, audience totals for the previous year's intercollegiate forums are included in each budget request submitted to student government and the academic affairs office. In the 1989–90 school year, three debates drew audiences totally 2,500 students. The expenditure per student benefitted for the intercollegiate forums was approximately twenty-five cents. On the other hand, the expenditure per student benefitted was about six hundred dollars for travel to and participation in student congresses, and debate and forensics tournaments.

Participating in intercollegiate, audience-style debates is thus generally cheaper than participating in tournament-oriented forensics activities. [...] Of course, if the adversary is not too distant, the travelling team can return to campus the same day.

[...]

Conclusion

Intercollegiate, audience-style debating fulfills many needs of a college debating program. Audience-style debates provide speakers and listeners with opportunities to test their understanding of rhetorical principles. The student debater uses skills normally emphasized in basic courses in speech communication. In particular, the student applies the lessons of invention, arrangement, style, and delivery to the forensic situation. The audience's role in the debate is a distinctive characteristic of audience-style debate. The audience listens, learns, evaluates, and may determine the outcome of the debate.

Intercollegiate, audience-style debating attracts the attention of university administrators, faculty members, townspeople, and students, and it adds to the intellectual climate of a campus and its community. In terms of the cost spread over the number of student speakers and listeners, the verdict is compelling for intercollegiate, audience-style debates are economical forensic activities. [...]

ENDNOTES

1. See Potter. The Association of American Collegiate Literary Societies was formed in 1978 in order to revive collegiate literary societies, and it holds an annual congress in the spring.

[...]

4. "Constructive alternativism" clearly demonstrates the diversity of perspectives among audience members. See Kelly 14–15.

WORKS CITED

Boileau, Don M. "The Role of Department Chair as Forensic Promoter." National Forensic Journal 8 (1990): 87–94.

Kelly, George A. A Theory of Personality: The Psychology of Personal Constructs. 1955; New York; Norton, 1963.

[...]

Potter, David. "The Literary Society." A History of Speech Education in America. Ed. Karl R. Wallace. New York: Appleton-Century-Crofts, 1954. 238–58.

Wenzel, Joseph W. "Campus and Community Programs in Forensics: Needs and Opportunities" Journal of the American Forensic Association 7 (1971): 253–59.

---

*Charles DeLancey is an associate professor of speech at Furman University.

Halford Ryan is professor of English and public speaking and the director of forensics at Washington and Lee University.

DeLancey, Charles, and Halford Ryan. "Intercollegiate, Audience-style Debating: Quo Vadis." *Argumentation & Advocacy* 27 (1990): 49–58.

Used by Permission.

A Rationale for Intercollegiate Debate in the Twenty-first Century

*by Timothy O'Donnell**

INTRODUCTION

Democracy demands that people become citizens. It is a mandate that requires individuals to move from identities based in private interests to an engagement in civic life, speaking as members of a deliberative public. At the dawn of the twenty-first century, one of society's most pressing challenges lies in connecting public life to our various institutions, including those charged with cultivating an active and engaged citizenry.

Over the past ten years, a revolution has occurred, born of the realization that education alone is insufficient to produce capable citizens. These challenges are illustrated by recurrent calls for Americans to participate more consistently in the structures of public life. Predictably, in this environment, educators at all levels —irrespective of discipline or field—are increasingly concerned with creating and promoting programs that foster service learning, social responsibility, and civic engagement. A complex would be inundated by instant communication and overwhelming information flows demands the acquisition of "technologies" to mediate the simultaneous explosion of political speech.

Intercollegiate debate, positioned at the nexus of liberal learning, is uniquely located to rejoin the call to renew the promise of the American experiment. Debate is a technology that connects the explosion of political speech with a civic-oriented vision for the future as well as a mode of speech and inquiry that is constitutive of citizenship; people (students) become citizens both in and through their participation in debate.

Citizenship is both an identity and a skill—qualities that are cultivated through a liberal education that prizes debate. More than any other activity, debate prepares students to speak as citizens. Students must view themselves as participating in and being implicated by the vast systems of discourse that comprise civil society while at the same time imaginatively engaging in institutional decision making. In addition, they must have the skills essential to effective participation—skills to both consume public discourse and take part in it. In the present moment we need to emphasize these prerequisite proficiencies of democracy.

Debate is training for citizenship. As an essential tradition of democracy in the Western world, it possesses a rich pedagogy focused on preparing for and investing, in civic life. Such a conception of the role of argument in the civic imagination is loath traditional and contemporary:

> We ought, therefore, to think of the art of discourse just as we think of the other arts, and not to form opposite judgments about similar things, nor show ourselves intolerant toward that power which, of all the facilities which belong to the nature of man, is the source of most of our blessings. For in the other powers which we possess ... we are in no respect superior to other living creatures; nay, we are inferior to many in swiftness and in strength and in other resources; but, because there has been implanted in us the power to persuade each other and to make clear to each other whatever we desire, not only have we escaped the life of wild beasts, but we have come together and founded cities and made laws and invented arts; and, generally speaking, there is no institution devised by man which the power of speech has not helped us to establish. (Isocrates 1929, *Antidosis*, ii, 327–28)

Isocrates's paean to the place of speech and argument in human life has stood for 2,500 years as a touchstone of liberal education. It is an approach that acknowledges the linkage between speech and reason as a distinctive human characteristic, essential for the organization of human life and society. Even in a world rich with information and digital technologies, speech—the basic face-to-face interaction where people trade reasons in order to generate knowledge or reach decisions—even when mediated, stands at the core of what makes us human.

For a variety of reasons, recent years have been witness to a resurgence of interest in public deliberation and to the point of radical democracy. Advocates for public deliberation assert that policy wonks and interest-group politics are insufficient on their own to completing democracy's vision. Rather than mediate power struggles among interest groups, such advocates seek means of communication that are adequate to the task of (re)introducing meaningful discussion and debate to the policy process while at the same time empowering mass participation. In such an environment, at the dawn of the twenty-first century, the tools of the fifth century BCE seem more relevant than ever.

More than language is required to make democracy work. As Tocqueville concluded, the success of American democracy rests on structures of civil society that support it; democratic institutions in the United States rest on a massive understructure of civil society, sustained by forms of communication. From the school board to the neighborhood watch, the Rotary Club to the PTA and the Red Cross, people come together in nongovernmental groups. In their communion, such groups allow for the realization of what John Dewey called "the public"—groups of people (often dispersed across society) who share common concerns. As Dewey described it, democracy was more than a set of governmental institutions (plus voting); it was a mode of associated living. Every social interaction is a chance to enact the democratic ideals of debate, discussion, and rational argument, noncoercively producing agreement on solutions to problems. More recently, deliberative democrats, such as Benjamin Barber (2004) and James Fishkin (2009), have sought to take seriously this legacy of democracy as reasoned decision making.

Yet, participants in the movement for a return to deliberation realize there will be no simple return to the idyll of Athenian democracy (if, indeed, it ever existed) nor can it be accomplished by nostalgia for the mystic chords of memory wrought from the American experience. The world has changed. But so has debate education. In writing a rationale for debate in the twenty-first century, our purpose is to articulate how and why intercollegiate debate prepares students for civic participation, while also serving as a tool of civic change itself.

Debate trains the mind the way sports train the body, making it more powerful and capable. In daily life, in situations large and small, we are called upon to receive arguments and invent our own, as part of a process of collective inquiry. Cultivating the habits of mind and skills to advance, defend, and judge claims is the essence of liberal learning and the staple of knowledge production in the academy and beyond. We can no longer take for granted that the only essential skill of democratic life is mere speaking. Though there are certainly many varieties of speaking, informed speakers advancing critical arguments over issues that matter is the standard of democratic life.

Liberal education is the education of the "free" (*liber*) citizen to make decisions and engage others. Debate as a mode of liberal learning is incredibly powerful. And debate, especially in its highly developed contemporary form, as practiced through intercollegiate debate, is a technology of liberal education without equal; it is intrinsically cross-disciplinary, applicable to any field and able to connect any field to public life.

Despite changes in form and function, a constellation of values has connected and distinguished intercollegiate debate for over a century.

> Debate is a cross-disciplinary method of collaborative inquiry and intentional learning, focused on the controversial pub-lic policy issues of the day, emphasizing the fundamentals of argument—reasoning, research, communication, and practical judgment—through the clash of competing ideas and the habits of mind that come from understanding others' arguments as well as one's own. Although intercollegiate debate is a highly

competitive activity, it is profitably viewed from a pedagogical perspective as a leadership laboratory designed to prepare the next generation for entry into the public sphere and the process of lifelong teaming. From public administration to community activism, from personal decision making to government policy, and across a wide variety of fields from business to education, intercollegiate debate provides a liberal education that is the foundation of civic engagement.

How does contemporary intercollegiate debate embody the values and goals of liberal education for a democratic society? At its core and from its earliest appearance in the American academy in the once wildly popular literary societies to its contemporary manifestation in national championship tournament competition, intercollegiate debate is a well-established and highly successful educational practice with substantial educational benefits for all students (O'Donnell 2008a). It is, in every sense, what George Kuh (2008) refers to as a "high-impact educational practice." [...] The literature selected for review focuses predominantly on research concerning intercollegiate debate. [...]

1. Critical Thinking

Developing critical-thinking skills is one of the primary goals of American education. A survey by the Higher Education Research Institute (2009) of 22,562 full-time college and university faculty members reported that 99.6% of them viewed critical-thinking skills as paramount to undergraduate education. Several national reports (Association of American Colleges and Universities 1985; National Educational Goals Panel 1991; National Institute of Education Study Group 1984) have identified critical thinking as a major goal of higher education.

Many have written about the importance of critical thinking to achieving a free, safe, and prosperous society. Richard Franke, a fellow of the National Academy of Sciences, observes: "the value of critical thinking is incalculable. From assessing markets to identifying the salient features of a policy to decisions about life, liberty, and the pursuit of happiness, critical thinking clears a path for rational judgment" (2009, 22). Argumentation professors Douglas Ehninger and Wayne Brockriede recognize that in the nuclear age, it is imperative for society to develop leaders with strong critical-thinking skills: "in an age when a single bomb can wipe out a great city, critical thinking is not a luxury but a necessity" (1978, 3). Edward Panetta and Date Herbeck argue that critical-thinking skills developed by policy-debate training "will help resolve impending geo-political crises" (1993, 25).

John Dewey considered critical-thinking skills to be an essential characteristic of good citizenship, and subsequent work has demonstrated this connection. Critical-thinking skills are a precondition for citizenship engagement and deliberation about public affairs (Owen 2004). For example, Jack Rogers (2005) shows that debaters are more likely than nondebaters to vote in elections and to participate in social and political campaigns.

Debate scholars claim that the teaching of critical-thinking skills is one of debate's greatest educational achievements. Enhancing critical thinking is "the most frequently cited educational merit of debate" (Omelicheva 2007, 163). Glenn Capp and Thelma Capp (1965) list critical thinking as one of the seven educational benefits to debate training. James McBath argues that debate provides an educational laboratory for training students in "critical thinking skills through the discovery of lines of argument and their probative value" (1984, 10). Edward Inch, Barbara Warnick, and Danielle Endres state "that intercollegiate debate provides students with an intensive and exciting method for developing their debating skills and critical thinking abilities" (2006, 354). Austin Freeley and David Steinberg contend, "since classical times, debate has been one of the best methods of learning and applying the principles of critical thinking" (2005, 2).

Lived experience is reflected in the opinion of former debaters' assessment of acquiring critical-thinking skills. Several demographic surveys (Katsulas and Bauschard 2000; Matlon and Keele 1984; Williams, McGee, and Worth 2001) reveal overwhelming support from former debaters that the activity sharpened their critical-thinking skills. In response to the survey by John Katsulas and Stefan Bauschard, Daniel Sutherland, the National Debate Tournament (NDT) winner in 1982, replied, "debate significantly enhanced my development as a lawyer. I think the major area is in critical thinking—understanding my own arguments, coming to grips with my opponents' arguments and forecasting how the judge might evaluate both positions" (Katsulas and Bauschard 2000, 7). Cynthia Leiferman, an NDT finalist in 1984, agreed, writing that debate training taught her how "to think outside the box." Creative critical thinking is the lifeblood for a successful litigator" (ibid.).

Additionally, empirical research demonstrates that debate training increases critical-thinking skills. Several studies comparing debaters to nondebaters substantiate this link. Kent Colbert's (1987) study of NDT and Cross Examination Debate Association (CEDA) debaters found that they scored substantially higher than nondebaters on the Watson-Glaser Critical Thinking Appraisal (WGCTA). This research tool measures critical-thinking ability in five areas: "inference, recognition of assumptions, deduction, interpretation, and evaluation of arguments" (Colbert 1987, 199). Colbert's study validated the results of prior studies (Cross 1971; Howell 1943; Jackson 1961; Williams 1951) showing a link between debate participation and critical thinking.

Using a different measuring technique, studies by Kenny Barfield (1989) and Kip McKee (2003) also demonstrate a positive link between debate and critical thinking. Barfield and McKee found that high school debaters scored substantially higher than nondebaters in reading comprehension and thinking skills on the Stanford Achievement Test (SAT). Because research proves that higher reading comprehension scores on the SAT correlate well with higher critical-thinking skills on the WGCTA, Barfield and

McKee's findings prove that debate participation enhances critical thinking.

The most definitive evidence comes from a meta analysis by Mike Allen et al. (1999), which examined data from 22 studies over 50 years that had explored the link between communication skills and critical thinking. Most of these studies used the WGCTA as their measurement instrument. The cumulative evidence indicated that communication skill instruction increased critical-thinking ability by 44%. However, "participation in forensics demonstrated the largest improvement in critical thinking whether considering longitudinal or cross-sectional designs" (Allen et al. 1999, 27). Allen et al. conclude that competitive debate enhances critical thinking more effectively than argumentation classes and public speaking. This study provides powerful support for the value of competitive debate to improve critical thinking.

Given all of the above evidence, Colbert's assessment that "the preponderances of defendable evidence suggests competitive debate experience can indeed improve critical thinking skills" is a valid conclusion (1995, 60). He also correctly points out that the few studies (e.g., Whalen 1991) not demonstrating a link stiffer from flaws in "design limitations, instrument ceiling, sampling, teaching method, or statistical procedures" (Colbert 1995, 60).

How does debate reach effective critical-thinking skills? There are numerous ways. Debate teaches analytical skills, whereby students practice identifying errors in reasoning and proof, recognizing, inconsistencies in arguments, assessing the credibility of sources, challenging assumptions, and prioritizing the salience of points (Murphy and Samosky 1993). Critical thinking requires that decision makers arrive at conclusions based on a careful examination of the facts and reasons, which is the heart of the methodology taught by debate. Jeffrey Parcher (1998) argues that the devil's advocacy approach to debating, whereby students argue both sides of a controversy, improves critical thinking. Research also shows that critical-thinking skills are developed through consistent practice, which debate tournament competitions afford to students (McKee 2003).

2. Leadership Training and Career Advancement
[...]

A plethora of evidence exists to support the claim that participation in debate facilitates the professional careers of students. Numerous surveys of former debaters have overwhelmingly found that debate participation was a positive influence in advancing their careers. Ronald Matlon and Lucy Keele's survey of 703 debaters who participated in the NDT found that "successful attorneys, educators, legislators, businesspersons, and consultants" stated unequivocally "that debate was as important as the total of the rest of their education, or more so" (1984, 205). A survey of former debaters by Jeffrey Hobbs and Robert Chandler (1991) arrived at similar findings, with 86% of the respondents recommending debate as beneficial training, including 75% of lawyers, 85% of managers, 97% of ministers, and 84% of teachers. David Zarefsky, a past president of the National Communication Association, a distinguished professor of communication at Northwestern, and an immensely successful debater and coach, says, "It's hard for me to imagine a profession for which debate is not a valuable kind of preparation" (Wade 2006).

Evidence from two longitudinal studies comparing the employment success of debaters and nondebaters provides empirical support for the claim that debate participation enhances career skills (Rogers 2002, 2005). In the first longitudinal study, Jack Rogers (2002) tracked the performance of 100 freshmen who were debaters versus 100 nondebaters over four years. The results showed that upon graduation, the debaters received job offers superior to those of the control group. Rogers concluded there is "a strong correlation between debate experience and involvement in professional internships," which resulted in the debaters receiving a higher rate of job offers upon graduation as compared with the nondebaters (2002,

16). In a follow-up study, Rogers (2005) examined the performance of this same group of students over four additional years. Once again, the results showed the debate group with superior career advancement. The study found that debaters received more job offers in their field, more positive evaluations from their supervisors, and slightly higher pay increments.

Especially in the field of law, debate training is overwhelmingly beneficial. A survey of 98 law school deans found that 70% of them recommended that students should participate in intercollegiate debate (Freeley and Steinberg 2005). Most prelaw academic counselors also advise undergraduates to take courses in argumentation and debate (Pfau, Thomas, and Ulrich 1987). A survey directed to 82 prominent lawyers who were former debaters asking about the benefit of collegiate debating revealed strong support for the belief that debate taught them skill in oral advocacy, critical thinking, brief writing, research, and listening (Katsulas and Bauschard 2000). Law school dean Erwin Chemerinsky credits his debate training for teaching him skills in analysis, research, and public speaking and he claims that "not a day goes by that I do not use the skills and lessons I learned in debate in my teaching, my writing, and my advocacy in courts" (2008, A11).

While the law remains the preferred career choice for many debaters, the skills taught by debate are just as necessary and useful for debaters who want to succeed in the world of business. Employers recognize this and perceive debating experience as a valuable asset. Bill Lawhorn, an economist with the Bureau of Labor Statistics, speaks about the value of debate training for employers: "Debaters must have strong research skills, be able to think quickly, and be able to communicate well. In addition, debaters must be comfortable performing in front of an audience—and having the confidence to do so is a valuable workplace skill, especially when it comes to making presentations to coworkers or superiors" (Lawhorn 2008, 19).

[...]

3. Academic Achievement in the Classroom

College educators overwhelmingly believe that participation in debate increases students' academic achievement. [...]

In fact, there is considerable empirical evidence to prove that academic debate boosts academic achievement. Several studies show that debaters achieve higher average grade point averages than nondebaters (Barfield 1989; Collier 2004; Hunt, Garard, and Simerly 1997; K. Jones 1994). It is also the case that almost three-quarters of debaters believe that involvement in debate benefits them academically (Hunt, Garard, and Simerly 1997). Jack Rogers (2002) found that debaters maintained higher grade point averages than nondebaters, matriculated at the same rate as nondebaters, and enjoyed a higher acceptance rate into graduate school programs. In another study, Rogers (2005) determined that debaters were more successful than nondebaters in completing their graduate studies and achieving higher scores on their LSATs and GREs.

Debate participation improves academic performance because it promotes numerous skills that are essential to realizing a high level of educational proficiency. The educational benefits of debate include teaching research skills, acquiring cross-disciplinary knowledge about the world, teaming how to organize and construct arguments, improving writing skills, enhancing listening and note-taking skills, increasing student self-confidence, and improving time-management skills.

A. RESEARCH

One of the obvious benefits of policy debate is that it teaches research skills in a manner "unparalleled in the world of academics" (Fritch 1993/1994, 7). No undergraduate college class assignment requires as much research as debate does. Robert Rowland argues that "debate, more than perhaps any other educational activity at the university level, teaches students about both the importance of research and the wealth of material that is available" (1995, 101). The research effort undertaken by debaters over the course of a single year's topic is often greater than the work to obtain a law degree or dissertation (Parcher 1998). Many debaters spend as many as 20 to 30 hours per week doing research (ibid.). A typical debate team gathers enough evidence to write thousands of pages of argument briefs.

[…]

Because doing research is so integral to competitive success, debaters have a strong incentive to acquire excellent research skills. Unlike most undergraduates who specialize in doing research in their own area of academic study, debaters require expansive research skills. Even when a debate topic is confined to a particular subject area, for example, reducing U.S. agricultural subsidies, debate arguments will emerge requiring research in the fields of economics, political science, law, international relations, the environment, and philosophy. This means debaters must learn to use all available library databases as well as locate evidence from books, government documents, newspapers, and the Internet.

[…]

c. Argument Construction and Organization

Argumentation is one of the important skills for maintaining a vibrant society. This is because "argumentation occurs everywhere, and we deal with it as readers, listeners, writers and speakers on a daily basis" (Inch, Warnick, and Endres 2006, 8). Every professional endeavor involves constructing arguments. Lawyers make arguments in support of their clients. Businesses make arguments to sell products and services. Legislators make arguments to advocate policy changes. Politicians make arguments for why they should be elected. Academics make arguments when they teach and publish scholarship. Argumentation is the lifeblood of society.

Competitive debate is an ideal laboratory for training students in the study of argumentation. Through it, students acquire fundamental skills in argumentation, beginning with how to analyze complex problems. Students team how to analyze a proposition by identifying the various issues on multiple sides of controversies. Students learn how to construct valid arguments and are taught that sound reasoning and appropriate evidence must support claims. In addition, students learn techniques of refutation in order to defeat poorly constructed arguments, and they are taught how to expose flaws in evidence or reasoning. Students acquire skills in organizing arguments such as prioritizing the placement of arguments as well as packaging them for consumption by multiple audiences. Finally, students learn how arguments interrelate and potentially conflict.

d. Writing

Debate participation improves writing skills in two ways. First, research shows that students who become more fluent speakers develop improved writing skills (Sperling 1996). By improving the oral communication skills of students, debate indirectly enhances their writing skills. This is borne out by research demonstrating that debaters achieve higher scores on writing exams than nondebaters (Peters 2008). Second, the process of crafting briefing papers and preparing speeches enables debaters to practice their writing skills on a regular basis. Writing debate briefs and cases teaches students how to structure and organize arguments. These skills are beneficial to students who are required to write term papers or to answer essay exam questions. Research shows that debate is beneficial in improving students' writing skills (Matlon and Keele 1984; Rothenberg and Berman 1980) and organizational skills (Hill 1982; Semlak and Shields 1977; Williams, McGee, and Worth 2001). College educators claim that the argumentation and organization skills they learned through debate are useful for making arguments to administrators and colleagues, and also help them with their scholarship and teaching (Srader 2006).

e. Oral Communication, Active Listening, and Note-taking

Debaters consistently rank improved oral communication skills as one of the top benefits of participation in debate (Huston 1985; Lybbert 1985; Matlon and Keele 1984; Oliver 1985; Williams, McGee, and Worth 2001). Debate develops oral communication skills in a number of ways. The first, and perhaps most obvious, is that it develops students' ability to deliver speeches in public, as has been observed by coaches and former debaters (Bernard 1999; Giesecke 1981; Pemberton-Butler 1999; Sowa-Jamrok 1994), and demonstrated empirically (Semlak and Shields 1977). Debate provides extensive public-speaking practice and improves self-confidence (Matlon and Keele 1984; Pemberton-Butler 1999; Sowa-Jamrok 1994), two of the most important factors in reducing public-speaking anxiety and improving performance (Lucas, 1998). The sheer number of critiqued speeches a debater presents in a typical debate season is not insignificant. Assuming a moderate travel schedule consisting of ten tournaments per year, with six debates (at minimum) at each tournament and two speeches per debate easily yields a tally of 120 unique speeches in an academic year. Most do many more, to say nothing of practice speeches with coaches and teammates both before and after tournaments.

[...]

Equally compelling is the extent to which debate develops listening skills. Studies have long established that active listening skills are important, but that most people are passive listeners, retaining only 25% of what is heard (Nichols and Stevens 1957). Active listening has been cited as an important prerequisite for engaging in productive dialogue and for engaging other skills (Goleman 2000). Improved listening and note-taking ability are frequently cited benefits of participation in debate (Freeley and Steinberg 2009; Goodnight 1993; Wood and Goodnight 2006). Competing successfully in debates requires effective responses, and effective responses are possible only when a student has listened carefully and taken thorough notes on their counterparts' arguments.

In addition to presenting and listening to speeches, intercollegiate debate offers a unique opportunity to refine advanced communication skills through cross-examination—a practice that involves interviewing someone with an opposing viewpoint, and thereby engages both listening and speaking skills. Conducting a productive and respectful cross-examination is difficult to learn but is invaluable to public discourse (Hill and Leeman 1997). Further, cross-examination provides a unique opportunity for critical listening—evaluative listening—the type of listening that results in a judgment, which is particularly useful in preparing and executing a cross-examination (Hill and Leeman 1997). As noted by Lawrence Norton, "Selecting the properly worded question to ask at the right time and arranging a meaningful series of questions is a real challenge to the thought process. Knowing how to select the right answer also is based on listening" (1982, 35).

[...]

E. SELF-CONFIDENCE AND TIME MANAGEMENT

There are also a number of indirect ways that debate participation helps to improve students' academic achievement. There is evidence that debating experience makes students feel more confident in their ability to communicate, both orally and verbally (Freeley and Steinberg 2005; Rogers 2002, 2005). This self-confidence may encourage students to participate more actively in class discussions and improve their performance when they give oral presentations or write term papers. Debate also teaches students useful time-management skills. Debaters learn to multitask and process information faster and more efficiently than nondebaters (Parcher 1998). Better time-management skills allow students to complete their schoolwork in a timely fashion.

[...]

5. Community Building

Intercollegiate debate has a long history of outreach to a variety of local, national, and international communities, although efforts to foster alignment with constituencies outside of the competitive arena have gathered momentum in recent years. Public debates represent one mode of outreach and community building and are an active and visible aspect of many intercollegiate debate programs. Such forums allow students who have honed their knowledge and skills through competition to bring the benefits of a debate education to larger audiences—both on the campus and beyond. The CEDA actively encourages intercollegiate debate programs to build community, with a yearly award for the intercollegiate program that best realizes these objectives. Countless examples emanate from intercollegiate debate programs across the country, and many have been backed by strong administrative support—support that recognizes the centrality of debate to the mission of the university. One of the signature events involving multiple institutions in a public debate competition is the James Madison Commemorative Debate and Citizen Forum. Held annually for the past decade, the event is adjudicated by lay judges and is attended by large audiences froth university and the broader community. With financial backing from the university, this forum is indicative of the power of intercollegiate debate to extend the reach of competition to foster civic engagement and public deliberation in local and regional communities.

[. . .]

Internationally, several organizations merge debate with community building. The International Debate Education Association focuses on bringing the methods of debate to societies where democracy is in its infancy, while the National Communication Association's Committee for International Discussion and Debate sponsors long-running debate tours between intercollegiate debate teams in the United States and debating teams from both Britain and Japan. On a different tack, several U.S. State Department international youth programs integrate debate training into curricular design (SEEYLI, Ben Franklin). Research testifying to the impact of such initiatives reveals that students who participate in such programs are better positioned to push for increased democratic accountability in these postcommunist states (Mitchell et al. 2006).

Although not always formally tied to the organs of intercollegiate debate, perhaps the most powerful evidence of the benefits of a debate education emanates from the urban debate movement. Spearheaded by intercollegiate debate programs, this effort has matured over the past two decades to bring colleges, middle and high schools, as well as community organizations and philanthropic organizations together in fruitful collaborations designed to bring the virtues of a debate education to underserved urban communities. With outposts in more than 20 of the nation's largest cities and tens of thousands of graduates, the results have been astonishing. As Will Baker notes, "there is no doubt that urban debate leagues using policy debate produce results and engage students that other resources have failed to reach" (1998, 69–70). Linda Collier's (2004) empirical study of urban debate students establishes a strong link between participation in debate and improvements in reading, self-esteem, decision making, GPA (grade point average), and prospects for attending college. Similarly, Carol Winkler's (2010) empirical assessment of urban debate league programs in Atlanta finds even stronger correlations between debate and a variety of academic, behavioral, and social benefits. These students also experience the empowering potential of debate. As Edward Lee, a graduate of the Atlanta league, explains, debate "allows students to take control of their educational destiny and at once make it a site of resistance" (1998, 96).

[...]

6. Fostering Modes of Inquiry

A. ACTIVE LEARNING

Active learning is a mode of instruction that focuses the responsibility for learning on the learner. Charles Bonwell and James Eison (1991) suggest that learning is maximized when learners work in pairs, discuss materials while role-playing, debate, engage in examinations of case studies, and take part in cooperative learning,

L. Dee Fink explains that active learning occurs when learning activities "involve some kind of experience or some kind of dialogue" (1999, para. 3)—dialogue with self, dialogue with others, observing, and doing.

Intercollegiate debate fosters each of these learning activities. Dialogue with self involves thinking reflexively about topics, including what a person ought to think about a topic, and includes self-evaluation of the thinking, writing, and speaking, as well as consideration of the role of the knowledge in his or her own life. In order to decide what arguments to advance in a given debate, debaters must think critically about the topic they will be debating. To evaluate their opponent's arguments (as well as to select their own), debaters need to assess their own thinking on the topic as well as research and prepare briefs and speeches. Finally, debaters consider the ways in which the things they learn have impacted their own lives, particularly when the topics involve social issues. Dialogue with others involves "intense" discussion about the issue at hand. Debaters engage in these intense discussions not only in their individual debates but also with coaches and teammates, with frequent spillover outside of the tournament context into a variety of formal and informal social situations. Observation includes listening to someone else doing something that is related to what they are learning about. Debaters are involved in observation when they are listening to the speeches of their opponents, listening to practice debates, and listening to others debate at tournaments. Lynn Goodnight explains that debaters learn to become active listeners, concentrating on the speaker, mentally reviewing what has been said, trying to anticipate what will come next, and noting the kind of evidence that is being used (1987, 6). Doing simply involves a learning activity where the participant "does something." Debaters are involved in doing the debating, analyzing the material, writing the speeches, presenting the arguments, and making the choices that will win debates (Bellon 2000).

[...]

B. COOPERATIVE LEARNING

There are five essential elements of cooperative learning: positive interdependence; face-to-face interaction; interpersonal and small-group skills; individual accountability and personal responsibility, and frequent use of group processing (Johnson et al. 1991). Each of these elements is thrust upon participants in intercollegiate debate. It is unavoidable.

In order to experience positive interdependence, students must perceive that they "need each other." Participants in intercollegiate debate are competitively interdependent. Given the tremendous research, argument preparation, and scouting burdens, it would be very difficult, if not impossible, for individuals to succeed in debate without the support of the larger team, let alone their debate partner (Shelton 1995). As Ehninger and Brockriede explain, "In this respect debate may be compared with a group of mountain climbers concerned with their mutual safety" (1978, 15). Positive interdependence is manifest in intercollegiate debate because students share research resources and strategies and perform individually assigned roles that contribute to the collective good. To be successful, debaters and coaches must work together in a variety of group processes to share information, coordinate research assignments, and work as a squad at tournament competitions. Similarly, to be a member of a successful team requires a large degree of individual accountability and personal responsibility.

[...]

Interpersonal and small-group skills, such as decision-making, trust-building, communication, and conflict-management skills are also critical because students debate in teams of two. [...] This requires building trust and effective communication between partners. And, when conflicts arise—as they inevitably do—debaters must work to manage conflicts in order to be successful.

C. INTENTIONAL LEARNING

For Carl Bereiter and Marlene Scardamalia, intentional teaming is characterized by "processes that have learning as a goal, rather than an incidental outcome" (1989, 363). Marlene Francis, Timothy Mulder, and Joan Stark sharpen this perspective by focusing on its essential attributes. Intentional teaming is "learning with self-directed purpose, intending and choosing to learn and how and what to team, Intentional learning involves five attributes of teaming: questioning, organizing, connecting, reflecting, and adapting" (1995, para. 2). Success in intercollegiate debate depends crucially on maintaining each of these aspects.

To begin with, debaters need to learn not only to question arguments made by their opponents but also to question the strength of their own arguments before they decide to advance them in debates. At the same time, debaters need to organize and synthesize arguments and opinions advanced by myriad sources to coherent and concise positions. They must also organize their own research, the work of their teammates, and scouting information collected by tournament participants. Furthermore, developing arguments and preparing them for presentation in debates requires making connections between arguments and opinions derived from many different literatures, connecting arguments with those advanced by ones partner, developing a full understanding of the relationships between arguments in order to synthesize positions for rebuttal speeches, as well as cultivating an awareness of the contested relationships between arguments—arguments presented in any particular debate as well as those advanced by others throughout the academic year.

[...]

7. Student Empowerment

In addition to cultivating educational skills, participation in debate has long been recognized as having positive benefits in shaping the personality of students (Mayer 1936). Because debate requires students to debate both sides of controversies, they become more flexible arguers and more tolerant of opposing viewpoints (Bellon 2000; Muir 1993). There is also evidence that debaters are more socially tolerant and less likely to accept conventional social norms (Rogers 2002, 2005). This is a unique benefit to switch-side debating. Rogers explains: "as debaters become exposed to various resolutions and topics for debate, conduct research on both sides of usually controversial social subjects, organize and write briefs for both sides, and go through the process of arguing those positions, they have the opportunity to develop a wider view of differing social perceptions" (2002, 13–14). Research also shows that debaters are more inclined to become members of intercultural organizations and enroll in cross-cultural classes (Rogers 2005). These tendencies are improved and enhanced when debate programs engage in community outreach. Beth Breger observes that these programs "encourage a dialogue" that not only results in "profound learning" but also "becomes the bridge across the chasms of difference" (1998, 67). This finding is consistent with empirical research that has linked service teaming with building citizenship (Morgan and Streb 2001).

Empirical research proves that debate involvement enhances beneficial argumentative skills, while reducing verbal aggression (Colbert 1993, 1994). Debate helps students deal with other types of aggression as well. Reflecting on the Open Society Institute's lengthy experience, Breger reports that "debate teaches students to command attention with words, provides students with an alternate outlet for day-to-day conflicts, and gives them a tool with which they can combat physical aggression" (1998, 66–67). As Melissa Wade explains, "If one knows how to advocate on one's own behalf in a way that will be acknowledged by the listener, one does not have to resort to violence to get the attention of decision-makers" (1998, 63). This contention has been confirmed by empirical research that documents a link between debate participation and a sharp decline in disciplinary referrals (Winkler 2010).

[...]

CONCLUSION

In addition to its many tangible benefits and time-honored virtues, debate is fun. The pleasure that students take in the development and exercise of their speaking and reasoning abilities is a major motivation for why they participate; debate is exciting, challenging, and enjoyable. Both the competitive and collaborative nature of debate combine to create the conditions for participation in an activity that is as intense and satisfying as any in the academy—including intercollegiate athletics. Along the way, participants form lifelong relationships and gain entry to a networked community that is unparalleled in the history of American higher education.

REFERENCES

Allen, M.; S. Berkowitz; S. Hunt; and A. Louden. 1999. "A Meta-analysis of the Impact of Forensics and Communication Education on Critical Thinking. *Communication Education* 48: 18–30.

[...]

Association of American Colleges and Universities. 1985. Integrity in the College Curriculum. Washington, DC.

Baker, W. 1998. "Reflections on the New York Urban Debate League and 'Ideafest II.'" *Contemporary Argumentation and Debate* 19: 69–71.

Barber, B. 2004. *Strong Democracy: Participatory Politics for a New Age.* Berkeley: University of California Press.

Barfield, K.E. 1989. "A Study of the Relationship Between Active Participation in Interscholastic Debating and the Development of Critical Thinking Skills with Implications for School Administrators and Instructional Leaders." *Dissertation Abstracts International,* 50-09: 2714.

[...]

Bellon, J. 2000. "A Research-based justification for Debate Across the Curriculum." *Argumentation and Advocacy* 36: 161–75.

Bereiter, C., and M. Scardamalia. 1989. "Intentional Learning as a Goal of Instruction." In *Knowing, Learning, and Instruction: Essays in Honor of Robert Glaser,* ed. L.B. Resnick, 361–92. Hillsdale, NJ: Lawrence Erlbaum.

Bernard, P. 1999. "A Way with Words; Florida Forensics Institute Gives Teens a Verbal Boost." *Sun-Sentinel,* Community News, August 25, p. 1.

Bonwell, C., and J. Eison. 1991. "Active Learning: Creating Excitement in the Classroom." ERIC Document Reproduction Service, #ED336049.

[...]

Breger, B. 1998. "Building Open Societies Through Debate." *Contemporary Argumentation and Debate* 19: 66–68.

Capp, G.R., and T.R. Capp. 1965. *Principles of Argumentation and Debate.* Englewood Cliffs, NJ: Prentice Hall.

[. . .]

Chemerinsky, E. 2008. "Inner-city Schools Suffer When 'Debaters' Go Silent." *USA Today*, January 31, p. A11

[. . .]

Colbert, K.R. 1987. "The Effects of CEDA and NDT Debate Training on Critical Thinking Ability." *Journal of the American Forensic Association* 23: 194–201.

———. 1993. "The Effects of Debate Participation on Argumentativeness and Verbal Aggression." *Communication Education* 42: 206–14.

———. 1994. "Replicating the Effects of Debate Participation on Argumentativeness and Verbal Aggression." *Forensic of Phi Kappa Delta* 79: 1–13.

———. 1995. "Enhancing Critical Thinking Ability Through Academic Debate." *Contemporary Argumentation and Debate* 16: 52–72.

Collier, L. 2004. "Argumentation for Success: A Study of Academic Debate in the Urban High Schools of Chicago, Kansas City, New York, St. Louis and Seattle." Paper presented at the Hawaii International Conference on Social Sciences. Honolulu, HI, June 16–19.

[. . .]

Cross, G. 1971. "The Effects of Relief Systems and the Amount of Debate Experience on the Acquisition of Critical Thinking." Dissertation Abstracts International, 32-06: 3461.

[. . .]

Ehninger, D., and W. Brockriede. 1978. *Decision by Debate.* 2d ed. New York: Harper and Row.

Fink. L. Dee. 1999. "Active Learning." http://honolulu.hawaii.edu/intranet/committees/FacDevCom/guidebk/teachtip/active.htm (accessed June 7, 2009).

Fishkin. J.S. 2009. *When the People Speak: Deliberative Democracy and Public Consultation.* New York: Oxford University Press.

Francis, M.C.; T.C. Mulder; and J.S. Stark. 1995. "Intentional Learning: A Process for Learning to Learn in the Accounting Curriculum." Sarasota, FL: American Accounting Association. http://aaahq.org/aecc/intent/cover.htm (accessed July 28 2009).

Franke, R.J. 2009. "The Power of the Humanities and a Challenge to Humanists." *Daedalus* 138: 13–23.

Freeley, A.J., and D.L. Steinberg. 2005. *Argumentation and Debate: Critical Thinking for Reasoned Decision Making.* 11th ed. Belmont. CA: Thomson Wadsworth.

———. 2009. *Argumentation and Debate: Critical Thinking for Reasoned Decision Making.* 12th ed. Belmont, CA: Thomson Wadsworth.

Fritch, J. 1993/1994. "What's Right with Forensics: The Perspective of a College Forensic Educator." *Forensic Educator* 8: 6–8.

Giesecke, N. 1981. "Who Spends 15 Hours a Week Studying in the Library?" *Christian Science Monitor*, December 14, p. 17.

Goleman. D. 2000. *Working with Emotional Intelligence*. New York: Bantam.

Goodnight, L. 1987. *Getting Started in Debate*. New York: McGraw-Hill.

———. 1993. *Getting Started in Debate*. 2d ed. New York: Glencoe.

[…]

Higher Education Research Institute. 2009. "The American College Teacher National Norms for 2007–2008." HERI Research Brief, March. http://www.heri.ucla.edu/PDFs/pubs/briefs/briefpro30508-08faculty.pdf (accessed June 2, 2009).

Hill, B. 1982. "Intercollegiate Debate: Why Do Students Bother?" *Southern Speech Communication Journal* 48: 77–88.

Hill, B., and R.W. Leeman, 1997. *The Art and Practice of Argumentation and Debate*. Mountain View, CA: Mayfield.

Hobbs, J.D., and R.C. Chandler. 1991. "The Perceived Benefits of Policy Rebate Training in Various Professions." *Speaker and Gavel* 28: 4–6.

[…]

Howell, W. 1943. "The Effects of High School Debating on Critical Thinking." *Speech Mimeographs* 10: 96–101.

[…]

Hunt, S.K.; D. Garard; and G. Simerly, G. 1997. "Reasoning and Risk: Debaters as an Academically At-risk Population." *Contemporary Argumentation and Debate* 18: 48–56.

Huston, D. 1985. "What Should Be the Goals of High School Debate? An Examination and Prioritization." Paper presented at the National Forensic League Conference on the State of High School Debate, Kansas City, MO. ERIC Document Reproduction Service, #ED272942.

Inch, E.S.; B. Warnick; and D. Endres. 2006. *Critical Thinking and Communication: The Use of Reason in Argument*, 5th ed. Boston: Allyn and Bacon.

Isocrates. *Antidosis*, trans. by George Norlin. Cambridge: Cambridge University Press, 1929.

Jackson, T. 1961. "The Effects of Intercollegiate Debating on Critical Thinking." Dissertation Abstracts, 21-11: 3556.

Johnson, D. et al. 1991. *Cooperation in the Classroom*. Edina, MN: Interaction Book.

[…]

Jones, K. 1994. "Cerebral Gymnastics 101: Why Do Debaters Debate?" *CEDA Yearbook* 15: 65–75.

Katsulas, J., and S. Bauschard. 2000. "Debate as Preparation for the Legal Profession; A Survey of Debaters from the 1970s to 1990s." Paper presented at the annual meeting of the Southern States Communication Association, New Orleans, LA, March 29–April 2.

Kuh, G. 2008. *High-Impact Educational Practices*. Washington, DC: Association of American Colleges and Universities.

Lawhorn, B. 2008. "Extracurricular Activities: The Afterschool Connection." *Occupational Outlook Quarterly* 52: 16–21.

Lee, E. 1998. "Memoir of a Former Urban Debate League Participant." *Contemporary Argumentation and Debate* 19: 93–96.

Lucas, S.E. 1998. *The Art of Public Speaking*. 6th ed. Boston: McGraw-Hill.

Lybbert, B. 1985. "What Should Be the Goals of High School Debate?" Paper presented at the National Forensic League Conference on the State of High School Debate, Kansas City, MO. ERIC Document #ED272941.

Matlon, R.J., and L.M. Keele. 1984. "A Survey of Participants in the National Debate Tournament, 1947–1980." *Journal of the American Forensic Association* 20: 194–205.

Mayer, J.E. 1936. "Personality Development Through Debate." *Quarterly Journal of Speech* 22: 607–11.

McBath, J.H. 1984. "Rationale for Forensics." In *American Forensics in Perspective: Papers from the Second National Conference on Forensics*, ed. D.W. Parson, 5–11. Annandale, VA: Speech Communication Association.

McKee, K. 2003. "The Relationship Between Debate and Critical Thinking with Advanced Placement Teacher Perceptions of That Relationship." *Dissertation Abstracts International*, 64-08, 2766.

[...]

Mitchell, G.R.; Pfister, D.; Bradatan, G.; Colev, D.; Manolova, T.; Mitkovski, G.; Nestorova, I.; Ristic, M.; & Sheshi, G. 2006. "Navigating Dangerous Deliberative Waters: Shallow Argument Pools, Group Polarization and Public Debate Pedagogy in Southeast Europe." *Controversia* 4: 69–84.

Morgan, W., and M. Streb. 2001. "Building Citizenship: How Student Voice in Service-learning Develops Civic Values." *Social Science Quarterly* 82: 154–70.

[...]

Muir, S.A. 1993. "A Defense of the Ethics of Contemporary Debate." *Philosophy and Rhetoric* 26: 277–95.

Murphy, S.K., and J.A. Samosky. 1993. "Argumentation and Debate: Learning to Think Critically." *Speaker and Gavel* 30: 39–45.

National Education Goals Panel. 1991. *The National Education Goals Panel: Building a Nation of Learners*. Washington, DC: U.S. Government Printing Office.

National Institute of Education Study Group. 1984. *Involvement in Leaning: Realizing the Potential of American Higher Education*. Washington, DC: National Institute of Education, U.S. Department of Education

Nichols, R.G., and L.A. Stevens. 1957. *Are You Listening?* New York: McGraw-Hill.

Norton, L.E. 1982. "Nature and Benefits of Academic Debate." In *Introduction to Debate*, ed. C. Keefe, T B. Harte, and L. E. Norton, 24–40. New York: Macmillan.

O'Donnell, T.M. 2008a. "The Great Debaters: A Challenge to Higher Education." *Inside Higher Education*, January 7. http://www.insidehigered.com/views/2008/01/07/odonnell (accessed August 4, 2009).

[…]

Oliver, P. 1985. "How Well Are We Meeting the Goals of High School Debate?" Paper presented at the National Forensic League Conference on the State of High School Debate, Kansas City, MO. ERIC Document Reproduction Service, #ED272943.

Omelicheva, M.Y. 2007. "Resolved: Academic Debate Should Be Part of Political Science Curricula." *Journal of Political Science Education* 3: 161–75.

Owen, D. 2004. "Citizenship Identity and Civic Education in the United States." Paper presented at the Conference on Civic Education and Politics in Democracies sponsored by the Center for Civic Education and the Bundeszentrale fur Politische Bildung, San Diego, CA, September 26–October 1.

[…]

Panetta, E.M., and D.A. Herbeck. 1993. "Argument in a Technical Sphere: Incommensurate Rhetorical Visions." In *Argument and the Postmodern Challenge: Proceedings of the Eighth SCA/AFA Conference on Argumentation*, ed. R.E. McKerrow, 25–30. Annandale, VA: Speech Communication Association.

Parcher, J. 1998. "Evaluation Report: Philodemic Debate Society." http://groups.wfu.edu/NDT/Articles/gtreport.html (accessed June 2, 2009).

Pemberton-Butler, L. 1999. "Flexing Forensic Muscles—Auburn High School Debate Teams Compete Nationally Thanks to the Districts Commitment and Inspiration of Longtime Teacher." *Seattle Times*, February 2, p. B1.

Peters, T. 2008. "An Investigation into the Relationship Between Participation in Competitive Forensics and Standardized Test Scores." Master's thesis, Regis University.

Pfau, M.; D.A. Thomas; and W. Ulrich. 1987. *Debate and Argument: A Systems Approach to Advocacy.* Glenview, IL: Scott, Foresman.

Rogers, I.E. 2002. "Longitudinal Outcome Assessment for Forensics: Does Participation in Intercollegiate Competitive Forensics Contribute to Measurable Differences in Positive Student Outcomes?" *Contemporary Argumentation and Debate* 23: 1–27.

————. 2005. "Graduate School, Professional, and Life Choices: An Outcome Assessment Confirmation Study Measuring Positive Student Outcomes Beyond Student Experiences for Participants in Competitive Intercollegiate Forensics." *Contemporary Argumentation and Debate* 26: 13–40.

[. . .]

Rothenberg, I.F. and J.S. Berman. 1980. "College Debate and Effective Writing: An Argument for Debate in the Public Administration Curriculum." *Teaching Political Science* 18: 21–39.

Rowland, R.C. 1995. "The Practical Pedagogical Functions of Academic Debate." *Contemporary Argumentation and Debate* 15: 98–108.

Semlak, W., and D. Shields. 1977. "The Effects of Debate Training on Students Participation in the Bicentennial Youth Debates." *Journal of the American Forensic Association* 13: 193–96.

Shelton, M.W. 1995. "Squad as Community: A Group Communication Perspective on the Debate Workshop." Paper presented at the annual meeting of the Southern States Communication Association, New Orleans, LA, March 29–April 2.

Sowa-Jamrok, C. 1994. "High School Students Can't Say Enough About Debate Experience." *Chicago Tribune*, April 24, p. C9.

Sperling. M. 1996. "Revisiting the Writing-Speaking Connection: Challenges for Research on Writing and Writing Instruction." *Review of Educational Research* 66: 53–86.

Srader, D. 2006. "The Impact of Prior Experience in Intercollegiate Debate upon a Postsecondary Educator's Skillset." Paper presented at the annual meeting of the National Communication Association, San Antonio, TX, November 16–19. http://northwestchristian.academia.edu/documents/0011/5331/Paper.pdf (accessed May 22, 2009).

[. . .]

Wade, M. 1998. "The Case for Urban Debate Leagues." *Contemporary Argumentation and Debate* 19: 60–65.

———. 2006. "The Value of Debate: A Report for Tom Jenkins." http://www.debatecoaches.org/wp-content/ev/08-09/jenkinsmemo.doc/(accessed May 28, 2009).

Whalen, S. 1991. "Intercollegiate Debate as a Co-curricular Activity: Effects on Critical Thinking." In *Argument in Controversy: Proceedings of the Seventh SCA/AFA Conference on Argumentation*, ed. D.W. Parson, 391–97. Annandale, VA: Speech Communication Association.

Williams, D. 1951. "The Effects of Training in College Debating on Critical Thinking Activity." Master's thesis, Purdue University.

Williams, D.; B. McGee; and D. Worth. 2001. "University Student Perceptions of the Efficacy of Debate Participation: An Empirical Investigation." *Argumentation and Advocacy* 37: 198–209.

Winkler, C. 2010. "The Impact of Policy Debate on Inner-city Schools: The Milwaukee Experience." In *The Function of Argument and Social Context*, ed, D. Gouran, 565–571. Annandale, VA: National Communication Association.

Wood, R.V., and L. Goodnight. 2006. *Strategic Debate*. New York: Glencoe.

[. . .]

*Timothy O'Donnell** is an associate professor and director of debate at the University of Mary Washington.

O'Donnell, Timothy. "A Rationale for Intercollegiate Debate in the Twenty-first Century." In *Navigating Opportunity: Policy Debate in the 21st Century*, edited by Allan D. Louden, 27–56. New York: IDEBATE Press, 2010.

PART 2

Skills Learned through Debate

Part 2 presents eight articles that detail the different types of skills gained through debate participation. All but one of these articles offer social scientific studies to support their claims that debate, indeed, generates valuable skills. The first article, "A Meta-analysis of the Impact of Forensics and Communication Education on Critical Thinking," by Mike Allen et al., is perhaps the most referenced study in debate literature. The article details the significant impact debate has on the development of critical thinking skills. In "Academic Debate and Critical Thinking: A Look at the Evidence," Robert Greenstreet also discusses critical thinking skills and how debate fosters the enhancement of critical thinking. One of the complaints about competitive academic debate is that it encourages verbal aggressiveness. "The Effects of Debate Participation on Argumentativeness and Verbal Aggression," by Kent R. Colbert, and "Argumentativeness, Verbal Aggressiveness, and Relational Satisfaction in the Parliamentary Debate Dyad," by Crystal Lane Swift and Christina Vourvoulias, discuss the relationship between debate and verbal aggressiveness. Additionally, Donald J. Bingle examines the value and importance of parliamentary debate in "Parliamentary Debate Is More Serious Than You Think: Forensics at the University of Chicago." He argues that parliamentary debate provides unique advantages over other formats of debate, particularly for university students. More specifically, these articles report how debate promotes advocacy and argument skills, rather than verbal confrontation. In fact, as many of these studies suggest, debate tends to help participants know how to reduce verbal conflict, instead of inflaming it. Given that academic debate involves the clash of arguments, Don Faules in "Measuring Refutation Skill: An Exploratory Study" argues that debate teaches vital refutation skills.

While not very many studies report on the value of debate in an international context, Narahiko Inoue and Mika Nakano, in "The Benefits and Costs of Participating in Competitive Debate Activities," study the comparative merits of debate in Japan and the United States. In so doing, they argue that the costs and benefits of debate are generally similar in both national contexts, but the study goes on to report exactly what those costs and benefits are. Not surprisingly, the authors argue that the value of debate far outweighs any perceived disadvantages. Finally, in "University Student Perceptions of the Efficacy of Debate Participation: An Empirical Investigation," David E. Williams et al. focus on the benefits of debate that are perceived by the participants themselves. Although some will undoubtedly argue that self-reporting among debaters contributes to biased results, we should heed the results of this study, since the participants report what they actually receive from their debate experiences, as opposed to what might be otherwise speculated.

A Meta-analysis of the Impact of Forensics and Communication Education on Critical Thinking

by *Mike Allen, Sandra Berkowitz,*
*Steve Hunt, and Allan Louden**

[...]

One of the central arguments for instruction in public speaking, argumentation, persuasion, and debate is the belief that such training improves the critical thinking ability of the participants (for a complete discussion of the range goals of forensics that would apply to other public communication instruction, see Hunt, 1994). Hill (1993) points out that demands for educational accountability require that forensics (as well as other communication courses) document the degree to which those activities meet educational goals. The increasing need for university programs to provide "proof of service" creates a need for communication courses and activities to document the improvements generated. Such claims can be supported with testimonials, [anecdoctal] stories, and examples from participants. However, systematic and more objective indications of improvement would provide an additional level of support more persuasive to some critics.

Garside (1996) surveyed the impact of group discussion teaching strategies on the development of critical thinking skills and concluded that:

> the literature suggests at least four defining aspects of thinking
> that make it *critical*: (a) thinking that is clear, precise, accurate,
> relevant, logical, and consistent; (b) thinking that reflects a con-
> trolled sense of skepticism or disbelief of any assertion, claim, or
> conclusion until sufficient evidence and reasoning is provided to
> conclusively support it; (c) thinking that takes stock of existing

information and identifies holes and weaknesses, thereby certifying what we know or don't know; and (d) thinking that is free from bias, prejudice, and one-sidedness of thought. (p. 215)

Instructors of public speaking, discussion, and argumentation, as well as those advocating participation in competitive forensics, have argued that such activities improve critical thinking. Unbridled by the limitations found within the traditional lecture-oriented classroom situation, participants must learn to invent, organize, and articulate thoughts subject to scrutiny by others. The student learns to improve the quality [of] thinking and how to critique the arguments and conclusions of others. The process of participation as a communicator originating the argument and as a critical consumer provides a "hands on" experience that should improve critical thinking ability.

Assuming that such improvement occurs, the conclusion is that the educational advantages of a person able to both generate and critique conclusions provides the basis for quality participation in the society and the academic environment. The conclusion offered is simple: participation in forms of public communication involved in public speaking, forensics (debate, mock trial, individual events), and argumentation requires attention to argument and counterargument.

[...]

Justification for Using Meta-analysis

A previous meta-analysis (Follert & Colbert, 1983) concludes that "the results of this analysis cast substantial doubt on the claimed relationship between debate training and critical thinking skill improvement" (p. 2). The conclusion derived from five studies indicates no significant correlation exists between participation in debate and subsequent critical thinking gains. The meta-analysis form Follert and Colbert used generated a set of 47 individual comparisons. Of the 47, 28 demonstrated a gain in critical thinking for debate while 19 did not. The conclusion they offer is that there is no consistent body of evidence for a gain in critical thinking skill.

The previous meta-analysis employed a technique using a binomial test of the results of individual significance tests. Unfortunately, the binomial test fails to consider the impact of Type II error and treats each trial as a separate outcome. The result is that the failure to achieve significance does not consider the impact of the separate incidence of Type II error for each sample.

In short, the technique used by Follert and Colbert (1983) did not seek to establish an average effect; instead, the effort was made to create a common metric and then to look for consistency among the results of individual significance tests. Rather than averaging effects, the analysis is conducted at the level of individual units employing a vote-counting method. The form of meta-analysis used by Follert and Colbert has been replaced by the other forms of meta-analysis (particularly variance-centered forms, Bangert-Drowns, 1986).

METHOD

Literature Search
Manuscripts were obtained by searching the available electronic data bases (COMINDEX, DISSERTATION ABSTRACTS, ERIC, INDEX TO COMMUNICATION JOURNALS, PSYCHLIT), various bibliographies available on the topic (Colbert, 1995; Follert & Colbert, 1983; Hill, 1993), as well as the reference section of manuscripts obtained.

To be included in the analysis a manuscript had to meet the following conditions:

(a) contain quantitative data,
(b) some type of communication skill improvement exercise (this could be in the form of a course or participation in competitive forensics), and

(c) some method of assessing critical thinking skill improvement (either using a cross-sectional or longitudinal design).

Coding of Study Features

Study features were coded as potential sources of moderating influences. If the average results of the investigations are heterogeneous, then the search for moderator variables (particularly design differences) could serve as an explanation for such inconsistencies.

Type of Research Design

The investigations included in this analysis used two types of research designs to estimate the impact of communication skill training on critical thinking improvement: longitudinal and cross-sectional designs. Some studies used both types of designs and contributed to both sets of analyses. This information and associated statistical effects appear in Table 1.

Type of Communication Skill Experience

The type of communication skill improvement approach differed both between and within investigations. The experiences involved competitive forensic participation as well as courses designed to improve the skill of the student in accomplishing some communication task. The longitudinal experience was coded into the following categories: (a) public speaking class, (b) argumentation, debate, and discussion class, and (c) competitive forensics participation (this includes debate, discussion, individual events, mock trial, or other types of participative competitive events). The division represents the type of experiences available to the participant. The coding for individual studies is found in Table 2.

The cross-sectional comparisons were divided into three types of comparisons: (a) communication skill activity (forensics, public speaking class, or argumentation class) to a control group, (b) a public speaking or argumentation class to forensics, and (c) an argumentation class (or "special" public speaking class that included a

TABLE 1: LISTS OF STUDIES WITH ASSOCIATED TECHNICAL AND OTHER INFORMATION

Study	Date	Longitudinal			Cross-Sectional			Measure
		r	r'	N	r	r'	N	
Allen	1995	.092	.096	104	.210	.229	138	Watson-Glaser
Baumgartner	1965	.345	.380	34	.286	.296	77	Watson-Glaser
Beckman	1955	.066	.066	293				Watson-Glaser
Beihl	1963	.083	.092	106				Watson-Glaser
Brembeck	1947	.196	.196	202	.136	.136	413	Watson-Glaser
Bursack	1961	.217	.275	328				Sarett Test
Colbert	1987	.303	.329	285	.342	.373	285	Watson-Glaser
Colbert	1995	.005	.006	148				Watson-Glaser
Cross	1971	.072	.078	136				Watson-Glaser
Douglas	1951	.392	.426	11	.512	.557	20	Combination
Frank	1964	.105	.111	103	.429	.451	206	Watson-Glaser
Green	1990	.671	.671	11	.449	.449	23	Graded Essays
Howell	1942	.207	.225	213	.051	.055	415	Watson-Glaser
Hurst	1962	.169	.180	87	.343	.367	157	California
Jackson	1961	.118	.126	123	.172	.179	249	Watson-Glaser
Ness	1967	.172	.180	164	-.045	-.049	331	Watson-Glaser
Smith	1942				.143	.155	34	Watson-Glaser
Tame	1958	.164	.164	309				Combination
Whalen	1991				.458	.475	49	Watson-Glaser

Note. The designation "r" indicates the uncorrected effect. The designation "r'" indicates the effect after correcting for error due to attenuated measurement, restriction in range, and regression to the mean. All averages are calculated using the effects after they have been corrected for the appropriate errors.

section on argumentation and debate) compared to a public speaking class. The information for individual studies appears in Table 3.

The divisions between types of courses or activities based on content provide some type of assessment about whether a particular type of content would most improve critical thinking skills. Competitive forensics is often given academic credit and the provision

TABLE 2: LIST OF EFFECTS BY TYPE OF
LONGITUDINAL COMPARISON

Study	Date	Size of the Effect			Type of Experience
		r	r'	N	
Allen	1995	-.035	-.038	37	Public Speaking
		.041	.044	32	Argumentation Class
		.257	.285	35	Forensics
Baumgartner	1965	.354	.380	34	Public Speaking
Beckman	1955	.066	.066	293	Argumentation Class
Beihl	1963	.083	.092	106	Public Speaking
Brembeck	1947	.196	.196	202	Argumentation Class
Bursack	1961	.217	.275	328	Forensics
Colbert	1987	.303	.329	285	Forensics
Colbert	1995	.005	.006	148	Forensics
Cross	1971	.072	.078	136	Forensics
Douglas	1951	.392	.426	11	Argumentation Class
Frank	1964	.105	.111	103	Public Speaking
Green	1990	.671	.671	11	Argumentation Class
Howell	1942	.207	.225	213	Forensics
Hurst	1962	.169	.180	87	Public Speaking
Jackson	1961	.118	.126	123	Forensics
Ness	1967	.172	.180	164	Public Speaking
Tame	1958	.164	.164	309	Forensics

for such credit is based on critical thinking improvement as well as skill at public presentation. Demonstrating the relative size of the improvements offered in critical thinking for each type of activity provides educators with information on what approach(es) can be expected to generate particular outcomes.

Statistical Analysis

The data were analyzed using the variance-centered form of meta-analysis developed by Hunter and Schmidt (1990) reflected in the computer programs METACOR (Hamilton & Hunter, 1990) and

TABLE 3: LIST OF STUDY EFFECTS AND CODING WHEN USING CROSS-SECTIONAL DESIGNS

Study	Date	r	r'	N	Type of Comparison
Allen	1995	.133	.145	71	Control/Public Speaking
		.115	.125	69	Public Speaking/Argumentation
		.432	.470	72	Forensics/Public Speaking
		.245	.266	66	Control/Argumentation
		.327	.355	67	Forensics/Argumentation
		.486	.528	69	Control/Forensics
Baumgartner	1965	.286	.296	77	Control/Public Speaking
Brembeck	1947	.136	.136	413	Control/Argumentation
Colbert	1995	.342	.373	285	Control/Forensics
Douglas	1951	.512	.557	20	Public Speaking/PS+A
Frank	1964	.429	.451	206	Public Speaking/PS+A
Green	1990	.449	.449	23	Control/Forensics
Howell	1942	.051	.055	415	Control/Forensics
Hurst	1962	.343	.376	157	Control/Public Speaking
Jackson	1961	.172	.179	249	Public Speaking/Forensics
Ness	1967	.099	.113	227	Control/Public Speaking
Smith	1942	.143	.155	34	Public Speaking/PS+A
Whalen	1991	.168	.185	34	Argumentation/A+F
		.440	.458	32	Public Speaking/A+F
		.402	.417	33	Public Speaking/Argumentation

ATTEN (Hamilton & Hunter, 1991).[1] The technique takes the statistical information from investigations and converts the information to a common metric. The form recommended is the correlation coefficient. The estimates for each study are statistically transformed into a correlation. The conversion creates a common metric from each investigation that can be averaged.

Transformed data are corrected for a variety of statistical artifacts and possible design limitations. Correction to the data for attenuated measurement (Hunter & Schmidt, 1990) or restriction in range (Hunter & Schmidt, 1990) is possible. This correction can consider the impact of selection artifacts that reflect the possibility of self-selection artifacts for debaters. The impact of both sets of conditions is to systematically *underestimate* the size of the effect (Allen, Hunter, & Donohue, 1989; Hunter & Schmidt, 1990). Consequently, these corrections serve to increase the size of the existing effect, not reduce it. The average effect is therefore slightly larger after the corrections and the estimate of the variance is larger as well. Each table provides the corrected correlations (r') as well as the uncorrected correlations (r). A confidence interval can be estimated for the average effect (Hunter & Schmidt, 1990, p. 208).[2]

The transformed data are then averaged using a formula that weights each correlation by the corresponding sample size. The reason that a weighted average is used is that the assumption is that larger samples provide more accurate estimates of the population effect than do small samples. The level of Type II error is less with larger sample sizes. A study using a small sample size has a larger amount of sampling error and is therefore a less accurate estimate of the population parameter. Weighting by sample size is a recognition of this variability in the accuracy of the estimate. A moderator variable produces subsets where a comparison of the mean effect of each subset demonstrates differences between the groups.

No data appear more than once in any particular subgroup, although data sets are used in multiple subgroups. This creates a problem of the data lacking statistical independence. A Monte Carlo test of the impact of lack of independence demonstrates, however, that estimates of both the mean and standard deviation are unaffected by this problem (Tracz, 1984).

RESULTS

The comparisons in the overall analysis (as well as moderator analysis) consider the two basic types of designs (longitudinal and cross-sectional) separately. The results of the longitudinal designs illustrate that communication skill exercises improve critical thinking (*average r* = .176, *var.* = .010, *k* = 17, N = 2657, 95% Confidence Interval [C.I.] ± .037). Cross-sectional designs find that a communication skill exercise improves critical thinking (*average r* = .196, *var.* = .028, *k* = 13, N = 2395, 95% C.I. ± .038). The summary data for this and all other sections appear in Table 4.

A comparison of the difference in the size of the correlations demonstrates that while the effects observed in cross-sectional designs are larger than those reported by researchers employing longitudinal design (*d* = .055), the difference is relatively small. The most important finding is that the effects are both positive, indicating that critical thinking improved when either using a longitudinal or cross-sectional comparison.

[...]

This improvement in critical thinking ability indicates a large substantial positive influence of public communication training relating to critical thinking.

Type of Critical Thinking Measurement Instrument

The studies fell into two basic groups: (a) studies that used some version of the Watson-Glaser Critical Thinking Appraisal (1951) or (b) some other measure of critical thinking. Table 1 provides a list of the measures used in each investigation. This analysis for the two different types of measurement instrument groups presents the results separately for the longitudinal and cross-sectional designs.

[...]

The results indicate that the Watson-Glaser method of measuring critical thinking improvement produces smaller effects than other measures. However, the effect is consistent in direction, if not magnitude, to all the other measures. The evidence suggests the possibility of differential validity for scales, but the consistent pattern indicates convergent validity for the measures.

	Type of Design	
	Longitudinal	Cross-Sectional
average r	.176	.196
variance	.010	.028
k	17	13
N	2657	2395
95% CI	±.124	±.291

	Type of Measurement			
	Longitudinal		Cross-Sectional	
	Watson-Glaser	Other	Watson-Glaser	Other
average r	.160	.217	.192	.226
variance	.010	.007	.029	.013
k	12	5	10	3
N	1875	782	2105	290
95% CI	±.124	±.150	±.303	±.123

	Effects when Comparing Types of Experience					
	Cross-Sectional			Longitudinal		
	CS v. C	F v. A or PS	A/PS v. PS	PS	A	F
average r	.241	.271	.364	.145	.129	.203
variance	.025	.015	.022	.066	.012	.010
k	10	5	5	6	5	8
N	1526	455	362	531	549	1577
95% CI	±.270	±.190	±.206	±.460	±.107	±.152

Note. For type of skill comparison, CS = Communication Skill, PS = Public Speaking Class, C = Control, A = Argumentation Class, and F = Forensics.

Type of Communication Skill Experience

The longitudinal investigations examined the critical thinking gain associated with three different types of skill experiences: (a) public speaking class, (b) argumentation class, and (c) competitive debate/

forensics. The longitudinal design makes it possible to measure the improvement for each condition separately and compare effect sizes.

Participation in a public speaking course improves the critical thinking skill of students (*average r* = .145, *var.* = .066, *k* = 6, *N* = 531, 95% C.I. ± .082).

Argumentation classes result in improvement in critical thinking ability (*average r* = .129, *var.* = .012, *k* = 5, *N* = 549, 95% C.I. ± .081).

Competitive forensics participants demonstrated improvement in critical thinking across the investigations (*average r* = .203, *var.* = .010, *k* = 8, *N* = 1577, 95% C.I. ± .047).

The results indicate that all methods of communication skill training improvement generate gains in critical thinking. The largest effect, however, was observed for competitive forensic participation when compared to a public speaking class (*d* = .89) or an argumentation class (*d* = 1.14).

[...]

CONCLUSIONS

Unfortunately, this summary cannot adequately address the concerns about the reliance on the Watson-Glaser measure of critical thinking. While other measures of critical thinking [Bursack (1961) used Sarett's (1951), "How Do You Think Test?"; Douglas (1951) used Johnson's (1942) measure of reflective thinking; Green & Klug (1990) evaluated written essays; Howell (1942) used the California Analogies and Reasoning Test; Tame (1958) used a combination of Bradley's Logical Reasoning Test, Henning's (1946) Problem Recognition Test, and Sarett's measure] were utilized by investigations, the bulk of existing data rely on the Watson-Glaser measure (in all of its forms). This limitation requires additional research that both develops and utilizes alternative devices. However, while the investigations primarily relied on a single measurement instrument, a comparison to the other measurement efforts produced consistently larger effects. That is, the other devices demonstrated improvement in critical thinking for all the public communication skill efforts, which argues for the generalizability of the conclusion. While primary reliance on the Watson-Glaser instrument may undermine the results should limitations exist in the instrument, use of alternative measurement devices generates similar conclusions. Future research should consider whether instrumentation could be improved or alternative instruments to Watson-Glaser contain similar flaws.

The most important outcome of the present meta-analysis is that regardless of the specific measure used to assess critical thinking, the type of design employed, or the specific type of communication skill training taught, critical thinking improved as a result of training in communication skills. The findings illustrate that participation in public communication skill building exercises consistently improved critical thinking. Participation in forensics demonstrated the largest improvement in critical thinking scores whether considering longitudinal or cross-sectional designs.[3]

The forensics community needs to consider whether the integration of these practices into departmental instruction would be an improvement. The central issue regarding communication, as a field, involves the fact that the process is an action necessary to living. Our field is a *lived* experience that every person enacts each day. Regardless of the area (organizational, interpersonal, rhetorical, mass, technological, small group, etc.), there exists an aspect of performance and/or competence within that area which is a part of the ongoing theoretical and research tradition. One result, in the cross-sectional comparison, demonstrates that public speaking instruction may be improved by incorporating more aspects of argumentation into the curriculum. The central issue is to what degree the need to develop critical thinking skills plays an important part of the expectations for this or any course.

The results demonstrate the value of forensics' participation in improving critical thinking. The effects point to a possible additional advantage that debate and forensics' participation can provide to training solely in public speaking for those interested in the development of critical thinking. The companion activities of engaging in both argument and counterargument, whether required in public speaking, discussion, argumentation, and/or forensics competition better prepare students to become full participants in society. This evidence provides a partial answer to charges of "anti-humanism" in the last few years (Roth, 1996). Competitive forensics, particularly debate, may require the development of critical listening skills, an often underdeveloped part of the practice that is important.

This paper provides some evidence for meeting the calls of those asking for evidence of educational accountability. Forensic participation (as well as other forms of public communication instruction) can be justified on the basis of the critical thinking improvement offered. These results provide important evidence to support the maintenance of forensics and other communication skills training programs in an era of increased educational accountability, downsizing, and budgetary cutbacks.

Public communication (forensics, argumentation, public speaking), as a part of this larger endeavor, has a contribution to make both to the research, theory, and practice. The forensics community needs to contribute to the issues regarding how to improve the practice. Knowing that our contributions are positive should encourage confidence in our ability to experiment and to evaluate. The challenge is to integrate these experiences as a part of our overall curriculum rather than to view public communication skill training as a separate component. After all, improving critical thinking skills should benefit all students, regardless of the major or which class they next enroll.

[...]

The impact of public communication training on the critical thinking ability of the participants is demonstrably positive. This summary of existing research reaffirms what many ex-debaters and others in forensics, public speaking, mock trial, or argumentation would support: participation improves the thinking of those involved.

ENDNOTES

1. A comparison of this method with other methods of meta-analysis (Johnson, Mullen, & Salas, 1995) demonstrates that this method differs from methods used by Hedges and Olkin (1985) or Rosenthal (1984). Johnson, Mullen, and Salas (1995), demonstrate little difference on the question of mean effect as demonstrated in or on issues of variability. The differences are found in the use of significance testing of the mean effect and moderator prediction. The Hunter and Schmidt (1990) technique demonstrates no improvement in power as the sample size or number of studies increases. The Hunter and Schmidt procedure provides a technique less sensitive to sample size; therefore, it is consistent with the design of the technique to differ from methods that increase in power as sample size increases. Consequently, the estimates in this report are conservative with regard to interpretations of statistical significance. Hunter and Schmidt recommend that the use of the significance test be discontinued, and reliance on confidence intervals be substituted. This report follows that recommendation.

2. There are a number of methods for constructing confidence intervals for mean correlations in meta-analysis (see other methods in Hunter & Schmidt, 1990 as well as Cooper & Hedges, 1994; Hedges & Olkin, 1985). The Hunter and Schmidt (1990) procedure followed treats the mean correlation much as any correlation is treated; thus, the confidence interval is influenced by the number of participants on which the average correlation is based and does not consider directly the variability among the studies or number of studies. Other procedures use different considerations when calculating the confidence interval. Each method of calculation of confidence intervals has different implications for the interpretation of the mean correlation.

3. While the effect is largest for forensics, it should be noted that the confidence intervals with forensics and other types of communication skill exercises overlap. In traditional terms this would indicate that the two groups are not "significantly" different at the .05 level. The use of that term or technique is avoided in this particular form of meta-analysis, which instead relies on confidence intervals. The reader is encouraged to inspect the particular effects and associated confidence intervals provided and apply the relevant standard of assessment in making a decision about how to describe the difference.

REFERENCES

*indicates manuscripts contributing data used in the statistical portion of the meta-analysis.

*Allen, M., Berkowitz, S., & Louden, A. (1995). A study comparing the impact of communication classes and competitive forensic experience on critical thinking improvement. *The Forensic, 81,* 1–7.

Allen, M., Hunter, J., & Donohue, W. (1989). Meta-analysis of self-report data on the effectiveness of public speaking anxiety treatment techniques. *Communication Education, 38,* 54–76.

Bangert-Drowns, R. (1986). Review of developments in meta-analytic method. *Psychological Bulletin, 99,* 388–399.

*Baumgartner, A. (1965). *An experimental study of speech fundamentals unit in public speaking upon organization skill and critical thinking ability.* Unpublished master's thesis, University of Nebraska, Lincoln.

*Beckman, V. (1955). *An investigation of the contributions to critical thinking made by courses in argumentation and discussion in selected colleges* Unpublished doctoral dissertation, University of Minnesota, Minneapolis

*Beihl, E. (1963). *An analysis of the critical thinking ability of speech I students at the University of Kansas in the summer of 1963.* Unpublished master's thesis, University of Kansas, Lawrence.

*Brembeck, W. (1947). *The effects of a course in argumentation on critical thinking ability.* Unpublished doctoral dissertation, University of Wisconsin, Madison.

[…]

*Bursack, L. (1961). *The effect of high school debating on knowledge of subject, attitude toward issue, and critical thinking.* Unpublished master's thesis, Washington State University, Pullman.

*Colbert, K. (1987). The effects of CEDA and NDT debate training on critical thinking ability. *Journal of the American Forensic Association, 23,* 194–201.

[…]

Colbert, K. (1995). Enhancing critical thinking ability through academic debate. *Contemporary Argumentation and Debate, 16,* 52–72.

Cooper, H., & Hedges, L. (Eds.). (1994). *The handbook of research synthesis.* New York: Russell Sage Foundation.

*Cross, G. (1971). *The effects of belief systems and the amount of debate experience on the acquisition of critical thinking.* Unpublished doctoral dissertation, University of Utah, Salt Lake City.

*Douglas, J. (1951). *An experimental study of training in problem-solving methods.* Unpublished doctoral dissertation. Northwestern University, Evanston, IL.

[…]

Follert, V., & Colbert, K. (1983, November). *An analysis of the research concerning debate training and critical thinking.* Paper presented at the annual meeting of the Speech Communication Association, Washington, DC. (ERIC Document #ED 238 058)

*Frank, A. (196·4). *An experiment in teaching critical thinking in a high school speech fundamentals course.* Unpublished doctoral dissertation, University of Wisconsin-Madison, Madison.

Garside, C. (1996). Look who's talking: A comparison of lecture and group discussion teaching strategies in developing critical thinking skills. *Communication Education, 45*, 212–227.

*Green, C., & Klug, H. (1990). Teaching critical thinking and writing through debates: An experimental evaluation. *Teaching Sociology, 18*, 462–471.

[…]

Hamilton, M., & Hunter, J. (1990). *META-COR.* Unpublished computer program for conducting meta-analysis on correlations, East Lansing, MI.

Hamilton, M., & Hunter, J. (1991). *ATTEN.* Unpublished computer program for correcting correlations for artifacts. East Lansing, MI.

Hedges, L. & Olkin, I. (1985). *Statistical methods for meta-analysis.* Orlando, FL: Academic Press.

Henning, J. (1946). *An experimental study of the role of presumption and the burden of proof in problem solving.* Unpublished doctoral dissertation, Northwestern University, Evanston, IL.

Hill, B. (1993). The value of competitive debate as a vehicle for promoting development of critical thinking ability. In A. Gill (Ed.), *CEDA yearbook 14* (pp. 1–22). Dubuque, IA: Kendall/Hunt Publishing Company.

[…]

Hunt, S. (1994). The values of forensic participation. In T. Winebrenner (Ed.), *Intercollegiate Forensics* (pp. 1–19). Dubuque, IA: Kendall/Hunt Publishing Co.

Hunter, J., & Schmidt, F. (1990). *Methods of meta-analysis: Correcting for error and bias in research results.* Beverly Hills, CA: Sage.

*Hurst, C. (1962). *Speech and functional intelligence: An experimental study of education implications of a basic speech course.* Unpublished doctoral dissertation, Wayne State University, Detroit, MI.

*Jackson, T. (1961). *The effects of intercollegiate debating on critical thinking.* Unpublished doctoral dissertation. University of Wisconsin-Madison, Madison.

Johnson, A. (1942). *An experimental study in the analysis and measurement of reflective thinking.* Unpublished doctoral dissertation, Northwestern University, Evanston, IL.

*Ness, J. (1967). *The effects of a beginning speech course on critical thinking ability,* Unpublished doctoral dissertation, University of Minnesota, Minneapolis.

Roth, M. (1996, January/February). On the limits of critical thinking. *Tikkun, 33*, 85–86.

Sarett, L., Foster, W., & McBumey, J. (1951). *Speech.* Boston: Houghton Mifflin Company, Inc.

*Smith, D. (1942), *Experiment in teaching critical thinking in a high school speech class.* Unpublished master's thesis, University of Wisconsin-Madison, Madison.

*Tame, E. (1958). *An analytical study of the relationship between ability in critical thinking and ability in contest debate and discussion.* Unpublished doctoral dissertation, University of Denver, CO.

Tracz, S. (1984). *The effect of the violation of the assumption of independence when combining correlation coefficients in a meta-analysis.* Unpublished doctoral dissertation, Southern Illinois University, Carbondale.

Watson, G., & Glaser, E. (1951). *Critical thinking appraisal, Form YM.* New York: Harcourt, Brace, & World, Inc.

*Whalen, S. (1991). Intercollegiate debate as a cocurricular activity: Effects on critical thinking. In D. Parson (Ed.), *Argument in controversy: Proceedings of the 7th SCA/AFA Conference on Argumentation* (pp. 391–397). Annandale, VA: Speech Communication Association.

---

*Mike Allen is an associate professor in the Department of Communication at University of Wisconsin–Milwaukee.

Sandra Berkowitz is an instructor in communication at Minneapolis Community and Technical College.

Steve Hunt is professor in the department of communication at Lewis and Clark College.

Allan Louden is an associate professor in the Department of Speech Communication and director of forensics at Wake Forest University.

Allen, Mike, Sandra Berkowitz, Steve Hunt, and Allan Louden. "A Meta-analysis of the Impact of Forensics and Communication Education on Critical Thinking." *Communication Education* 48 (1999): 18–30. Reprinted by permission of the publisher (Taylor & Francis Group, http://www.informaworld.com).

Academic Debate and Critical Thinking: A Look at the Evidence

*by Robert Greenstreet**

Competitive debate and the study of debating occupied Americans involved in higher education before America became an independent nation (Greenstreet, 1989). However, despite the longevity the activity has enjoyed, little empirical evidence exists to support the notion that debating is of value to participants. While it is true that every now and then a public figure provides an unsolicited testimonial to the value of debating or a survey of former debaters reveals support for the educational value of the activity, this irregular stream of testimonials is neither sufficient to convince the unbelieving nor an acceptable substitute for reliable data that debate moves practitioners toward desired objectives. Such data should be gathered by any group of professionals concerned with assessing the worth of their endeavors. It should certainly be available in a field so thoroughly focused on the uses and abuses of evidence as debate. Unfortunately, while most contemporary debate texts claim study of and/or experience in debate enhances the critical thinking skills of practitioners, little empirical evidence exists in support of that claim.[1] Most of the evidence cited as support for debate in contemporary texts fails to meet the standards for evidence reflected in those very texts. This paper (1) explores the frequently proposed claim of currently available texts in debate and forensics that debating enhances the critical thinking skills of participants, (2) examines the evidence on which such claims are based,[2] and (3) concludes there is little support for the widely espoused belief that study of or participation in debate enhances a student's ability to think critically. This paper does not challenge the claim itself, but it does reject the validity and/or reliability of the empirical evidence cited to support it.

This paper focuses on currently available texts for several reasons. Initially, many of the texts reviewed have been available for some time. Several are revisions and, as such, should represent a distillation and clarification of the author's best work. Further, debate has changed a great deal in the past two decades. The changes have been substantial and have resulted in debate-1992 bearing only marginal resemblance to debate-1965. Intercollegiate forensics directors commonly refer to the "theory explosion" of this time period, an explosion which has tremendously expanded both affirmative and negative options in debating policy propositions. Still more basic is the shift to cross-examination in all forms of debate. In addition, more than 330 colleges and universities annually debate propositions of judgment through the Cross Examination Debate Association, an option only sporadically available prior to this period. Earlier texts would not be expected to consider non-policy proposition debating; for a contemporary text, ignoring such debate would represent a serious oversight.[3] Lincoln-Douglas debate over propositions of judgment has become commonly accepted and nationally endorsed on the high school level during this time. While prior to the period in question a researcher could reasonably assume some similarity of experience shared by all debaters, such an assumption today would be true only on the most rudimentary and fundamental level. Finally, debating today is wholly different due to the tremendous proliferation of summer institutes and pre-season analysis clinics, and the widespread acceptance of and reliance on handbooks, externally prepared briefs and cases, and prepackaged evidence. This paper will not assess the worth of these changes. They are noted as indicators that a contemporary debater experiences a substantially different world from that which prevailed only two decades ago.

[...]

The essence of the claims cited in support of academic debate as an educational activity is that *a strong and causal relationship exists between study of argumentation and debate, participation in competitive debate, and improved critical thinking ability*. Empirical support for this claim demands that the experience of debating and/or the experience of studying argumentation and debate in a formal course be isolated as a causal agent. It further requires debaters demonstrate an increase in critical thinking ability after exposure to debate experience and/or coursework. As we shall see in the next section of this paper, those conditions have not been met by the studies cited.

THE EVIDENCE

The authors who endorse the causal relationship between debate and improved participant critical thinking ability cite one of three sources in support of that claim: Gruner, Huseman and Luck (1971); Huseman, Ware and Gruner (1972); and Colbert and Biggers (1985). Each of these articles attempts to explore the relationship between critical thinking ability and academic debate by measuring the critical thinking abilities of participants in debate or of college students exposed through coursework in argumentation and debate.

Probably the most significant study, at least in terms of the frequency with which it is cited in other works, is the one conducted by Huseman, Ware and Gruner (1972).[5] This study is most frequently cited to support the claim that participation in debate improves students' ability to reason critically (Norton, 1982; Sayer, 1980; Freeley, 1986, 1990). The study compares high school debaters' scores on the Watson-Glaser Critical Thinking Test (now the Watson-Glaser Critical Thinking Appraisal [WGCTA]), and discovers students perceived to be excellent debaters outscore those perceived to be much less effective debaters on this test. The WGCTA offers a reasonable (though apparently not spectacular) level of reliability, as it assesses critical thinking through reading and selection from multiple choice responses (Mitchell, 1985; Woehlke, 1985).[6] The use of the WGCTA for purposes of attempting to link critical thinking with another behavior on the basis of group scores appears entirely consistent with the nature of the instrument (Woehlke, 1985, p. 683). Further, the WGCTA appears to be the best instrument available to assess the complex construct of critical thinking (Woehlke, 1985, p. 685; Berger, 1985, p. 1693).[7] This study supports only the notion that excellent debaters score highly on this test of critical thinking ability. It does not support the claim that coursework or participation in debate causes a difference in the students' critical thinking ability, or to demonstrate any improvement by participants in the study. Huseman, Ware and Gruner (1972) argue a reasonable interpretation of their study to be that high achievers in critical thinking are more likely to be successful in debate (p. 265). McGlone (1974) explains, "There is a rather large number of investigations which demonstrate that debate improves certain cognitive abilities and a large body of criticism of these studies which points out that people who have these abilities are simply attracted to debate" (p. 140). The inability to resolve this chicken/egg question continues to plague research investigating the relationship between debating experience and critical thinking ability. An unmentioned but underlying concern is that improvement in cognitive abilities is the thrust of a student's education. To claim any single activity or course of study achieves that effect by itself is simply inappropriate (if only because that activity or course occurs in a context of similarly targeted activities and courses).

Gruner, Huseman and Luck (1971) studied high school students participating in a summer debate institute. As in the previously discussed study, debaters completed the WGCTA on the first day of the workshop, and after the workshop those who had coached or judged the debaters rated the subjects according to perceived debate ability. Scores on the WGCTA were compared with perceived debating ability. Higher rated debaters performed better on the WGCTA overall and in all five subcategories (Gruner, Huseman and Luck, 1971, pp. 64–65).[8] As with the previous study, it is impossible to demonstrate a causal link between debate and critical thinking or to claim improvements in critical thinking ability. What this study appears to demonstrate is that better critical thinkers are perceived as more effective debaters. McGlone (1974) commented, "It may be that critical thinking is a characteristic already possessed by debaters, rather than an affect [sic] of debate training" (p. 143).

The remaining piece of evidence cited by authors of contemporary debate texts, a report by Colbert and Biggers (1985), is actually a survey of the literature rather than a scientific study. The claims for improved critical thinking ability are referenced to Norton (1982), who the reader will recall bases his conclusions on Huseman, Ware and Gruner (1972). While citation of this article represents an interesting piece of documentary circumlocution, the claim remains subject to evidentiary concerns raised in the previous two paragraphs.

OTHER EVIDENCE

While hard empirical evidence supporting the claim that debate enhances critical thinking abilities is lacking, there appears to be an abundance of other support. Even a casual reader may reasonably conclude the authors cited above endorse the validity of the claim. As these authors include some highly regarded names in both forensics and the field of speech communication, such endorsement might be considered expert (if biased) testimony. There is also considerable solicited and unsolicited testimonial evidence, often (but not always) from surveys.

Both solicited and unsolicited testimony are quoted with abandon in texts and articles purporting to endorse the value of debating. Several sources cite a survey published by Union and Freedom magazine in 1960 (Freeley, 1986; Klopf and Lahman, 1973; Colbert and Biggers, 1985). This survey reports "a very high percentage of persons who have achieved leadership positions have had school or college debate experience, and they regard that experience as a significant factor in their attainment of those positions" (Freeley, 1986, pp. 19–20). Future debate texts and opinion pieces may well replace the now-dated Union and Freedom survey with a survey conducted by Matlon and Keele (1984). This survey is limited to participants in the National Debate Tournament between 1947 and 1980.[9] Of the 703 respondents, nearly forty percent had earned law degrees and more than twenty percent held doctorates. Six hundred and thirty-three of 703 had at least one advanced degree, with 209 holding more than one (Matlon and Keele, 1984, p. 195). Clearly, these respondents continued the level of achievement they attained in intercollegiate debate. The respondents also list a number of advantages to participation in debate, including improved critical thinking, organizational abilities, the ability to think quickly, and improved open-mindedness/objectivity (Matlon and Keele, 1984, p. 197). Respondents to this survey clearly feel they benefited significantly from their intercollegiate policy debating experiences. Hill (1982) provides a refreshing use of survey data, albeit on a limited scale, as he seeks reasons students participate in debate. He surveyed students at three tournaments in the Southeastern U.S. to find out what draws them to debate. Their answers may not be applicable everywhere, but they are enlightening nonetheless. Reasons listed by a large proportion of the respondents include improved analytical skills, opportunity for educational/learning experiences, and improved argumentation skills (Hill, 1982, p. 82). This survey provides an indicator of typical student expectations from debate. It also reflects student perceptions of the outcomes they are experiencing as a result of participation in competitive debate.

Unsought testimonials from former debaters abound. Freeley (1986) quotes John F. Kennedy, who says "I think debating in high school and college a most valuable training for politics, the law, business, or for service on community committees such as the

PTA and the League of Women Voters" (Freeley, 1986, pp. 19–20). McBath (1975) includes a number of ringing testimonials to the value of debate, including this frequently-cited excerpt from Helen M. Wise, former president of the National Education Association:

> No college freshman can project twenty-five years to decide what he needs to learn—subject matter is easily forgotten and in today's world, the knowledge explosion makes constant learning an inevitability. But all adults today need to be able to communicate with clarity, to articulate ideas, to reason, to separate key facts from the barrage of ideas we all are exposed to every day. No single activity can prepare one better than debating—the ability to think on one's feet, to form conclusions rapidly, to answer questions logically and with clarity, to summarize ideas are all processes which forensic activities develop and develop well (p. 82).

McBath (1975) also includes testimonials from individuals who attribute their success to debate experience, as in the following from Richard Markus, past president of the American Trial Lawyer's Association:

> While the skills of oral presentation were necessarily developed during my forensic training, I consider those skills clearly secondary to the skills of organization and analysis which were finely honed during that training. They involved the ability to evaluate a general topic with minute care over an extended interval, followed by the ability to organize a concise persuasive argument on that subject, followed by the ability to apprehend and organize material presented by an adversary in a short time, followed by the ability to respond in a tightly knit and well-supported structure in a similar short time interval (p. 100).

A tremendous variety of former high school debaters attest to the value of debate training on their thinking as well as their communication abilities. Even Lee Iacocca (1984) jumped on the bandwagon in his autobiography. Testimonial and survey support appear consistent that debate experience equates with positive changes in participant thinking behavior.

[...]

Conclusion

What is needed is a study which examines the nature of the well-established link between debate and critical thinking ability. The unresolved chicken/egg question may be researchable through the relatively recent evolution of the summer debate institute. A two-week institute offers an opportunity to pre- and post-test subjects over a short but intense period of time devoted almost exclusively to study of and practice in competitive debate. Such institutes are held throughout the nation at all levels of debating, from novice through champion. It would be possible to pre- and post-test subjects at several institutes throughout the country and generate data which would allow comparison of improvement on Watson-Glaser scores by region, size and nature of workshop curriculum, length of workshop, and level of debate experience. Such data may be expected to address the issue of causality in the relationship between data and critical thinking ability.

Freeley (1986) suggests debate demands students develop proficiency in critical thinking: (1) to create an argument, a student is required to research issues (which requires knowledge of how to use libraries and data banks), organize data, analyze the data, synthesize different kinds of data, and evaluate information with respect to the quality of conclusions it may point to; (2) to form an argument after this process, a student must understand how to reason, must be able to recognize and critique different methods of reasoning, and must have an understanding of the logic of decision making; (3) the successful communication of arguments to audiences reflects another cognitive skill: the ability to communicate complex ideas clearly with words; (4) finally, the argumentative interaction of students in a debate reflects an even more complex cognitive ability—the ability to process the arguments of others quickly and to reformulate or adapt or defend previous positions (pp. 27–28). Is debate better than other ways a student may derive such benefits? Freeley does not claim experience in debate is superior to other methods, only that it is different. His argument is not that debate is the only way, only that it offers a unique set of characteristics which set it apart from other methods of stimulating student growth along the lines indicated above. He says, "debate is distinctive because of its unique dialectical form, providing the opportunity for intellectual clash in the testing of ideas" (Freeley, 1986, p. 27).

Finding fault with the support offered to endorse the claim that debate enhances critical thinking ability does not disprove the claim such evidence is meant to support. The *a priori* assumptions underlying the claims, the hasty conclusions of scientific studies, and the misinterpretation of such studies are merely bad support. Their problems do not support the conclusions drawn, it is true, but neither do they disconfirm those claims. No serious research doubts debate is an activity from which students may derive tremendous benefit. Unfortunately, the debate community has failed to adequately document claims of such benefit. Productive research in the immediate future should be directed toward discovering the immediate effect of participation in debate on the critical thinking ability of the participants. That a relationship between these variables exists is well supported; future research should address the nature of that relationship. Anderson (1974) warns lack of such research may soon become intolerable.

> In an age of educational accountability, the forensics community is and will increasingly be called upon to tell what it seeks to do, how well it accomplishes its goals, and what other effects it has. Surprisingly, there seems little interest in such research at this time (p. 155).

Measuring progress on definable outcomes, discovering specific behaviors and abilities, is the first step toward accountability. When we deal with what is measurable, we deal with what is possible to verify and validate. If the outcomes of debate are as incontrovertibly positive as surveys and testimony suggest, there appears to be no reason to expect empirical research not to find a causal relationship between participation in debate and enhanced critical thinking ability.

NOTES

1. Indeed, most currently available intercollegiate debate textbooks do not bother to cite a source for the claim of improved critical thinking ability. Freeley (1986, 1990), Norton (1982), Sayer (1980) and Pfau, Thomas and Ulrich (1987) are the exceptions.

2. As this paper reports material readily available to other researchers, it relies on the most recent *Index to Journals in Communication Studies Through 1985* (Matlon and Facciola, 1987) as the primary index consulted to locate journal articles in related refereed journals.

3. Several of the authors cited in this paper focus exclusively on nonpolicy debate. Among them are Bartanen & Frank (1991), Church & Wilbanks (1986, 1991), Corcoran (1988) and Pelham & Watt (1989).

[…]

5. The use of this article to claim debate improves critical thinking ability is questionable. The authors appear more concerned with helping coaches identify potentially effective debaters. They conclude, "it would seem to follow, from a pedagogical point of view, that coaches and directors can best improve their charges' debating performance by attempting to develop in them the abilities measured by the tests in this study: logical thinking, reflective thinking and the ability to organize ideas" (Huseman, Ware and Gruner, 1972, p. 265).

6. Some critics claim a large judgmental component on the Watson-Glaser "inference" subtest impunes the value of this standardized test (Helmstadter, 1985, pp. 1693–1694; Berger, 1985, pp. 1692–1693).

7. Helmstadter (1985) would like to see more direct comparison with the Cornell Critical Thinking Test and the A.C.E. Test of Critical Thinking (p. 1694).

8. The lone exception occurred in the "Evaluation of Arguments" sub-category, where third quartile (next to lowest) debaters outscored those in the second quartile (Gruner, Huseman and Luck, 1971, pp. 64–65).

9. Matlon and Keele (1984) offer two justifications for such a restriction: (1) it was possible to locate these participants, and (2) the authors presume these subjects had devoted a considerable "proportion of their academic careers to debate" (p. 194).

[…]

REFERENCES

Anderson, K.E. (1974). A critical review of the behavioral research in argumentation and forensics. *Journal of the American Forensic Association*. 10(3), 147–155.

Bartanen, M.D., and Frank, D.A. (1991). *Debating values*. Scottsdale, AZ: Gorsuch Scarisbrick.

Berger, A. (1985). Review of the Watson-Glaser Critical Thinking Appraisal. In J.V. Mitchell, Jr. (Ed.), *The ninth mental measurements yearbook.* Vol. 2 (pp. 1692–1693), Lincoln, NE: The Buros Institute of Mental Measurements.

Church, R.T. and Wilbanks, C. (1986). *Values and policies in controversy: An introduction to argumentation and debate.* Scottsdale, AZ: Gorsuch Scarisbrick.

Colbert, K. and Biggers, T. (1985). Why should we support debate? *Journal of the American Forensic Association.* 21(4), 237–240.

Corcoran, J. (1988). *An introduction to non-policy debating.* Dubuque, IA: Kendall/ Hunt.

[…]

Freeley, A.J. (1986). *Argumentation and debate: Critical thinking for reasoned decision making* (6th ed.). Belmont, CA: Wadsworth.

Freeley, A.J. (1990). *Argumentation and debate: Critical thinking for reasoned decision making* (7th ed.). Belmont, CA: Wadsworth.

[…]

Greenstreet, Robert W. (1989). Student interest and higher education: lessons from the literary societies. *Journal of the Oklahoma Speech Theatre Communication Association.* Fall, 1989, 17–30.

Gruner, C.R., Huseman, R.C. and Luck, J.I. (1971). Debating ability, critical thinking ability and authoritarianism. *Speaker and Gavel.* March, 1971, 63–65.

Helmstadter, G.C. (1985). Review of the Watson-Glaser Critical Thinking Appraisal. In J.V. Mitchell, Jr. (Ed.). *The ninth mental measurements yearbook.* Vol. 2 (pp. 1693–1694), Lincoln, NE: The Buros Institute of Mental Measurements.

Hill, B. (1982). Intercollegiate debate: Why do students bother? *The Southern Speech Communication Journal.* 48(1), 77–88.

Huseman, R., Ware, G. and Gruner, C. (1972). Critical thinking, reflective thinking and the ability to organize ideas: A multi-variate approach. *Journal of the American Forensic Association.* 9(4), 261–265.

Iacocca, L. (1984). *Iacocca: An autobiography.* New York, NY: Bantam Books.

Klopf, D.W., & Lahman, C.P. (1973). *Coaching and directing forensics.* USA; National Textbook Co.

Matlon, R.J. and Facciola, P.C. (Eds.) (1987). *Index to journals in communication studies through 1985.* Annandale, VA: Speech Communication Association.

Matlon, R.J., & Keele, L.M. (1984). A survey of participants in the national debate tournament 1947–1980, *American Forensics Association Journal,* 20, 194–205.

McBath, J.E. (Ed.)(1975). *Forensics as communication: The argumentative perspective.* Skokie, IL: National Textbook.

McGlone, E.L. (1974). The behavioral effects of forensics participation. *Journal of the American Forensic Association.* 10(3), 140–146.

Mitchell, J.V. Jr. (Ed.)(1985). *The ninth mental measurements yearbook.* Lincoln, NE: The Buros Institute of Mental Measurements.

Norton, L.E. (1982). Nature and benefits of academic debate. In Keefe, C, Harte, T.B. and Norton, L.E. (Eds.) *Introduction to debate* (pp. 24–40). New York: Macmillan.

[…]

Pelham, W.D. and Watt, W. (1989). "Profile of academic debate." In Wood, S. and Midgley, J. (Eds.). *Prima facie: A guide to value debate* (pp. 3–15). Dubuque, IA: Kendall/Hunt.

Pfau, M., Thomas, D.A. and Ulrich, W. (1987). *Debate and argument: A systems approach to advocacy.* Glenview, IL: Scott, Foresman.

[…]

Sayer, J.E. (1980). *Argumentation and debate: Principles and applications.* Sherman Oaks, CA: Alfred.

[…]

Watt, S. and Pelham, W.D. (1986). Profile of academic debate. In S. Wood and J. Midgley (Eds.), *Prima facie: A guide to value debate* (pp. 3–14). Dubuque, IA: Kendall/Hunt.

Woehlke, PL. (1985). Watson-Glaser Critical Thinking Appraisal. In DJ. Keyser and R.C. Sweetland (Eds.), *Test critiques.* Vol. III (pp. 682–685), Kansas City, MO: Test Corporation of America.

[…]

---

*Robert Greenstreet is professor of communications studies and director of forensics at East Central University

Greenstreet, Robert. "Academic Debate and Critical Thinking: A Look at the Evidence." *National Forensic Journal* 11 (1993): 13–28, http://cas.bethel.edu/dept/comm/nfa/journal/vol11no1-2.pdf.

Used by Permission.

The Effects of Debate Participation on Argumentativeness and Verbal Aggression

by Kent R. Colbert*

[...]

Competitive academic forensics offers a unique educational experience. Besides team debate, forensic tournaments often offer Lincoln-Douglas debate; oratory; dramatic, oral, duo, and humorous interpretation; and extemporaneous, persuasive, and impromptu speaking. Some even have events in negotiations, listening, and thematic reading. Few educational opportunities like forensics exist where teachers can mentor students on an individual basis for several years (Ziegelmueller, 1968). As a result, debate and public speaking competitions motivate students to conduct extensive research, develop critical thinking abilities, and refine communication skills (Colbert & Biggers, 1986).

In addition to training superior communicators and providing excellent preprofessional experience (Colbert & Biggers, 1986), 50 years of research correlates debate training with the enhancement of critical thinking skills (Beckman, 1957; Brembeck, 1949; Colbert, 1987; Cross, 1971; Howell, 1943; Jackson, 1961; Williams, 1951). A neglected area of pedagogy research, however, involves the effects that forensic tournament training could have on student traits. Although early research reported positive effects for those participating in debate (King & Phifer, 1968; Tucker, Koehler, & Mlady, 1967), Simons (1990) observed that, "research into the area of debater's personality has ceased during the past decade. Yet circumstances have arisen which seem to justify a further look into the area" (p. 4). Such circumstances include the growing popularity of individual speaking events (IE); a shift from problem-solution (policy paradigms) to non-policy approaches (value paradigms); faster than usual rates of delivery by debaters (Colbert, 1991); and criticism regarding the possible overemphasis on competition (Frank, 1991; Horn & Underberg, 1991). Inch (1991) suggested. "Forensics is in a period of transition. While the number of programs is stable, institutions have begun to make sweeping decisions about the long term direction and philosophy of programs" (pp. 49–50).

At least three reasons justify additional examination into the effects of teaching forensics on the participants. First, it is important that forensic educators identify and emphasize activities that are most beneficial to their students. Even in ideal situations, students typically are limited to a few co-curricular activities. [. . .]

Second, a major shift from traditional policy style debating to non-policy (value) debating occurred in the 1970s. Corcoran (1988) explained, "Over the past two decades, non-policy debate has overtaken policy debate as the predominant intercollegiate activity. . . . CEDA has risen to a current membership level of approximately 300 universities and colleges" (p. v). Many universities no longer offer policy debating (NDT) and many participate in non-policy (CEDA) debate (Cardot, 1991). At the high school level, a dramatic increase in Lincoln-Douglas (LD) debate (non-policy) also has occurred, while NFL (policy) participation has declined (Cox, 1991). The effects of the shift from policy paradigms, largely adapted from Dewey's (1910) problem-solving principles to more abstract models focusing on value conflicts have not been investigated empirically. Much of the research associating debate training with increased critical thinking scores was reported before the emergence of non-policy debate formats. A recent study of debate training effects suggested that NDT (policy) debaters scored higher than CEDA (non-policy) debaters on the Watson-Glaser Critical Thinking Appraisal instrument (Colbert, 1987). While not conclusive, this finding raises concern about the effects of abandoning problem-solving paradigms (policy) without empirical support for this decision.

Third, many observers complain that the competitive aspects of forensic activities dominate educational goals, and that tournament debating often tolerates and even rewards hostile or verbally aggressive behavior. For example, Steinfatt (1990) reported, "a good deal of hostility was sometimes generalized, sometimes aimed specifically at an opponent, and sometimes aimed at the judge" in debates that he observed (p. 67). Steinfatt is not alone in asserting that some debaters exhibit verbal behavior interpreted as aggressive. [...] Frank (1991) wrote, "the virtual disappearance of civility in modern debate can be traced to the belief that debate not only shares some characteristics of a game, but that debate is a game" (p. 6). [...] Despite these observations, little empirical research measuring the effects of various types of contemporary debate participation on argumentativeness (ARG) and verbal aggression (VA) has been reported.

Given the research associating debate training with critical thinking development, it is possible this activity also could develop argumentation skills. For example, important critical thinking skills developed by debating include the ability to define a problem, select pertinent information for the solution of a problem, recognize stated and unstated assumptions, formulate and select relevant and promising hypotheses, and draw valid conclusions and judge the validity of inferences (Watson & Glaser, 1980).

This study focused on the effects of debate participation on two specific traits related to arguing—argumentativeness and verbal aggression. Infante and Rancer (1982) explained:

> the locus of attack may be used for distinguishing argument from verbal aggression.... [A]rgument involves presenting and defending positions on controversial issues while attacking the position taken by others on the issues. Verbal aggression... denotes attacking the self-concept of another person instead of, or in addition to, the person's position on a topic of communication. (p. 62)

VA includes character attacks, competence attacks, insults, maledictions, teasing, ridicule, profanity, threats, background attacks, physical appearance attacks, and nonverbal indicators (Infante, 1987; Infante & Wigley, 1986). Research suggest VA precedes a range of effects including damage to self-concepts (Infante, 1988), physical violence in families (Gelles, 1974), and criminal violence (Toch, 1969).

Typically, the use of VA is indicative of (a) psychopathology, (b) disdain for others, (c) social learning, and (d) argumentative skill deficiency (Infante, 1988). Given the view that forensic tournaments are co-curricular educational experiences, it is reasonable to expect that such training, especially debate, reduces argument skill deficiency. Infante (1988) reasoned:

> If the parties in an argument are skillful arguers, VA is less likely. Skillful arguers will rarely run out of things to say when defending and attacking positions. In fact, they typically think of so many things to say that they do not have enough time to reach their final thought on the controversial issue. Verbal aggression is also less likely because skillful arguers have a clear conception of the difference between genuine argument and verbal aggression. (p. 27)

Infante and others suggest social learning and argumentative skill deficiency are two major causes of verbal aggression.

An "argumentative approach involves informative and persuasive aspects. In addition, each person attacks the other's position on the issue in order to establish the superiority of one's position" (Infante, 1988, pp. 5–6). It is, therefore, reasonable to expect forensic participation to enhance individual ARG. Although Infante (1982) found that those with the most high school training in argumentation were the most argumentative, he reasoned it is possible that "students who are initially high in argumentativeness [elect] the most high school training in argumentation" (p. 146). He concluded, "Research at the high school level is needed to determine what the speech communication curriculum and extracurricular activities do to the student's level of argumentativeness" (p. 146). The present study attempted to replicate Infante's study and extend his findings regarding argumentativeness and debating. In addition, this study investigated the effects of debate on VA.

It is important to establish the effects of forensic training on participants, especially if these activities diminish positive traits or reinforce negative traits. If some forensic training increases VA or reduces ARG, serious rethinking of these approaches may be justified on those grounds. Because of the lack of research supporting specific relationships between forensic competition and ARG and VA, two non-directional hypotheses were tested:

H_1: Students who participate in competitive debate differ in their level of VA from students who have not yet participated in debate.

H_2: Students who participate in competitive debate differ in their level of ARG from students who have not yet participated in debate.

Method

Respondents
Respondents were 332 high school students participating at a large Western forensic tournament at the beginning of the 1990 academic year. Forty-four respondents failed to complete the ARG or VA questionnaire and were excluded from the sample. Some IE participants who did not complete the instrument typically wrote "not a debater," and returned the questionnaire. They seemed to perceive the instruments as measuring constructs unrelated to them and relevant to argumentation only. Seventeen additional respondents were excluded because of their clearly systematic methods of marking question items.

The final sample consisted of 158 males, 113 females, and 7 who did not indicate their sex, ranging in age from 13 to 18 (18 = 7%; 17 = 32%; 16 = 28%; 15 = 22%; 14 = 8%; and 13 = 2%). The birthplaces of the respondents represented over 25 states and 6 countries. Both private and public schools were included in the study. Overall, the experienced debaters and those beginning their debate experience appeared to represent a wide cross-section of ethnic, cultural, and racial diversity.

[...]

Instruments

Each student completed Infante and Rancer's (1982) Argumentative Scale and Infante and Wigley's (1986) Verbal Aggression Scale. Each scale consists of 10 approach items and 10 avoidance items. Examples of questions from the ARG questionnaire include. "I enjoy avoiding arguments" and "Arguing creates more problems for me than it solves." Examples of questions from the VA questionnaire include, "When I attack a person's idea, I try not to damage their self-concepts" and "I like poking fun at people who do things which are very stupid in order to stimulate their intelligence." The 20 statements on each scale are rated on a five-point scale ranging from "almost never true" to "almost always true."

[...]

Procedure

Data were collected at the beginning of the academic year so the forensic students without debate experience could be contrasted with those having prior experience. The ARG and VA instruments were given to judges before the fifth and sixth rounds of the tournament. The judges distributed the instruments, answered questions, and collected and returned the completed instruments after the round (with their ballots). The process of filling out questionnaires at forensic tournaments is common and there was no reason to believe any of the participants felt threatened.

Results

Tests of Hypotheses

First, do those with participation experience in competitive debate (value and/or policy) differ in their level of VA from those who have not yet participated? The mean level of VA for the group of experienced debaters was statistically significantly less than the group without debate experience, $t(270) = 2.31$, $p < .05$. Table 1 presents the ns, means, standard deviations, t-test results, and, for significant results, their associated squared point-biserial correlations (r_{pb}) for the VA instrument. The squared correlations provide an indication of the variance accounted for by the t-test, that is, the *importance* (as opposed to the statistical significance) of the results (Cohen, 1977).

The n in the experienced debate category represents students with a year or more of debate experience, while the no experience category represents those with no value or policy debate experience.

TABLE 1: MEANS, STANDARD DEVIATIONS, t-SCORES, AND POINT BISERIAL CORRELATIONS FOR VERBAL AGGRESSION SCORES

	N	M	SD	t	r
Debate					
No experience	130	51.83	12.38	2.31*	.02
Experienced	141	48.55	11.02		
Policy Debate					
No experience	191	49.88	12.67	−.35	
Experienced	79	50.43	9.77		
Value Debate					
No experience	216	51.09	11.56	2.74**	.03
Experienced	54	46.13	12.42		
Gender					
Male	158	52.20	11.38	3.43**	.04
Female	113	47.28	11.99		

*$p < .05$.
**$p < .001$.

TABLE 2: MEANS, STANDARD DEVIATIONS, *t*-SCORES, AND POINT BISERIAL CORRELATIONS FOR ARGUMENTATIVENESS SCORES

	N	M	SD	t	r
Debate					
No experience	131	75.05	12.74	-2.45^*	.02
Experienced	141	78.61	11.22		
Policy Debate					
No experience	191	75.72	12.31	-2.49^*	.02
Experienced	79	79.70	11.10		
Value Debate					
No experience	216	76.60	12.20	$-.79$	
Experienced	54	78.04	10.97		
Gender					
Male	158	78.16	12.04	-1.99^*	.01
Female	113	75.21	11.98		

$^*p < .05.$

$^{**}p < .001.$

The *n* in the policy experience category represents students with a year or more of policy debate experience, while the no experience category represents those with value debate experience, no debate experience, or only IE experience. The *n* in the value debate category represents students with a year or more of value debate experience, and the no experience category represents students with no policy debate experience, no debate experience, or only IE experience.

The second hypothesis predicted that students with competitive experience in academic debate differ in their level of ARG from forensic students without debate experience. Those without debate experience scored statistically significantly lower than the experienced debate group, $t(279) = -2.45$, $p < .05$. Table 2 presents the results. A correlation between debate experience and ARG was $r = .17$, $p < .01$.

Post-hoc Tests

Post-hoc data analysis indicated that the experienced value debaters scored significantly lower than forensic students without value debate experience on the VA scale, $t(268) = 2.74, p < .05$. The correlation between value debate experience and VA was $r = -.17, p < .01$.

Those without policy experience scored significantly lower than experienced policy debaters on the ARG scale, $t(268) = -2.49, p < .05$. The correlation between policy debate experience and ARG was $r = .15, p < .05$.

[...]

DISCUSSION

Findings of this study suggest some noteworthy conclusions. First, they are consistent with Infante's (1982) work reporting a positive correlation between ARG and high school debating experience. Moreover, this study better accounts for the self-selection feature that may have affected Infante's study. Because all respondents had chosen to compete in forensics, the difference was probably not a function of their attraction to the activity. Comparing forensic students (often high on ARG and VA) with non-forensic students (often lower than forensic students on ARG and VA) may reflect the preexisting differences in the traits of the groups being compared. By comparing groups with similar predispositions, it was possible to isolate the specific effects attributed to forensic training.

Second, this study extends Infante's (1982) research by investigating the effects of specific types of forensic experience. Findings suggest that specific methods of debate training may be more effective at reducing VA and enhancing ARG; specifically, policy debate training may enhance ARG trait development, a constructive personality characteristic, without affecting VA, and value debate training may reduce VA, a typically destructive trait, without affecting ARG development. This discovery has implications for those who set the educational agenda of each activity. Those subscribing to a rhetorical stylistic approach (value debate) may have more effect on reducing student VA. Educators emphasizing critical thinking skills (policy debate) may enhance student ARG traits. Obviously, not all forensic directors or programs fall neatly into "value" or "policy" camps; indeed, exposure to both styles of debating may yield optimal results with regards to ARG and VA.

Findings of this investigation dispute anecdotal claims that participation in tournament debating is counterproductive, that is, that it negatively impacts ARG and VA. Additional research should determine the optimal levels of policy and value debate experience that are most effective at reducing VA and enhancing ARG.

Despite the small sample of students with IE and no debate experience, results indicated these students scored significantly lower on ARG than every other comparison group, including those with no prior forensic experience. This finding suggests that forensic directors who eliminate debate in favor of IE are not justified when increased ARG is the objective. If forensic educators adopt the goal of increasing ARG, findings suggest that debate training may be a more effective strategy than IE. Given these results, future research needs to document the benefits of IE participation.

[...]

The present study provides an optimistic perspective of tournament debate as an academic activity. Findings suggest that policy debating increases ARG and value debating reduces VA. Future research should attempt to replicate these findings to provide educators the information needed to maximize the potential of the forensics experience. This study, like several before it, suggests that forensic training can produce positive results. Hopefully, the critics will pause long enough to permit researchers an opportunity to document fully the effects of forensics.

REFERENCES

Beckman, V. (1957). *An investigation of the contributions to critical thinking made by courses in argumentation and discussion in selected colleges.* Unpublished doctoral dissertation, University of Minnesota, Minneapolis, MN.

Brembeck, W. (1949). The effects of a course in argumentation on critical thinking ability. *Speech Monographs, 16,* 172–189.

[…]

Cohen, J. (1977). *Statistical power for the behavioral sciences* (rev. ed.). New York: Academic Press.

Colbert, K. R. (1987). The effects of CEDA and NDT debate on critical thinking. *Journal of the American Forensics Association, 23,* 194–201.

Colbert, K. R. (1991). A study of CEDA and NDT speaking rates. *CEDA Yearbook, 12,* 88–94.

Colbert, K. R., & Biggers, T. (1986). Why should we support debate? *Journal of the American Forensics Association, 21,* 237–240.

Corcoran, J. (1988). *Non-policy debating.* Dubuque, IA: Kendall Hunt.

Cox, E. S. (1991). Assessing and re-positioning the educational function of collegiate debate. In S. Roden (Ed.), *Proceedings of the 1991 Pi Kappa Delta Professional Development Conference* (pp. 139–159). Eatontown, NJ: University of Central Arkansas Professional Development.

Cross, G. (1971). *The effects of belief systems and the amount of debate experience on the acquisition of critical thinking.* Unpublished doctoral dissertation, University of Utah, Salt Lake City, UT.

[…]

Frank, D. A. (1991, August). *Debate as rhetorical scholarship: Changing delivery practices in CEDA.* Paper presented at the CEDA Assessment Conference, St. Paul, MN.

Gelles, R. J. (1974). *The violent home.* Beverly Hills, CA: Sage.

Horn, G., & Underberg, L. (1991, August). *Educational debate: An unfulfilled promise?* Paper presented at the CEDA Assessment Conference, St. Paul, MN.

Howell, W. (1943). The effects of high school debating on critical thinking. *Speech Monographs, 10,* 96–103.

Inch, E. S. (1991). Forensics, ethics, and the need for vision. In S. Roden (Ed.), *Proceedings of the 1991 Pi Kappa Delta Professional Development Conference* (pp. 47–57). Eatontown. NJ: University of Central Arkansas Professional Development.

Infante, D. A. (1982). The argumentative student in the speech communication classroom: An investigation and implications. *Communication Education, 31,* 141–148.

Infante, D. A. (1987). Aggressiveness. In J. C. McCroskey & J. A. Daly (Eds.), *Personality and interpersonal communication* (pp. 157–192). Newbury Park, CA: Sage.

Infante. D. A. (1988). *Arguing constructively.* Prospect Heights, IL: Waveland Press.

[…]

Infante, D. A., & Rancer, A. S. (1982). A conceptualization and measure of argumentativeness. *Journal of Personality Assessment, 46,* 72–80.

Infante, D. A., & Wigley, C. J. (1986). Verbal aggressiveness: An interpersonal model and measure. *Communication Monographs, 53,* 61–69.

Jackson, T. (1961). The effects of intercollegiate debating on critical thinking. *Dissertation Abstracts International, 21,* 3556.

King, T. R., & Phifer, G. (1968). The college debater as seen by himself and his peers. *Journal of the American Forensics Association, 5,* 48–52.

[…]

Simons, B. K. (1990, November). *What makes us tick?: An exploratory analysis of the personality characteristics of the CEDA debater.* Paper presented at the meeting of the Speech Communication Association, Chicago.

Steinfatt, T. M. (1990). College debate a quarter century later. *CEDA Yearbook, 11,* 66–71.

Toch, H. (1969). *Violent men.* Chicago: Aldine.

Tucker, R. K., Koehler, J. W., & Mlady, L. (1967). The image of the college debater. *Journal of the American Forensic Association, 4,* 1–9.

Watson, G., & Glaser, E. (1980). *Critical thinking appraisal manual for forms A and B.* New York: Harcourt Brace Jovanovich.

Williams. D. (1951). *The effects of training in college debating on critical thinking ability.* Unpublished master's thesis. Purdue University, Lafayette, IN.

Ziegelmueller, G. (1968). The role of the coach. In D. F. Faules & R. D. Rieke (Eds.), *Directing forensics: Contest and debate speaking.* (pp. 79–94). Scranton, PA: International Press.

---

*Kent R. Colbert is an assistant professor of speech communication and director of forensics at East Tennessee State University.

Colbert, Kent R. "The Effects of Debate Participation on Argumentativeness and Verbal Aggression." *Communication Education* 42 (1993): 206–214. Reprinted by permission of the publisher (Taylor & Francis Group, http://www.informaworld.com).

Argumentativeness, Verbal Aggressiveness, and Relational Satisfaction in the Parliamentary Debate Dyad

*by Crystal Lane Swift and Christina Vourvoulias**

[...]

Forensics competition is a rhetorical institution in which students are trained to argue effectively. School participation in intercollegiate parliamentary debate has been on the rapid rise for some time now (Bingle, 1978; Crossman, 1996), and schools are continuously looking to expand their parliamentary debate programs (Dittus, 1998; Kuster, Olson & Loging, 2001). One of the primary goals of communication education is to equip students with the ability to communicate and to argue effectively (Dannels, 2001). Research shows that one of the most positive traits of an effective communicator is argumentativeness, whereas one of the most negative traits is verbal aggressiveness (Anderson & Martin, 1999; Beatty, Zelley, Dobos, & Rudd, 1994; Infante, Riddle Horvath, & Tumlin 1992; & Martin & Anderson, 1997). For instance, communication research has indicated a link between high levels of verbal aggressiveness and low levels of relational satisfaction (Anderson & Martin, 1999). Specifically, Teven, Martin, and Neupauer (1998) concluded that verbal aggressiveness makes a significant, detrimental impact on sibling relationships and how siblings communicate. In this study, we are interested in discovering the associations between argumentativeness, verbal aggressiveness and relational satisfaction in parliamentary debaters.

Distinctions between Argumentativeness and Verbal Aggressiveness

It is important to understand how argumentativeness and verbal aggressiveness affect debaters. We can start by making the distinction between these two concepts that people tend to mistakenly conflate. Martin & Anderson (1997) explained that verbal aggressiveness is destructive, whereas argumentativeness is constructive. Moreover, "verbally aggressive individuals attack the self concepts of others, attempting to cause psychological pain" (Infante and Wigley, 1986 as cited in Daly, 2002, p. 150). This idea is supported by Infante, Trebing, Shepherd, & Seeds (1984) when they explained that "Infante and Rancer . . . conceptualized argumentativeness as a personality trait which predisposes an individual to recognize controversial issues, to advocate positions on them, and to refute other positions. In contrast, in their model, verbal aggressiveness is a personality trait which leads one to attack the self-concept of others instead of, or in addition to, refuting their positions on issues" (p. 68). Daly (2002) explained that a vast amount of scholarship has been conducted on argumentativeness and verbal aggressiveness. Since verbal aggressiveness has been determined to be such an undesirable trait, it is imperative to explore some of the reasons highly verbally aggressive people behave in this manner.

Verbal Aggressiveness

The reasons that verbally aggressive people give for being verbally aggressive seem to put the blame on others for their behavior. While these can be valid reasons, they are not always the root of verbal aggressiveness. "Reasons people give for being verbally aggressive include reciprocity and socialization-being taught to be verbally aggressive" (Infante, et al., 1992; Martin, Anderson, & Horvath, 1996, as cited in Martin & Anderson, 1997, p. 303). The most commonly given reasons by people who are high in trait verbal aggressiveness were wanting to appear tough, being in rational discussions that degenerate into verbal fights, wanting to be mean to the message receiver and wanting to express disdain for the message receiver (Infante, et al., 1992).

People who are verbally aggressive tend to blame society or say that they were countering the attack of someone else. Alternatively, Infante (1989) explained that the four feasible reasons for verbal aggressiveness—psychopathology, disdain, social learning, and argumentative skill deficiency—may or may not be inherently linked. Looking at these possible reasons can help us better understand the verbal aggressiveness that is encountered in debaters' relationships with their partners.

Infante (1987) helped to categorize verbal aggressiveness by explaining that it comes about as a part of hostility, which is an intrinsic aspect of personality. Infante's categorization is supported by the findings of McCroskey, Heisel, & Richmond (2001), who assert that both neurotic introverts and psychotics tend to report high levels of verbal aggressiveness. It has been explained that "there are numerous types of verbally aggressive messages . . . : character attacks, competence attacks, insults, maledictions, teasing, ridicule, profanity, and nonverbal emblems" (Infante & Wigley, 1986, p. 61). Additionally, Infante et al. (1992) explained that:

> High verbal aggressives can be distinguished: (1) by their more frequent use of competent attacks, teasing, swearing, and nonverbal emblems; (2) by their beliefs in the less hurtful nature of competence attacks, physical appearance attacks, and threats; (3) by their reasons for being verbally aggressive which include wanting to appear tough, wanting to be mean to the message target, having disdain for the receiver, and being unable to keep a rational discussion from degenerating into a verbal fight (p. 125).

Generally, scholars agree that verbal aggressiveness is a negative trait. There is a vast body of literature about this trait (e.g., Infante et al., 1992; Anderson & Martin, 1999; and Beatty, Zelley, Dobos,

& Rudd, 1994). For instance, Edwards, Bello, Brandau-Brown, and Hollems (2001) found that when presented with ambiguous messages, people high in verbal aggressiveness are more likely to perceive them as negative messages, and are more likely to have difficulty communicating. The authors also noted that it is possible that people high in verbal aggressiveness may not perceive difficulty in communication. They may achieve their communicative goals while it is the partner in the interaction who feels the difficulty. Levels of verbal aggressiveness strongly influence interpersonal interaction.

Verbal aggressiveness and argumentativeness differ in a number of ways. For example, Ifert and Bearden (1998) concluded that verbally aggressive individuals reported a greater number of non-evidentiary appeals than evidentiary appeals, meaning that they were more likely to make a statement or a claim and not back it up with any support. They also concluded that argumentative individuals were more likely to use evidentiary appeals, meaning that they were more likely to back up a claim they made with some type of support.

[...]

ARGUMENTATIVENESS

Whereas verbal aggressiveness is considered to be destructive, argumentativeness is considered to be constructive. Erwin (1989) developed a typology of argumentativeness. There were two types that were developed; avoiders and arguers. Avoiders were people who disliked confrontation and arguers were people who liked argumentativeness and disliked verbal aggressiveness. Avoiders tested low on the Argumentativeness Scale and disliked using or being subjected to argumentativeness or verbal aggressiveness. Arguers agreed with argumentative behavior and disagreed with or disliked verbally aggressive behavior.

Furthermore, Schullery and Schullery (2003) suggested that the older a person is, the less argumentative, and the more educated one is, the more argumentative. In men, the decrease in argumentativeness began in the mid-twenties and stabilized near forty-five. For women, argumentativeness slowly decreased around thirty and the decrease accelerated into the fifties. The effect of education is more significant in men than in women, and there is very little effect from age or education on high-argumentatives.

In terms of flexibility, Neer (1994) indicated that argumentative flexibility, which is the willingness to participate in an argument, did not correlate with intention to select argumentative responses. Females and high trait arguers both tended to have strong intentions to respond argumentatively. High flexibility arguers tended to have stronger intentions to avoid aggressive responses than high trait arguers and males had strong intentions to choose aggressive responses. High trait arguers, female arguers and high flexibility arguers all avoided punishing responses. Males, high trait arguers and high flexibility arguers all tended to avoid rewarding responses. High trait arguers and high flexibility arguers seemed to have a bit stronger tendency than others to continue an argument, and high flexibility arguers seemed to have a bit more tendency than others to discontinue an argument over relational conflict. Finally, high flexibility arguers had a stronger desire to accept a strategy than others. Overall, flexibility in argument seemed to be a positive trait.

Verbal Aggressiveness and Argumentativeness in the Communication Classroom

The conceptual distinction between verbal aggressiveness and argumentativeness is important to understand. These concepts have been studied frequently, generally and less frequently in relation to students of communication. Friedley (1972) used the Watson-Glaser scale to survey students in a speech 210 course. The Watson-Glaser scale measures inference, recognition of assumptions, deduction, interpretation and evaluation of arguments. Parliamentary debate is primarily concerned with critical thinking skills because of the lack of research used, as opposed to traditional forms of academic debate (Crossman, 1996; Galizio & Chuen, 1995; Kuster, 2002; O'Niell, 1986; Puchot, 2002; Stris, 1996; Theodore, Sheckels, & Warfield, 1990; Williams, & Guajardo, 1998).

Additionally, Infante (1982) conducted a study on traits of the communication student. The variable that most distinctly differentiated between high and low argumentativeness was time of argument training in high school. Students with higher levels of argumentativeness were born earlier in their family birth order and had higher GPAs. Males tended to be more argumentative than females. Moreover, Myers and Knox (2000) studied perceived instructor argumentativeness and verbal aggressiveness and found that argumentativeness did seem to increase students' satisfaction with their course as well as the instructor. Additionally, perceived instructor verbal aggressiveness tended to decrease students' satisfaction with their course as well as the instructor.

[...]

RATIONALE

The literature leads us to conclude that debaters will have high levels of argumentativeness because of their training. Argumentation training also seems to decrease verbal aggressiveness. We would expect that debaters would score low in verbal aggressiveness. The literature also supports a strong connection between high levels of verbal aggressiveness and low levels of relational satisfaction. This link leads us to expect that if there are high levels of verbal aggressiveness reported within the dyad, the level of reported relational satisfaction will be low. While there have been studies on debaters versus the general population, there is no current research on debaters perceptions of each other or debaters versus other debaters. Within debate, students frequently encounter argumentativeness and verbal aggressiveness. These concepts, along with relational satisfaction, are well established. Hence, we pose the following hypotheses and research questions:

Hypotheses and Research Questions

H1: Debate dyads with similar levels of self-report and perceived partner argumentativeness and verbal aggressiveness will have higher levels of relational satisfaction than dyads with incongruent levels of self-report and perceived partner argumentativeness and verbal aggressiveness.

H2: Debate dyads that do not fit the aforementioned hypothesis will have low relational satisfaction if they have high levels of verbal aggressiveness and low levels of argumentativeness.

RQ1: Will biological sex have an impact on argumentativeness, verbal aggressiveness and relational satisfaction in debate dyads?

Methods

Variables, Conceptual, and Operational Definitions

In our study, we measured debate partner dyads' perceptions of argumentativeness, verbal aggressiveness, and relational satisfaction. We employed an adapted version of the Argumentativeness Scale, the Verbal Aggressiveness Scale, and the Interpersonal Solidarity Scale. In our research, we collected demographic data regarding biological sex, age, and forensics experience of both partners. We asked the participant about his or her own length of time in intercollegiate forensics competition and which individual events he or she had competed in or currently competes in. We also asked the participant to report the aforementioned demographics about his or her partner. Regarding the two debaters together, we asked the participant to report the type of institution the debate team competes for (community college or four-year college or university), which national forensics organization(s) their institution is associated with, whether the partners chose to be partners or were assigned to be partners, how long the partners competed as a team together, which format of debate the partners compete in primarily, and any other format of partner debate the partners compete in together.

The three concepts we measured in our research were argumentativeness, verbal aggressiveness, and relational satisfaction. We conceptually define "argumentativeness as a personality trait that predisposes an individual to recognize controversial issues, to advocate positions on them, and to refute other positions" (Infante, Trebing, Shepherd, & Seeds, 1984, p. 68). Verbal aggressiveness is conceptually defined as "an exchange of messages between two people where at least one person in the dyad attacks the self-concept of the other person in order to hurt the person psychologically" (Infante & Wigley, 1986, p. 67). Interpersonal satisfaction is being measured by the level of solidarity reported in the dyad. We have conceptually defined interpersonal solidarity according to Wheeless (1978) as "a global measure of closeness that captures several affective dimensions particularly relevant to friendship. . . . solidarity provides an appropriate and 'meaningful criterion by which to assess the importance of interpersonal communication phenomena in interpersonal relationships'" (p. 154, as cited in Cupach & Messman, 1999, p. 14). Operationally, we adapted Infante & Rancer's (1982) Argumentativeness Scale, Infante & Wigley's (1986) Verbal Aggressiveness Scale and Wheeless's (1978) Interpersonal Solidarity Scale.

Measurement Instrument Adaptation
We began the process with three distinct scales: the Argumentativeness Scale (Infante & Rancer, 1982), the Verbal Aggressiveness Scale (Infante & Wigley, 1986), and the Interpersonal Solidarity Scale (Wheeless, 1978). For each scale we adapted, the original scale was 20 questions in length, about half of which were reverse-coded.

We assessed the questions and chose what we felt were the five best straight forward prompts and the five best reverse-coded prompts from each scale. We then altered the language of the prompts so that they were congruent in weight and made the linguistic constructs of the relational scale debate-specific. Finally, we repeated the modified argumentativeness and verbal aggressiveness scales so that the prompts would ask for the participant's perception of their partner. We decided to use abbreviated versions of the aforementioned scales to avoid participant exhaustion and to assure that we were asking equally weighted questions for each variable.

[...]

RESULTS

Respondents

We surveyed 89 intercollegiate parliamentary debate competitors. There were 48 males and 41 females, ages 17–36 with a mean age of 19.94 years. There were 20 freshman, 31 sophomores, 13 juniors, and 25 seniors. The respondents' debate partners were 56 males and 33 females who ranged in age from 17–54 with a mean age of 20.33 years. The group of partners was comprised of 23 freshman, 28 sophomores, 16 juniors, and 22 seniors. The forensic competition experience for the participants and their partners ranged from 1 semester to 3 years. Very few respondents reported themselves or their partners competing in individual events; however, 40 of the respondents reported competing in impromptu, and 37 reported their partners competing in impromptu.

Of the participants, 18 reported competing for a community college and 71 reported competing for a university. In addition, 82 reported their school belonging to the National Parliamentary Debate Association (NPDA), 18 reported belonging to the National Educational Debate Association (NEDA), 17 reported belonging to Phi Rho Pi (PRP), 25 reported belonging to the American Forensic

Association (AFA), 16 reported belonging to the National Forensic Association (NFA), and 26 respondents indicated that their school belonged to the American Parliamentary Debate Association (APDA), American Debate Association (ADA), National Debate Tournament (NDT), Cross Examination Debate Association (CEDA), Pi Kappa Delta (PKD), Delta Sigma Rho (DSR), or the National Christian College Forensics Invitational (NCCFI).

There were 46 respondents who reported choosing to be partners with their current debate partner and 43 who reported being assigned by their coach to be partners. The time that the participants had been debating with their current partners ranged from 1 semester to 3 years. There were 76 partnerships of 1 semester, 11 of 1 year, 1 of 2 years, and 1 of 3 years. All respondents reported competing in NPDA, 83 indicated that NPDA was their primary format of debate in competition, and 6 indicated that NEDA was their primary format. Of the other formats of debate that the participants competed in with their current debate partners, 10 reported NEDA, 2 reported NDT, and 4 reported CEDA.

Reliability

Our scales demonstrated excellent reliability: The Argumentativeness scale (ARG) had 90% internal consistency (alpha=.90), the Verbal Aggressiveness scale (VA) had 92% internal consistency (alpha=.92), the Partner Argumentativeness scale (PARG) had 92% internal consistency (alpha=.92), the Partner Verbal Aggressiveness scale (PVA) had 92% internal consistency (alpha=.92), and the Relational Satisfaction (RS) scale had 95% internal consistency (alpha=.95).

Correlations and Differences

Our first hypothesis, that debate dyads with similar levels of self-report and perceived partner argumentativeness and verbal aggressiveness will have higher levels of relational satisfaction than dyads with incongruent levels of self-report and perceived partner argumentativeness and verbal aggressiveness, was partially supported by the data. We computed the difference between ARG and PARG to determine our Difference of Argumentativeness (DARG) scale. We did the same with VA and PVA to create our Difference of Verbal Aggressiveness scale (DVA). DVA and RS had no significant correlation. However, DARG and RS had a −.32 correlation, with a .01 significance level.

The second hypothesis, that debate dyads will have low relational satisfaction if they have high levels of verbal aggressiveness and low levels of argumentativeness, was also partially supported by the data. ARG and RS had no significant correlation. VA and RS had a −.21 correlation with a .05 significance level. PARG and RS had a .54 correlation with a .01 significance level. PVA and RS had a −.24 correlation with a .05 significance level.

In order to answer the first research question, which explored whether biological sex would have an impact on argumentativeness, verbal aggressiveness and relational satisfaction in debate dyads, we ran an independent sample t-test. For males, the mean of VA was 3.36 and for females, the mean of VA was 2.30 (t=4.26, p=.00). For males, the mean of ARG was 5.30 and for females, the mean of ARG was 5.82 (t=−2.51, p=.01).

DISCUSSION

Sample

Our sample consisted primarily of NPDA debaters who generally do not participate in many other forms of debate or individual events. Additionally, we only surveyed Southern Californian and Midwestern debaters and did not take regions into account as demographic factors. We speculate that these regions might discourage intercollegiate forensics competitors from competing in many genres of events (or at least not encourage variance in genre).

Difference in VA and ARG

Interestingly enough, the results indicate that disparity between levels of participant self-report of verbal aggressiveness and report of perceived partner verbal aggressiveness has no impact on the report of relational satisfaction. However, the results indicate that disparity between levels of participant self-report of argumentativeness and report of perceived partner argumentativeness does have an impact on the report of relational satisfaction. Intercollegiate parliamentary debate is a highly competitive activity. Our study does not take in to account the importance of competitive success to debaters. If this is more important to debaters than interpersonal harmony with their partner, it is possible that debaters would forgive verbal aggressiveness more readily than the general population, because of the goal of winning. Given that argumentativeness should be an indicator of success in debate, it is also feasible that parliamentary debaters simply generally value their partner's argumentation skill over their partner's personality. The fact that ARG and PARG were significantly correlated lends support to this proposition.

Conversely, the results suggest that self-reports of argumentativeness have no impact on levels of relational satisfaction, while higher levels of verbal aggressiveness were associated with lower levels of relational satisfaction. This finding is supported by Edwards, et al. (2001), who found that people who are high in verbal aggressiveness have a difficult time communicating. It may be the verbally aggressive debater or their partner who suffers from this difficulty. Perhaps more verbally aggressive parliamentary debaters are not as good at debating from their partner's perspective. Bearden (1998) reported that verbally aggressive individuals are not as good at distinguishing well-formed arguments as their less verbally aggressive counterparts. It is also conceivable that highly verbally aggressive debaters may be neurotic introverts who are simply hard to please interpersonally (McCroskey, et al., 2001).

Our results support previous findings that there is a difference in levels of verbal aggressiveness and argumentativeness correlated with biological sex (e.g., Infante 1989). In our sample, females scored an average of over a point lower than males in verbal aggressiveness and an average of nearly a point higher than males in argumentativeness. This finding is directly at odds with the findings of Infante, Rancer, and Jordan (1996), who reported higher levels of argumentativeness in males than females in their study. Perhaps because of patriarchal gender roles that carry over in to forensics competition, females learn that they must be more argumentatively skilled yet less aggressive than males in order to win. Future research would do well to further examine the effects of biological sex and gender on ARG and VA, especially among debaters.

Support for Existing Literature

Our findings indicate that a lack of argumentative skill may, indeed, lead to higher levels of verbal aggressiveness, which is supported by many previous studies (e.g., Daly, 2002; Infante, 1987; Infante, et al., 1984; Infante, et al., 1992; Infante & Wigley, 1986; Martin & Anderson, 1997; Martin, Anderson & Horvath, 1996; & McCroskey, Heisel, & Richmond, 2001). Therefore, our study further validates research in this area, while extending the extent of knowledge to another type of interpersonal relationship.

Unexpected Findings

Contrary to our expectations, when self-reports of verbal aggressiveness were higher, the reports of perceived partner verbal aggressiveness were higher (r=.24, p=.05). This may mean that debate partners closely identify with their partners or, perhaps, that debaters generally identify their partner as having similar flaws in personality (being verbally aggressive) as they perceive themselves to have.

Additionally, RS and time debate partners competed together (Time) had a .27 correlation with a .05 significance level. This finding seems to indicate that the longer debaters work together as partners, the more satisfied they are with their relationship with their partner. However, our sample was primarily comprised of debaters who had competed with their current partner as a team for only a semester. Therefore it is unclear whether this correlation would hold up over time. However, it is possible that future research could collect longitudinal data to test this relation.

Another unexpected finding concerned differences between community college and university competitors. Community college competitors scored an average of nearly a point lower in verbal aggressiveness than their four-year institution counterparts. For community college competitors, the mean VA was 2.13 and for four-year institution competitors, the mean VA was 3.05 ($t=-1.82$, $p=.08$). Additionally, community college competitors had a mean ARG report of 6.50 and for four-year institution competitors, the mean ARG was 5.31 ($t=5.00$, $p=.00$). The results indicate that community college competitors may be more argumentative than the four-year institution competitors. This difference could indicate that community colleges tend to be more effective in teaching argumentation skill or discouraging verbal aggressiveness.

[...]

CONCLUSION

By exploring how argumentativeness, verbal aggressiveness and relational satisfaction relate to the parliamentary debate dyad, we have found that there are many significant relationships. Our findings indicated that higher levels of verbal aggressiveness were correlated with lower levels of relational satisfaction. Higher levels of perceived partner argumentativeness and lover levels of perceived partner verbal aggressiveness both correlated with high levels of relational satisfaction. These findings support existing literature and further illustrate the detrimental effect that verbal aggressiveness can have on personal relationships. As a discipline, we can strive to promote a higher level of awareness and education in the area of argumentative skill in an attempt to lessen these negative effects. Another significant finding was that intercollegiate parliamentary debaters are most relationally satisfied when they are able to choose their own partner. Hopefully, future research will unveil whether relational satisfaction is important to debaters. If so, perhaps debaters ought to be given choice in their partnerships. This research can serve as an impetus for future studies that examine the unique relationship between debate partners as well as studies that look to improve the satisfaction in any interpersonal relationship.

The authors wish to thank Dr. Marcy Meyer of Ball State University for her contribution to their study.

REFERENCES

Anderson, C. M., & Martin, M. M. (1999). The relationship of argumentativeness and verbal aggressiveness to cohesion, consensus, and satisfaction in small groups. *Communication Reports, 12*(1), 21–31.

Beatty, M. J., Zelley, J. R., Dobos, J., A., & Rudd, J. E. (1994). Father's trait verbal aggressiveness and argumentativeness as predictors of adult sons' perceptions of fathers' sarcasm, criticism, and verbal aggressiveness. *Communication Quarterly, 42*(4), 407–415.

[...]

Bingle, D. J. (1978). Parliamentary debate is more serious than you think: Forensics at the University of Chicago. *Speaker and Gavel*, 36–40.

[...]

Crossman, M. (1996). The future of academic debate: CEDA's Decline and the growth of parliamentary debate. *The Forensic of Pi Kappa Delta, 82*(1), 27–33.

Cupach, W. R., & Messman, S. J. (1999). Face predilections and friendship solidarity. *Communication Reports, 12*(1), 13–19.

Daly, J. A. (2002). Personality and interpersonal communication. In Knapp, M. L., & Daly, J. A. (Eds.), Handbook of Interpersonal Communication (3rd ed., 133–180). Thousand Oaks, CA: Sage Publications, Inc.

Dannels, D. P. (2001). Time to speak up: A theoretical framework of situated pedagogy for communication across the curriculum. *Communication Education, 50*(2), 144–158.

Dittus, J. (1998). Building interest in parliamentary debate through demonstration. *Speaker Points, 5*(2). Retrieved December 7, 2004, from: http://www.phirhopi.org/prp/spkrpts5.2/dittus.htm

Edwards, R., Bello, R., Brandau-Brown, F., & Hollems, D. (2001). The effects of loneliness and verbal aggression on message interpretation. *Southern Communication Journal, 66*(2), 139–150.

Erwin, J. S. (1989). *Examination of the interrelatedness of argumentativeness and verbal aggressiveness.* Unpublished manuscript, Ball State University, Muncie, IN.

Friedley, S. A. (1972). *Study of the relationship between critical thinking ability and grades in public speaking class.* Unpublished manuscript, Ball State University, Muncie, IN.

Galizio, L., & Chuen, B. H. (1995). This house believes that parliamentary debate should be included in the Phi Rho Pi national tournament. *Speaker Points, 2*(2). Retrieved December 7, 2004, from: http://www.phirhopi.org/prp/spkrpts2.2/galizio.html

[…]

Ifert, D. E., & Bearden, L. (1998). The influence of argumentativeness and verbal aggression on responses to refused requests. *Communication Reports, 11*(2), 145–154.

Infante, D. A. (1982). The argumentative student in the speech communication classroom: An investigation and implications. *Communication Education, 31,* 141–148.

Infante, D. A. (1987). Aggressiveness. In McCroskey, J. C, & Daly, J. A. (Eds.), *Personality and interpersonal communication* (157–192). Newbury Park, CA: Sage Publications, Inc.

Infante, D. A. (1989). Response to high argumentatives: Message and sex differences. *The Southern Communication Journal, 66*(2), 139–150.

[…]

Infante, D. A, & Rancer, A. S. (1982). A conceptualization and measure of argumentativeness. *Journal of Personality Assessment, 45,* 72–80.

Infante, D. A, Rancer, A. S., & Jordan, F. F. (1996). Affirming and nonaffirming style, dyad sex, and the perception of argumentation and verbal aggression in an interpersonal dispute. *Human Communication Research, 22*(3), 315–334.

Infante, D. A., Riddle, B. L., Horvath, C. L., & Tumlin, S. A. (1992). Verbal aggressiveness: Messages and reasons. *Communication Quarterly, 40*(2), 116–126.

Infante, D. A., Trebing, J. D., Shepherd, P. A., & Seeds, D. E. (1984). The relationship of argumentativeness to verbal aggression. *The Southern Speech Communication Journal, 50,* 67–77.

Infante, D. A., & Wigley, C. J. (1986). Verbal Aggressiveness: An interpersonal model and measure. *Communication Monographs, 53,* 61–69.

Kuster, T. A. (2002). Appreciating the "public" nature of parliamentary debate: A dozen benefits. *Speaker Points, 9*(2). Retrieved December 7, 2004, from: http://www.phirhopi.org/prp/spkrpts9.2/kuster.html

Kuster, T. A., Olson, L. M., & Loging, J. L. (2001). Enlisting non professional judges in parliamentary debate. *Speaker Points, 7*(2). Retrieved December 7, 2004, from: http://www.phirhopi.org/prp/spkrpts7.2/kuster.html

Martin, M. M., & Anderson, C. M. (1997). Aggressive communication traits: How similar are young adults and their parents in argumentativeness, assertiveness, and verbal aggressiveness. *Western Journal of Communication, 61*(3), 299–314.

McCroskey, J. C., Heisel, A. D., & Richmond, V. P. (2001). Eysenck's big three and communication traits: Three correlation studies. *Communication Monographs, 68*(4), 360–366.

[…]

Myers, S. A., & Knox, R. L. (2000). Perceived instructor argumentativeness and verbal aggressiveness and student outcomes. *Communication Research Reports, 17*(3), 299–309.

Neer, M. R. (1994). Argumentative flexibility as a factor influencing message response style to argumentative and aggressive arguers. *Argumentation & Advocacy/Journal of the American Forensic Association, 57*(1), 17–33.

O'Niell, D. J. (1986). Recollections of university parliamentary debate: Irish style. *The Forensic of Pi Kappa Delta, 71*(3), 66–69.

Puchot, R. (2002). Empowering student governance and promoting activism through forensics. *Speaker Points, 9*(2). Retrieved December 7, 2004, from: http://www.phirhopi.org/prp/spkrpts9.2./craft2002/puchot.html

Schullery, N. M., & Schullery, S. E. (2003). Relationship of argumentativeness to age and higher education. *Western Journal of Communication, 67*(2), 207–223.

[…]

Stris, P. (1996). The American Parliamentary Debate Association. *Argumentation & Advocacy/Journal of the American Forensic Association, 33*(2), 98–100.

Teven, J. J., Martin, M. M., & Neupauer, N. C. (1998). Sibling relationships: Verbally aggressive messages and their effect on relational satisfaction. *Communication Reports, 11*(2), 179–186.

Theodore F., Sheckels, J., & Warfield, A. C. (1990). Parliamentary debate: A description and a justification. *Argumentation & Advocacy/ Journal of the American Forensic Association, 27*(2), 86–96.

[…]

Wheeless, L.R. (1978). A follow-up study of the relationships among trust, disclosure, and interpersonal solidarity. *Human Communication Research, 4,* 143–157.

Williams, D.E., & Guajardo, M. (1998). The use of example in parliamentary debate. *The Forensic of Pi Kappa Delta, 84*(1), 21–34.

[…]

*Crystal Lane Swift** is an instructor of speech communication and debate coach at Louisiana State University.

Christina Vourvoulias is an associate professor of speech in the Lone Star College System.

Swift, Crystal Lane, and Christina Vourvoulias. "Argumentativeness, Verbal Aggressiveness, and Relational Satisfaction in the Parliamentary Debate Dyad." *Parliamentary Debate: Journal of National Parliamentary Debate Association* 11 (2006): 1–25.

Parliamentary Debate Is More Serious Than You Think: Forensics at the University of Chicago

by Donald J. Bingle[*]

The University of Chicago, one of the youngest of the major American universities, was founded in 1890. Launched with a program of ambitious dimensions and with a faculty of remarkable distinction under the intellectual leadership of William Rainey Harper, it was "a new kind of institution, borrowing from the structure and aims of German and English universities, joining the gentlemanly tradition of zeal for good works of the New England colleges with the confidence and brashness of the Middle West."[1] Harper instituted the four-quarter system, established the first university extension program, and announced that the University would be primarily devoted to graduate studies. The University of Chicago became at once one of the leading universities of the world. John D, Rockefeller, who provided the financial base for the University's creation, remarked of it, "It's the best investment I ever made."

The University still maintains the broad patterns set by Harper. Of the approximately 8,000 students currently enrolled, 5,500 are students in the graduate or professional schools; the remaining 2,500 are undergraduates. The emphasis on academic research is paramount; more than two-thirds of Chicago's Ph.Ds go into college teaching, and over forty Nobel Prize winners have been associated with the University. In fact, the University has been accused of being too serious-minded. In the late '30s Chicago dropped out of the Big Ten and discontinued football altogether. Students and professors alike devoted themselves to the "life of the mind." This somber tone can be seen in the quadrangle's architecture, primarily grey gothic with looming gargoyles, and in the worn stone steps to the undergraduate library. Even the gymnasium has an intricately patterned stained-glass window in the lobby. With a preponderance of departmentalized and research-oriented graduate students and a distressing imbalance in the male : female ratio, campus social life has been rated from "poor" to "nonexistent." In fact, one campus group has tried to boost spirits by hawking t-shirts picturing a gargoyle doubled-up with laughter and the caption: "Ho, ho. The University of Chicago is funnier than you think."

While the Chicago Debating Society is part of the intellectual life and rational discourse of the University, it does not have the problem of being thought too serious-minded. In fact, Chicago's debate program has quite the opposite reputation on much of the midwestern debate circuit, for Chicago, embraces—in fact, dominates—intercollegiate parliamentary debate. No doubt, many Midwestern colleges regard parliamentary debate as not serious enough—something like a cross between a Johnny Carson monologue and a rowdy sideshow. Parliamentary debate and participation in the Chicago Debating Society are certainly not humorless, but on the other hand, they are more serious than many may think.

RULES, ROLE-PLAYING, AND THE REASONABLE MAN: THE PARLIAMENTARY PERSPECTIVE

Since the Chicago Debating Society engages in parliamentary debate and public forums to the virtual exclusion of all else, our program cannot be examined without an understanding of the substance and rationale of parliamentary debate. Parliamentary debate is a Canadian and English phenomenon which promotes debate of many varied topics in a parliamentary context. The parliamentary rules of the House of Commons apply, and role-playing is part of the exercise. There is no affirmative or negative team, but a Government (comprised of the Prime Minister and another minister appropriate to the topic) and Her Majesty's Loyal Opposition (comprised of the Leader of the Opposition and a "shadow" minister).

Generally, the resolution to be debated is announced 15–30 minutes before the debate begins. The debate itself is run under the normal parliamentary rules by a Speaker of the House (usually the judge). A Member of the House (either a debater or an audience member) may rise to state a Point of Order (pointing out an infraction of the rules, e.g., exceeding the time limits set), a Point of Privilege (e.g., a request for apology if he or the Queen has been insulted, a request that a person speaking speak louder, etc.), or a Point of Information (a question addressed to the person speaking which lie may accept or not at his choice). Heckling is not only permitted, but encouraged. The Government is given considerable latitude in interpreting the resolution. Some tournaments even allow the Government to set the date in time and space in any parliamentary context: the Chicago City Council, Roman Senate, College of Cardinals, Joint Chiefs of Staff, and so forth.

The advantages of parliamentary debate are numerous. It is at once more useful, more stimulating, more entertaining, more rational, and more rewarding than national-topic style. At the same time it is less time consuming and less petty. It can be thought of as a "gentleman's sport," a pleasurable form of intellectual exercise for the reasonable man or woman. Perhaps some particularized comparisons will help to convey this point.

First of all, the number and variety of topics in parliamentary debate provide considerable advantages over national-topic style. Varied topics make debate rounds more interesting and less repetitive. They allow the student to see different perspectives on a whole host of issues; economic, political, religious, and philosophical. The role-playing aspects in competitive rounds not only enforce this, but explode the stereotyped caricatures that exist in students' minds by making them explain and justify the views they set forth in the roles they have taken.[2] Instead of a specialized knowledge of a narrow field, a parliamentary debater must have a "working" knowledge of the general concepts in various fields of thought, and a knowledge of history and current events in order to apply these concepts and give adequate examples in support of his assertions. This varied background is the essence of liberal education. The fact that the topics are varied and are not announced long in advance also has the effect of shifting the emphasis of the debate from research to analysis. Thought predominates over sheer force of work. And again, it is much more important and intellectually stimulating for a university to teach its students to think, rather than to teach then) how to research what other people have thought. Of course, *good* research needs analytical ability and builds upon the past. But too often, quality falls to the side in national-topic debate and quantity takes over. File boxes and index cards become ends unto themselves. The argument "I have six cards, he has four: I win by two," has no persuasive force of itself and would never be heard in parliamentary debate.

The collective voices of skeptical "national-topic" debate coaches might respond: "But wait a minute. Isn't parliamentary debate just a childish game of buffoonery where the logic of 'I have six jokes, he had four: I win by two' prevails?" The answer is simply "No." First, not all parliamentary rounds are meant to be humorous. In fact, the bulk of the debates involve serious discussions of philosophical issues even though the resolutions themselves are occasionally somewhat whimsical. If we merely told jokes, the University of Chicago could not have won one world championship[3] and three North American championships in parliamentary debate in the past five years and still have made respectable showings at national topic events such as the University of Illinois Forensic Progression. Instead, we stress analysis and speaking ability. As a bonus, those with a quick wit van have some fun in some of the debate rounds.

If Chicago has a reputation on the national-topic "debate circuit" for humor or rowdiness, it's partly because when parliamentary debaters talk to other people about debates they have been in, they tend to emphasize the humorous rounds. "They do this for several simple reasons. First, it makes better small talk. Secondly, it's much easier to relate the outline of a funny case, or a couple of one-liners, or in effective heckle, than it is to explain the intricate subtleties of a serious debate and the intellectual satisfaction you got from participating in it. In 45 seconds a Chicago debater can outline the most outrageous debate be or she was ever in: the improbable setting, the amusing case, our amusing counterattack and our devastating punchline response that set the mood of the rest of the round. In 15 seconds be can relate the curious interpretation lie once took of a resolution that literally made his opponent's mouth drop open. But he cannot in such time explain the intricacies of the best debate lie was ever in—about the existence of an immutable spirit—or tile final debate in London three years ago—which dealt with tile issues of equality and especially if he is asked what evidence he quoted. Thus, a reputation for humor develops. It is reinforced when we go to the University of Illinois because of the good-natured rivalry which exists between our schools. and because at parliamentary events attended by large numbers of non-parliamentary schools, we are willing to take the lead in heckling, realizing that others may not ho experienced enough to have the necessary self-confidence or timing. We are proud of the lead we take in these matters, especially at events like the 1977 forensic progression at the University of Illinois, where some national-topic debaters refused to debate in the experimental parliamentary round because the competitive impetus of judging was not present. The overbearing pettiness of competitiveness can be lessened. Certainly we try hard to do well at every tournament we attend, but when one can have a good time debating, winning isn't the only reason to go.

It should be noted that heckling need not always be humorous, though it often is. Heckling, like cross-examination, allows one to devastate his opponent on his opponent's own time. A four word heckle, when issued at the proper moment, can devastate an opponent's case by pointing out a glaring counter example or flaw, by logical *reductio ad absurdum,* and so forth. Attacking an opponent's character or motives through heckling may deflate his role or demeanor. A pun or witticism may distract an opponent's train of thought or speaking fluency. Heckling and responding to heckles—in fact, parliamentary debate in general—teaches one to think on his feet, to use language precisely, and to speak with self-assurance. It conforms more to reality than does the sterile atmosphere of cross-examination questions to a recalcitrant opponent in a nearly deserted college classroom. It emphasizes the persuasive aspects of public speaking, by pointing out that audience impact is central; and this is essential to remember in the real world. It might even mundanely be pointed out that parliamentary debate is more practical. It at least teaches one the elements of public speaking necessary for politics, after-dinner events, and business affairs. The peculiar speaking style and terms of art used by national-topic debaters perhaps would train one to be a legislative assistant; however, the bureaucracy is already too large.

Finally, the lack of research in parliamentary debate means that a student's time can be devoted to his studies, yet he can still participate in debate. This means students from many varied disciplines often do join the Chicago Debating Society. This diversity greatly adds to the quality of discussions. On the parliamentary circuit, graduate students remain eligible to compete; they often continue to compete because parliamentary debate is enjoyable. That may be its most important advantage of all.

[. . .]

[The Chicago Debating Society]
[. . .]

Society debaters work continually on new ways to engage in parliamentary debate, while at the same time serving the University community. For instance, public forums have been held regarding such topics as the University's grading policies and affirmative action. In addition, the Debating Society has been negotiating with the campus radio station regarding weekly radio debates. Individual members of the Society have recently undertaken to tutor local high school students in public speaking. Such programs are an especially beneficial form of public service, as Chicago Public Schools would otherwise be unable to provide such "supplementary" instruction to students due to budgetary constraints.

Increasing numbers of Chicago students are becoming involved in parliamentary debate. The students attracted to the University of Chicago seem to do well naturally in parliamentary debate, but rather than rely merely upon their natural speaking ability, Society members have shown increasing willingness to receive instruction and to practice their craft extensively. The benefits they receive from parliamentary debate serve them well in whatever direction they pursue in the real world. Chicago debaters not only become lawyers and politicians, but have also become doctors, researchers, and economists. There is something to be said for a program, which like a liberal education, can be both beneficial and enjoyable, no matter what career one pursues.

ENDNOTES

1. *The University of Chicago Announcements, 1977.*

2. It should be noted that students participating in public debates hosted by the University of Chicago generally debate on the side consistent with their personal position on the resolution.

3. The Trans-Atlantic Universities Speech Association (TAUSA) English Speaking World Championships. This tournament is discussed later in the essay.

[…]

---

*Donald J. Bingle is a private attorney and coach of the Chicago Debating Society.

Bingle, Donald J. "Parliamentary Debate Is More Serious Than You Think: Forensics at the University of Chicago." *Speaker and Gavel* 15, no. 2 (1978): 36–41.

Measuring Refutation Skill: An Exploratory Study

by Don Faules*

Because the concepts of attack and defense are inherent to an understanding of argumentation theory, there is little question about the importance of refutation skill. The refutation process is dependent upon a person's ability to examine structural and logical adequacy of reasoned discourse. In other words, refutation skill may reveal one's capacity for critical thinking. A study by Russell M. Keeling revealed that the greatest difference in the scores of winning and losing debaters occurred in the area of refutation.[1] In addition, winning debaters were scored superior more frequently for refutation than any other item. Such evidence indicates that refutation skill may be a predictor for debate effectiveness.

PURPOSE

The above considerations prompted this investigator to search for a method of measuring refutation skill. The purpose of this study was to devise a method that would approximate the argumentation setting and yield results that could be quantified. It was felt that such a method should have qualities of economy as well as realism.

A method of measuring refutation skill may produce the following values:

(1) Such a method may point the way toward a measure which could be used to test students in the classroom or the extra-curricular situation.

(2) In addition to its use as a tool of discrimination, the measure could be utilized to teach refutation skill.

(3) The measure might be employed to predict debate effectiveness. In addition, students who wanted to debate but were uncertain as to their ability or what was involved, could determine their skill in a short period of time.

(4) If refutation skill is related to critical thinking, such an approach might be utilized to determine the value of debate training. In other words, does debate training teach students to ask the right questions?

[...]

Results and Analysis

The following questions were deemed important to this study and the accompanying statistical analysis was employed to provide at least partial answers to the questions.

(1) Was the difference in subject matter of the two cases a major contributing factor to refutation score? The two cases were examined for equivalence by computing the correlation between the scores on each test made by the sample of intercollegiate debaters. An application of the Pearson r resulted in a correlation of .77. This figure was statistically significant at the .01 confidence level. The result indicated that the subject matter probably had less influence on the outcome of the score than the total effect of the other factors contributing to the scores. The "university case" was selected for purposes of analysis.

(2) Does debate training make a difference in the refutation scores obtained by the respondents? In order to answer this question three comparisons were made.

A. Students in the argumentation courses were examined before and after the course. Because of the problems of pre and post tests, the "university case" was submitted to argumentation classes at the beginning of the first semester and to different argumentation classes at the end of the second semester. The argumentation course was a one semester course and this method assumed that both samples were drawn from the same population. An examination of the personal data about each subject indicated that the two samples were essentially the same in terms of age, class rank, sex, and prior experience with courses containing subject matter about reasoning and logic. If the student indicated that he had prior debate training, he was removed from the sample. The scores of ninety-five subjects from the classes were retained for the analysis.

B. A comparison was made between those who were just entering the argumentation classes and those who were finishing the argumentation classes. An application of the Chi-Square test of independence yielded a figure that was statistically significant between the .01 and .05 confidence levels. Those who had the course did significantly better on the refutation exercise.

C. The difference between the scores of the intercollegiate debaters and those who had the argumentation course was statistically significant at the .001 level, in favor of the intercollegiate debaters. This was also true of the difference between the intercollegiate debaters and those who were just starting the argumentation course. In the lat[t]er case the difference in score was even greater. The differences were determined with the Chi-Square test of independence. It would appear that the more debate training a student has the more likely he is to score high on the refutation exercise. However, this is not to be construed as a causal relationship.

(3) Does a relationship exist between refutation scores and debate effectiveness? After the papers were scored the coaches of the three intercollegiate debate squads were asked to rank their students in the order of debate effectiveness. A Spearman Rho correlation was applied to the ranking of students and to the rank of refutation scores. Correlations of .73, .70, and .54 were obtained. The first two figures were statistically significant at the .01 confidence level and the last figure at the .05 level. The same analysis was made of four of the argumentation classes. Each instructor was asked to rank his students in terms of their debate effectiveness.

Rank order correlations produced correlations of .56, .72, .68, and .65. The first figure was statistically significant at the .05 level and the rest statistically significant at the .01 level.

This evidence indicates that the refutation exercise may be a valuable tool for predicting debate skill. In addition, the validity of the exercise is strengthened by the fact that the better students actually achieve a higher score.

(4) Is there a relationship between the quality of arguments advanced and the quantity of arguments given? A Pearson r was applied to quality scores and quantity scores of the one hundred thirty-five subjects. The result was a figure of .619 which was statistically significant at the .001 confidence level. This finding suggests that the more capable debaters not only produce quality arguments but they also produce more arguments than debaters with less skill and experience. It is interesting to note that this finding is consistent with research in creativity. In other words those who produce a quantity of ideas also produce more unique ideas.[3] The pressure of the time limit may be the variable that determines the differences between those with various degrees of debate experience. Indeed, this may be one value of debate training.

Summary and Discussion

The search for a method of measuring refutation skill presents somewhat of a paradox. A multiple choice test might be devised that would meet all the rigors required of a measuring instrument. The major advantage of this approach would be the achievement of an objective scoring procedure. However, would this really represent what a debater is expected and trained to do? This writer believes that it is one thing to recognize a reasonable argument and quite another to produce one. However, this may not be true and such a test might be devised from the responses obtained from the hypothetical case method. Such a method would allow an examination of reliability, validity, and the establishment of test norms.

The method of measurement employed in this study has several limitations. First, cases must be constructed for each particular situation unless the subject matter is familiar to the respondents. Although some defects in reasoning can be detected without regard to subject matter, there are advantages to using familiar subject matter. First, the beginning student should realize that an understanding of the requirements of good reasoning is as important as an understanding of the subject matter. Secondly, it is unlikely that the beginning student will have specialized training in the reasoning process, i.e., symbolic logic. The scoring method relies on a single judge. This problem might be solved by having a panel of judges judge each argument on a linear scale. However, the time and expense of such a method makes it questionable, especially if new cases must be constructed each time the method is utilized. Nevertheless this panel approach would be more adequate to answer questions that pertain to the effect of debate training.

Although there are a number of limitations imposed on the method used in this study, it does have some advantages. The cases are easy to construct, they are representative of the debate setting, and they are more economical than judging a complete debate. What is lost in precision may be gained in realistic simulation.

Statistical analysis revealed that the method did make a distinction between the levels of debate effectiveness. This was true in the case of intercollegiate debaters as well as for students in argumentation classes. This indicates that the method might be used as a predictor and also as an index for selecting debaters. Such a method has its virtues for purposes of try-outs. Students might get an idea of what is expected of a debater and what the training is designed to do. In addition, the subject matter would not scare those who are uncertain of their ability.

The results of the study provide evidence that students do improve in refutation skill after a course in argumentation. Gerald Phillips refers to a number of studies that examine the effects of debate training. He concludes that "the studies seem to show that whatever critical thinking tests measure, participation in debate doesn't seem to improve it, although debaters seem to be above average in the amount of it that they possess initially."[4] This writer feels that one would be hard put to make a distinction between refutation skill and critical thinking. Phillips states, "...if debate does not teach or improve critical thinking ability, then we ought to devote more effort to those areas where debate has proven useful, or we ought to revise debate programming until it is able to improve critical thinking skill."[5] This investigator is not willing to concede that debate training does not teach or improve critical thinking ability. This study presents evidence to the contrary. In addition, the alternatives cited by Phillips are not the most reasonable ones available. Why should one change a program to fit a measure that may not be able to measure what is being done?

The finding that those who produce the most arguments also produce quality arguments suggests an interesting area of research. A body of research demonstrates that "creative problem solving courses" have the effect of producing gains in quantity of ideas and in quality of ideas.[6] Such experimentation in the area of creativity has led to institutes, grants, and special courses. The debate director may be obtaining the same results with debate training without demonstrating it or looking for a way to demonstrate it.

The value of the hypothetical case for teaching refutation should not be overlooked. Students tend to become involved in the subject matter of a resolution which causes them to give habituated responses. Every director is familiar with the student who memorizes stock evidence and responds with the same upon cue. When the thinking process is short circuited, students tend to read evidence at arguments rather than analyze them. When students do not have stock arguments and evidence at their disposal, they are forced to deal with the general reasoning of a case. If they can accomplish this with a familiar topic, this skill can be transferred to a more complex situation. Students can also be taught that some arguments are more potent than others and why some will do more damage than others. The nature of direct refutation can be demonstrated and the five minute limit serves to emphasize selection of arguments. It is apparent that more arguments can be leveled at the cases than the time allows. Therefore the concept of priority can be stressed. It is helpful for the beginning student to see how the experienced intercollegiate debater approaches the task of refutation. The device used in this study yields a body of material for comparative purposes. The instructor can utilize this material to explain differences in organization, reasoning, and language.

The purpose of this study was to devise a method of measuring refutation skill and explore its possible utility. Although the limitations of the method did not allow for the development of a precise measuring instrument, the method did show potential value as a means of testing refutation skill, teaching refutation skill, predicting debate effectiveness, and demonstrating the value of argumentation training. In addition this exploratory study suggested means for refinement of the method and also pointed to other areas of research that might be fruitful.

ENDNOTES

1. "An Analysis of Refutation and Rebuttal in Interscholastic Debate" (Unpublished M.A. Thesis, Department of Speech, Baylor University, 1959), 86–91.

[…]

3. See the test administration manual of the "AC Test of Creative Ability," Industrial Relations Center. The University of Chicago.

4. Gerald M. Phillips, "Experimentation and the Future of Debate," *The Gavel*, XLV (November 1962), 5.

5. Ibid., 5–6.

6. See Arnold Meadow and Sidney J. Parnes, "Evaluation of Training in Creative Problem Solving," *Journal of Applied Psychology*, XLIII (No. 3, 1959), 189–194; and Sidney J. Parnes, "Effects of Extended Effort in Creative Problem Solving," *Journal of Educational Psychology*, LII (June 1961), 117–122.

***Don Faules** is associate director of the Center for Communication Studies at Ohio University.

Faules, Don. "Measuring Refutation Skill: An Exploratory Study." *Journal of the American Forensic Association* 4, no. 2 (1967): 48–51.

The Benefits and Costs of Participating in Competitive Debate Activities: Differences between Japanese and American College Students

by Narahiko Inoue and Mika Nakano*

0. INTRODUCTION

For over decades now, debate (dibeeto in Japanese) has been the focus of much attention in Japan. This is reflected in the frequency of the word "debate" in major Japanese newspapers, which shows a clear increase for a period of about twenty years. As Table 1 and Figure 1 show, the number of articles containing the word "debate" was zero in 1987. In 2003, however, this figure had risen to 349 (Inoue, 1994; Nakano, 2004, p. 1). This shows that "debate" has rapidly gained popularity in Japanese society. One reason for this rise in popularity is that debate has been recognized as an important skill for Japanese to communicate effectively in the globalized world. Much has been discussed over the use of debate in classroom activities in such courses as sciences and social studies as well as language courses of Japanese and English from elementary school to university.

Out in the world today there are diversified styles of competitive debating in English available for students. Long time ago when debating was brought to the American continent from Britain, it was just debating. Then Britons and Americans followed different paths. British debating remained armature activities, which later became institutionalized as Parliamentary Debate spreading to the world. American educators and scholars developed their own so-called Academic Debate, or NDT. Only recently did American scholars turn to Parliamentary Debate as one of the alternative styles.

Against this background, the current paper will discuss the benefits and costs associated with participating in competitive debate activities by analyzing the perceptions collected from Japanese college students. It will also examine the features of Parliamentary Debate (PD hereafter)[1] in contrast to more traditional NDT-style debate.[2] The results will also be compared with a similar survey in the U.S. There are three reasons why this paper will discuss these themes.

Firstly, the available research, especially empirical research about PD, is scarce. In Japan, PD was first introduced in 1990 by the International Debate Institute (Kawahatsu, 1990, June 19). Because of its short history, there have been no studies on PD except for the series of work by Nakano. In the U.S. there have been a number of debate studies but most of them are concerned with the more traditional debate styles, such as NDT and CEDA. It is only recently that PD has been taken up as a research topic in the field of forensics and argumentation. Since most of the previous studies on PD were conducted in the U.S., some factors were ignored, for example, English as a second language and international comparisons. As debate becomes more diversified and globalized, research on debate should consider such factors as well.

Secondly, PD has several unique characteristics. It is unique in its orientation toward extemporaneous and audience-focused

TABLE 1: ARTICLES CONTAINING "DEBATE" IN MAJOR NEWSPAPERS 1985–2003

	1985	1986	1987	1988	1989	1990	1991	1992	1993
Yomiuri	NA	0	0	1	1	2	2	5	9
Asahi	0	0	0	2	3	11	10	15	27
Mainichi	NA	NA	0	0	0	6	8	15	11
Total	0	0	0	3	4	19	20	35	47

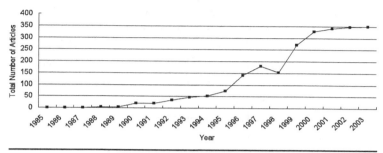

speeches, which is different from the styles many studies have centered on up until now. Moreover, PD is widely used all over the world, and the number of people participating in PD is increasing year by year. One of the reasons for this was made clear by the research on debate Nakano conducted in Asian countries. One of its findings points to the increasing need for education in English communication skills that has arisen as a result of globalization (Nakano, 2002).

Thirdly, an empirical approach has not been used much in debate studies in Japan. Apart from studies such as Inoue (1994), who discussed how English Speaking Societies conducted debates as an extracurricular activity in Japanese universities and Kamada (2000), who for over a decade researched the effects of debate

1994	1995	1996	1997	1998	1999	2000	2001	2002	2003
18	22	70	63	64	145	203	237	255	230
24	26	22	38	32	57	70	51	61	59
11	25	49	80	58	68	55	53	32	60
53	73	141	181	154	270	328	341	348	349

training on business people in Japan, the number of empirical studies that examine the costs and benefits of debate participation is quite small. Mikuma (2003) warns that the hasty introduction of debate into classrooms may be dangerous without considering the historical praxis of debate in extracurricular activities, which he claims were ignored by researchers (p. 138). While debate is advocated by some as a panacea to today's education problems, the costs as well as the benefits of debate need to be examined empirically. Such an empirical approach is also effective for examining the unique characteristics of PD.

Thus the problems of previous studies can be summarized as follows:

1. The number of studies covering PD is limited.
2. The characteristics of PD in English should be investigated, especially the perceptions of non-native speakers of English.
3. Empirical data are needed to assess the costs and benefits of debate participation.

This paper is intended to fill these gaps in research and will contribute to the discussion of the relative merits and demerits of different styles of debate across different cultural contexts. In order to allow the Japanese and American comparison, this research follows the method used by Williams, McGee, & Worth (2001), who compared the participants' perceptions in different debate styles in the U.S. [...]

1. Review of Previous Studies

[...]Discussions on introducing debate into education have been boosted in various school subjects such as Japanese, English, social studies, and sciences. PD, however, has rarely attracted attention until now. One of the earlier publications discussing PD, or British debating, was Milward (1983), who recommended British debate instead of American debate, which was dominant in Japan. [...]

Williams et al. (2001) stated the necessity of empirical studies on debate participation with two rationales (p. 198-99). Firstly, we should assess students' impressions of debate regularly since debaters' life is changing time to time as we have changes in coaching practice, method of collecting information, travel pattern and so on. The survey method also needs to be tested for validity. The past 10 years only saw two studies: Jones (1994), which is now about 10 yeas old, and Williams et al. (2001). Secondly, intercollegiate debate community has changed, and various styles should be compared. Especially PD has several points which are distinguished by NDT and CEDA. It was first empirically investigated by Williams et al., but in Japan no previous study has tried to account for PD. It is necessary to examine PD for more comprehensive understanding of competitive debating in particular and Speech Communication at large.

2. METHOD

2.1. Research Questions

This paper reports part of a larger study that tries to answer 7 research questions below. Numbers 1–4 are the same questions that Williams et al. (2001) used, and Numbers 5–7 were newly added for this study. This paper discusses research questions 1–5.

1. What benefits do students perceive from their participation in intercollegiate debate?
2. What disadvantages do students perceive from their participation in intercollegiate debate?
3. How do students' perceived benefits compare to those revealed in previous studies?

4. How do students' perceived disadvantages compare to those revealed in previous studies?
5. Do answers vary according to debate styles?
6. What motivations do students have from their participation in intercollegiate debate?
7. Are there any correlations between benefits and motivations?

2.2. Participants of the Survey

Respondents are the participants of NDT and PD. NDT-style debate and PD are the two styles of debate in the English language which are dominantly popular among college students in Japan. Williams et al. (2001) included other styles such as CEDA in addition to these two styles, but this survey in Japan does not include them since they are not practiced in Japan. For uniform sampling, the participants in one of the national tournaments for each style in 2003 were surveyed by gang survey when most of the participants gathered in one place: at the announcement of the qualifiers for the elimination tournament (NDT-style) and at the end of the final round (PD). The response rates of this survey are shown in Table 2.

Problems related to the methods used in previous studies include low response rates and problems with the validity of the mail survey technique. Williams et al. (2001) used mail survey in their study. But mail survey is not suitable for uniform sampling in ages, the years of experience, attributes and so on. The validity for comparison among debate styles is also questionable. The response

TABLE 2: RESPONSE RATES

	The number of sample	The number of effective sample	Response rate (%)
NDT-style	63	58	92.1
PD	120	109	90.8

rate is also quite low, around 19.5%. Although the response rate of mail surveys is around 20% in general, 19.5% is not enough for reliable surveys. Unfortunately, the low rate of response often remains a problem in forensics studies in general. To overcome these problems, this research used gang survey and succeeded in ensuring a more than 90% response rate.

2.3. Instrument (Questionnaire)

The questionnaire consisted of 2 sections: (1) demographic data and debate experience, (2) benefits, disadvantages and motivations of debate participation. The language used in the questionnaire was English. We will address the responses to Section (2) and will discuss the findings related to benefits and disadvantages. The questions in Section (2) are as follows:

Q1. Identify three benefits to your participation in debate.
Q2. Identify three disadvantages to your participation in debate.
Q3. Identify three motives to your participation in debate.

Following the method used by Williams et al. (2001), the answers were content-analyzed according to similarity and divided into their categories. When an answer didn't fit in with the existing categories, we asked one of the authors of the original study (Dr. D. E. Williams) to code it, and then set a new category. The results of the surveys are given in Table 3.

TABLE 3: OVERVIEW RESULTS OF THE SURVEYS

	Benefits	Costs	Motivation
Japan	341/29*	220/20*	361/32*
U.S.	735/49*	582/43*	NA

*the number of answers/the number of categories

3. RESULTS AND DISCUSSION

In 3.1, we will discuss the findings related to the benefits of debate. In 3.2 disadvantages of debate participation will be examined.

3.1 Benefits of Debate Participation

Firstly, what benefits do the students perceive from their participation in debate? From the characteristics of the two styles, it was predicted that the highest benefits of PD would be "English & communication skills" and the highest benefits of the NDT-style would be "logic" and "research". Table 4 reports the ranking of benefits in each style and Table 5 presents the raw number of responses and percentages by country and style of debate.

[...]

As we predicted from the characteristics of the NDT-style, "Analytical/Critical skills" which is the closest to the predicted "logic", occupies the highest position in the benefits of NDT. "Research", however, ranked low in Japan with only two participants giving "research" as a benefit of NDT. Since some answered "knowledge about particular topics" as a benefit, students have a tendency to report "research" not as a process, but "knowledge" as a result of "research" as benefits. On the other hand, there were answers such as "research and preparation take a lot of time", which reveals that "research" is considered more as a disadvantage than as a benefit by Japanese students. As was predicted about PD, "English

TABLE 4: RANKING OF BENEFITS (JAPAN)

Ranking	NDT-style (58)	PD (109)
1	Analytical/Critical skills	English skills
2	English skills	Speaking/Comm. Skills
3	Social life/Meeting people	Social life/Meeting people
4	Knowledge/Education	Knowledge/Education
5	Speaking/Comm. skills	Analytical/Critical skills

TABLE 5: BENEFITS BY STYLE AND COUNTRY

Benefit	Japan		U.S.	
	NDT-style (58)	PD (109)	NDT (55)	PD (122)
Speaking/Comm. skills	13	46	18	66
*	22.4%	42.2%	32.7%	54%
Research	2	5	16	9
*	3.4%	4.6%	29%	7.3%
Social life/Meeting people	22	42	20	36
*	37.9%	38.5%	36%	29.5%
Analytical/Critical skills	38	41	29	43
*	65.5%	37.6%	52.7%	35.2%
Knowledge/Education	16	42	NA	NA
*	27.6%	38.5%	NA	NA
English skills	27	62	NA	NA
*	46.6%	56.9%	NA	NA

*percentage of responses in respective debating styles

skills" and "Speaking/Comm. skills" are ranked top. This result supports a claim that PD is effective for English communication.

We will more closely look at "English skills" and "Speaking/Comm. skills". When we combine "English skills" & "Speaking/Comm. skills" as in Table 6, the NDT debaters' percentage is 69% while the percentage of PD debaters is 99.1%. In other words, 99.1% of PD debaters think "English skills" and/or "Speaking/Comm.

TABLE 6: ENGLISH & SPEAKING/COMM. SKILLS BY STYLE (JAPAN)

Benefit	NDT (58)	PD (109)
English & Speaking/Comm. skills	40	108
*	69.0%	99.1%

*percentage of responses in respective styles

skills" are derived from participating in PD. These numbers suggest that PD has the benefits of improving "English skills" and "Speaking/Comm. skills".

In the top five ranking of benefits, the same five categories were present in NDT and PD. This leads to the conclusion that these are the benefits that debaters perceive as deriving from participation in English debate in Japan, regardless of the debate style. Comparing each ranking of NDT and PD, "English skills" ranked high in both styles, the highest in PD (56.9%) and the second highest in NDT (46.6%), as is shown in Tables 4 and 5. The result is reasonable as the debate is conducted in English, but this does confirm Japanese debaters' perception that debate participation improves their English ability.

The ranking of "Knowledge/Education" is the same in NDT and PD, but the contents of the answers were different. Many NDT debaters replied "the depth of knowledge" as a benefit, while PD debaters frequently answered the "width" and "variety" of knowledge. This reflects each style's unique characteristics: NDT requires carefully prepared analysis based on the focused research on one topic while PD makes more varied and wide knowledge necessary for debaters to be able to talk about various resolutions in different rounds.

There is another implication on "Knowledge/Education". Some PD students answered "can know well about current events in the world" as a benefit, while others answered "frustration to always keep up with current events" as a disadvantage. However, one respondent's answer that "debate motivates me to study what I don't do by myself" shows that debate participation has a benefit of giving incentives to students to obtain broad knowledge.

Lastly, "Social life/Meeting people" uncovers an interesting feature of the Japanese. One of the answers found in both NDT and PD was: "it's impossible to debate with my friends. But in debate I can find a friend to debate with." This shows some Japanese students think it's hard to debate with friends in everyday life, but that they can find a different kind of friends in debate with whom they are able to debate or discuss various topics. If they want to enjoy intellectual discussion with friends, such friends may be hard to find in Japan but are likely to find in friends made through debating.

As for disadvantages, replies such as "(people who are) too critical become obnoxious," "when I argue back in daily life, people say 'don't debate,'" imply debate is not welcomed in daily life. A female student's answer "I was told that 'you are a girl... (why do you debate?)'" meaning that she was told that debating was not for girls. This shows a prejudice still present in Japanese society that females should not argue. Another answer "if I thrash an opponent logically, emotionally the relation gets worse" tells us that it is quite complicated to debate and maintain a good relationship at the same time, implying that attacking people's opinion is likely to be taken as an attack on their personality in Japanese society.

Next, we will compare the results of the original U.S. study with the current Japanese study (See Table 5).[5] The U.S. study did not identify "English skills" as an independent response for an obvious reason—"English" is taken for granted in speaking/communication. The percentages of "Speaking/Comm. skills" are 32.7% for NDT and 54.0% for PD, PD being higher than NDT. On the other hand, "Analytical/Critical skills" and "Research" show higher percentages for NDT than for PD. On "Analytical/Critical skills" NDT is 52.7%, while PD is 35.2%. On "Research" NDT is 29.0%, and PD is 7.3%. No clear difference is found on "Social life/Meeting people". These results explain that more PD debaters perceive "Speaking/Comm. skills" as a benefit derived from debate, while more NDT debaters perceive "Analytical/Critical skills" and "Research" as benefits in the U.S. In Japan, "Speaking/Comm. skills" shows the same tendency as in the U.S.; 42.2% for PD is higher than 22.4% for NDT. Similarly NDT shows higher percentages than PD in Japan on "Analytical/ Critical skills"; NDT is 65.5% and PD is 37.6%. In "Social life/Meeting people", there is no difference between PD and NDT in Japan.

However, Japanese NDT debaters ranked "Research" low (3.4%), even slightly lower than PD (4.6%). This shows that not only NDT debaters in Japan, but also Japanese debaters in general don't perceive "Research" as a benefit of debating. This is a noteworthy finding since evidence is indeed very important in NDT-style debate in Japan and research is supposed to be required. This may be because students see research as a burden rather than something they learn through debate. They may find research only a problem because Japanese libraries and other information systems are not adequate or because they are not systematically taught how to conduct research. Another possible interpretation is that some Japanese NDT debaters may see original research not as important as it should be because they find they can win debates with limited amount of evidence.

[...]

3.2 Costs of Debate Participation

In this section, we look into the results associated with the costs of debate. The responses related to costs are less varied and can be categorized into a few major disadvantages. Comparing the ranking of NDT and PD, the results turned out to be the same (as shown in Tables 7 & 8). The highest percentage is occupied by "Time" (for NDT, 82.8%; and for PD, 52.3) followed by "Health/sleep/frustration" (for NDT, 75.9%; and for PD, 38.5%), "Financial costs" (for NDT, 31.0%; and for PD, 21.1%), "Hurts academics"(extra burden

TABLE 7: DISADVANTAGES (NDT & PD, JAPAN)

Ranking	Disadvantage
1	Time
2	Health/sleep/frustration
3	Financial costs
4	Hurts academics
5	Affects social life

TABLE 8: DISADVANTAGES BY STYLE AND COUNTRY

Disadvantage	Japan		U.S.	
	NDT (58)	PD (109)	NDT (55)	PD (122)
Time	48	57	31	62
*	82.8%	52.3%	56.0%	50.8%
Health/sleep/frustration	44	42	10	23
*	75.9%	38.5%	18.1%	18.8%
Financial costs	18	23	4	24
*	31.0%	21.1%	7.2%	19.6%
Hurts academics	12	10	23	40
*	20.7%	9.2%	41.8%	32.7%
Affects social life	8	7	NA	NA
*	13.8%	6.4%	NA	NA
Others	28	39	NA	NA
*	48.3%	35.8%	NA	NA
Total	158	178	NA	NA
*	272.4%	163.3%	NA	NA

*percentage of responses in respective debating styles

academically) (NDT, 20.7%; PD, 9.2%), and "Affects social life" (NDT, 13.8%, PD, 6.4%).

As a total, the percentages for NDT (272.4%) are higher than those for PD (163.3%), which shows that a significantly greater number of disadvantages were reported for NDT than for PD. While most NDT debaters reported the maximum of three disadvantages allowed by the spaces, PD debaters on average reported only 1.6 disadvantages; actually there were some PD debaters who did not report any disadvantage.

PD debaters have fewer complaints about their activities than NDT debaters. Then, what is the factor that makes NDT debaters less happy than PD debaters? The relationship between "Research", "Time", and "Health/sleep/frustration" previously mentioned, offers an explanation. PD debaters conduct research individually about various topics, as they can't be fully prepared for debate rounds because the resolution is only given right before each round. On the other hand, in many cases NDT debaters' research is group-oriented with the aim of deepening analysis of the announced resolution as well as trying to find particular evidence to support the team's prepared arguments, which gives debaters a feeling of being pressed by time intensified by the sense of group obligation. Some NDT debaters actually related "Research" with "Health/sleep/frustration", saying that they "can't sleep because of research". Taking this into consideration, the higher percentages of NDT when compared to PD on "Hurts academics" and "Affects social life" can be explained by the time-consuming aspect of "Research". In conclusion, NDT debaters perceived the features of "Research" as disadvantages associated with debate. In comparison, PD debaters are less burdened by research, and have fewer factors to regard as disadvantages of debate participation.

Next, we will compare these results of Japanese with those of American debaters. Table 8 reports the disadvantages by countries and styles. In the survey conducted in the U.S., the disadvantage that shows the biggest difference between NDT and PD is "Financial costs" (NDT, 7.2%; PD, 19.6%). NDT (41.8%) is slightly higher than PD (32.7%) on "Hurts academics". On the other hand, there are few differences between different styles on "Time" and "Health/sleep/frustration". In summary, a difference between debate styles can be seen only in "Financial costs" in the U.S. In comparing this result with Japanese results, the percentage for PD debaters is found higher than that for NDT debaters on "Financial costs". Williams et al. (2001) described the reason for the higher percentages associated with financial costs for NDT when compared with PD in the U.S. as follows:

> One would expect that NPDA would be a less expensive form of debate because of lower photocopying costs and other expenses incurred in evidence acquisition. This finding may suggest that

NDT programs are typically better funded than programs sponsoring other types of debate. (p. 203)

However, in Japan the financial situation is almost the same in NDT and PD; therefore the difference in styles is not so large. This shows how well funded NDT debaters are in the U.S. Furthermore we can mention some factors that burden PD debaters apart from the cost for collecting data as in NDT. One example is traveling costs. In Japan, tournaments are often held in Tokyo and few others take place in other areas, when compared to NDT tournaments, which are more geographically diversified. In addition, it costs PD debaters a lot of money to participate in international tournaments, which are absent in NDT. Comparing the financial situations of Japan and the U.S., especially NDT, financial supports for students' debating in Japan are seriously lacking.

Looking at the overall ranking by country, it can be said that Japanese debaters are more likely to perceive "Health/sleep/frustration" as a cost than do American debaters: as both NDT and PD are below 20% in the U.S. while NDT is 75.9% and PD is 38.5% in Japan. As previously pointed out, Japanese debaters confront some prejudice and hardship when they are committed to debating, which may account for the higher percentage of Japanese debaters who feel stressed. As some studies have previously discussed, this result can be the reflection of the less argumentative predisposition of Japanese people. On "Hurts academics" American debater percentages are higher than Japanese debaters', which is likely to result from the difference in academic systems in higher education. That is, course requirements such as attendance and assignments are more demanding in American universities than in Japanese universities in general.

In the results for costs, the percentage for Japanese NDT is higher than that for PD, but the results for PD and NDT in the U.S. are similar. The percentages of cost items do not differ between styles in the U.S. In addition, "Time" and "Health/sleep/

frustration" which were previously discussed in connection with "Research" don't show any gap between styles in America. Does this mean American NDT debaters do not perceive "Research" as a disadvantage? To look further into this question, the benefits of "Research" need to be reviewed. The percentage of NDT debaters in the U.S. who perceive "Research" as a benefit is much higher than that of PD debaters (7.3%), while PD and NDT debaters in Japan show lower percentages (4.6% and 3.4%). This shows that many American debaters think "Research" is a benefit of debate, and fewer regard the problems caused by research as disadvantages. The above discussion clarifies the differences in perceptions between Japanese and American debaters. The support systems for research that are in place in each country may account for this difference. Libraries and other information systems are one possible factor. Another may be the difference of faculty support; i.e., forensic directors and coaches that some American squads enjoy are not at all available in Japan.

[...]

4. Conclusion

This paper examined the benefits and costs associated with debate participation from the results of the pioneering survey conducted on college students in Japan. Through a comparison of data, the unique characteristics of PD were illustrated. This will provide important databased suggestions for applying debate as part of English education in Japan. Comparison between the U.S. and Japan clarified some differences in the perceptions of American and Japanese debaters toward debate. Although these data are dependent on the individual perceptions of debaters, it is considered valid as empirical data.

[...]

ENDNOTES

1. There are several varieties of Parliamentary Debate used in students' competitions in the world. Since we do not get into differences among them, we simply use "Parliamentary Debate" in a generic sense.

2. What is being practiced in Japan is not exactly the same as the NDT debate in the U.S. but it has been directly or indirectly modeled after the NDT (Inoue, 1994). It is a style of debating with heavy emphasis on analysis and evidence using one policy resolution throughout the season. We call it NDT or NDT-style debate in this paper.

[…]

5. The original study (Williams et al., 2001) compared the difference of styles on "Speaking/Comm. skills", "Research", "Social life/Meeting people", "Analytical/Critical skills".

REFERENCES

[…]

Howes, R. F. (1925). American and English debating. *Quarterly Journal of Speech, 11,* 45–48.

Howes, R. F. (1928). The English debates. *Quarterly Journal of Speech, 14,* 112–116.

[…]

Inoue, N. (1994). *Ways of debating in Japan: Academic Debate in English Speaking Societies.* Ph.D. Dissertation, University of Hawaii (UMI Order Number 9519451). Dissertation Abstracts International, 56(02), 534.

Jones, K. T. (1994). Cerebral gymnastics 101: Why do debaters debate? *CEDA Yearbook, 15,* 65–75.

Johnson, E. A. (2003). *An early history of the NPDA.* Retrieved on December 31, 2003, from http://www.bethel.edu/college/dept/comm/npda/npdahistory.html.

[…]

Williams, D. E., McGee, B. R., & Worth, D. S. (2001). University student perceptions of the efficacy of debate participation: An empirical investigation. *Argumentation and Advocacy: The Journal of the American Forensic Association, 37,* 198–209.

[…]

[Literature in Japanese]

Kamada, H. (2000). *Nihon ni okeru syakaijin dibeeto kensyuu: Nihongo dibeeto kensyuu no eikyoo* [Debate training for business people in Japan: Influences of debate training in Japanese]. Unpublished M.A. thesis, Kyushu University, Japan.

Kawahatsu, M. (1990, June 19). *A prospectus of International Debate Institute, Japan.* (Distributed by the IDI Committee, College of International Relations, University of Tsukuba, Japan).

[...]

Mikuma, Y. (2003). *Eigo supiikingu gakusyuron: E.S.S. supiichi jissen no rekishiteki koosatsu* [Learning theory of speaking English: Historical analysis of praxis in public speaking in E.S.Ss.]. Tokyo: Sanshusha.

Milward, P. (1983). *Anata no Eigo o yuuben ni suru dibeeto no susume* [Invitation to debate which makes your English eloquent]. Tokyo: Eiyusha.

NAFA (The National Association of Forensics and Argumentation). (1985). *Gendai dibeeto tsuuron* [An introduction to contemporary debate]. Tokyo: NAFA Press.

Nakano, M. (2002, Oct). *Ajia shokokuno Parliamentary Debate katsudoo no jit-taichoosa* [A survey of parliamentary debate activities in Asian countries]. Paper presented at the 9th meeting of the Communication Association of Japan, Kyushu Chapter, Oita, Japan.

Nakano, M. (2004). *Kyooiku dibeeto ni okeru paaramentarii dibeeto no ichizuke: Ibunkakan kyooiku toshite no igi* [The locus of Parliamentary Debate in academic debate: Its value for intercultural education]. Unpublished M.A. thesis, Kyushu University, Japan.

Narahiko Inoue is a professor of languages and cultures at Kyushu University.

Mika Nakano is a graduate student at Kyushu University.

Inoue, Narahiko, and Mika Nakano. "The Benefits and Costs of Participating in Competitive Debate Activities: Differences between Japanese and American College Students." Paper presented at the Wake Forest University International Society for the Study of Argumentation, Venice, Italy, June 27–30, 2004.

Used by Permission.

University Student Perceptions of the Efficacy of Debate Participation: An Empirical Investigation

by David E. Williams, Brian R. McGee, and David S. Worth*

Complaints about the pedagogy and practice of interscholastic and intercollegiate debate in the United States have been legion over the last three decades. Despite the intuition of most scholars and ordinary citizens that competitive debate in both high schools and universities provides a good educational experience for students, many of those who know debate best have been quite critical of the norms that have developed over time in the debate community. For example, by 1990 Dale Herbeck, a longtime debate coach with a distinguished record concluded that "A growing body of evidence reveals that disparity may he developing between our educational objectives and [the] forensics experience that we are providing our debaters" (p. 4). The casual observer, after stumbling across our disciplinary journals, would be surprised at the ferocity of the criticism directed towards participation in debate.

Arguments to assess the efficacy of participation in debate, of course, are hardly new. For most of the last century, debate coaches have published essays devoted to defenses (e.g., McGee & Simerly, 1994; McKean, 1934; Stanfield, 1993; Steinberg, 1993) or critiques (e.g., Brooks, 1984; Frank, 1993; Howe, 1981; Rowland & Deatherage, 1988) of debate practice.

Many scholars have used survey instruments and/or interviewing methods targeting students in order to determine the most important benefits and the most significant drawbacks of debate involvement. With a few exceptions (e.g., Semlak & Shields, 1977), these studies have essentially relied on college students' (including former students') self-reports to evaluate the educational merits of academic debate (e g., Hill, 1982; Jones, 1994; Matlon & Keele, 1984; Wood & Rowland-Morin, 1989).

In this study, we follow the research tradition of asking students to report their own perceptions of the efficacy of debate practice. We see two rationales for doing so. First, to the best of our knowledge, only one study reporting student perceptions of debate efficacy has been published in the last decade, and [sic] that latest study is now six years old (Jones, 1994). To the extent that coaching practices and travel patterns may change over time, we should periodically assess whether students' impressions of debate have evolved as well.

Second, the intercollegiate debate community has changed dramatically in the last decade with the emergence of a variety of debate sponsoring organizations, yet no study has tried to compare the perceptions of students competing under the auspices of those organizations.[1] As an array of debate formats has become available, we should seek to determine whether or not those different formats are helpful in developing the same sorts of skills. Whatever the debate format in which students compete, an investigation of the current terrain where debate is concerned is required If we are to learn "why students become involved in forensics, why they stay in forensics, why they stay in the activity and [what] ... benefits they perceive they acquire by participating in forensics" (Porter, 1990, p. 99).

METHOD

The current study seeks to assess student perceptions of debate at the end of the 1990s. Surveys were mailed to directors of forensics of 358 debate programs in the United States. Mailing lists from intercollegiate debate organizations were used to secure these addresses. Each mailing included seven copies of the student questionnaire. Directors were asked to distribute the questionnaires to up to seven debaters, collect them, and return them via mail to the researchers

A cash incentive was provided to encourage a higher response rate. Each school was limited to seven surveys so that the sample would not over represent larger programs. Return postage was prepaid. A total of 70 institutions returned one or more student surveys, and 286 completed surveys were collected. Response rate was figured on the institutional responses for a rate of 19.5%, which, while not ideal, is consistent with expected response rates for mail surveys (e.g., Watt & Van Den Berg, 1995).[2] [...] The following research questions guided the analysis of the open-ended questions:

1   What benefits do students perceive from their participation in intercollegiate debate?
2   What disadvantages do students perceive from their participation in intercollegiate debate?
3   How do students' perceived benefits compare to those revealed in previous studies?
4   How do students' perceived disadvantages compare to those revealed in previous studies?

FINDINGS

Benefits of Intercollegiate Debate Participation

Question 22, on the benefits of participation, had a total of 735 responses that were compiled into 49 categories. The largest category of responses, speaking skills/communication skills, accounted for 136 responses or 18.6% of all responses. The smallest categories for benefits to debate participation involved a single response; there were 13 such categories. The 10 most frequently reported benefits are listed in Table 1.

The initial examination of the top 10 benefits identified by debaters reveals some familiar items. The first two items (speaking/ communication skills and analytical/critical thinking) are the same as the two most frequently identified benefits in the Matlon and

Item	Frequency	% of Total
Speaking skills/Comm. skills	136	18.6
Analytical/Critical skills	94	11.8
Social life/Meet people	77	10.4
Research skills	62	8.4
Knowledge/Education	46	6.2
Self-esteem/confidence	43	5.8
Argumentation	33	4.0
Travel	28	3.8
Learn about issues	28	3.8
Organizational skills	25	3.0
Thinking fast	21	2.8

Keele (1984) survey. In comparison, these two items were not rated as highly in the Wood and Rowland-Morin (1989) survey, in which improved communication skills and improved analytic skills were the sixth and eighth rated motivational elements for debaters. Also, in the Hill (1982) study the same items were the fourth and fifth most frequently identified motivations for participation. In comparing these studies, it could be argued that "benefits" of debate and "motivation" to debate are different concepts, thus accounting for the differences in the four studies. However, it is clear that the development of communication skills and critical thinking abilities has been and continues to be highly valued and consistently valued by intercollegiate debaters.

There were enough responses relevant to public speaking and communication skills to allow some examination by debate category (see Table 2). NDT (18), CEDA (54) and NPDA (66) debaters responding to this survey had a relatively high regard for the development of these skins when compared to other benefits of debate participation that were listed. Of potential interest is the percentage of debaters from each debate organization listing this benefit.

TABLE 2: SUMMARY BY ORGANIZATION

Benefits	NDT-55 debaters	CEDA-123 debaters	NPDA-122 debaters
Speaking/Comm— 171 responses	18 (10.5%)	54 (31.9%)	66 (38.5%)
*	32.7%	43.9%	54%
Research—76	16 (21%)	39 (51%)	9 (11.8%)
*	29%	31.7%	7.3%
Social—125	20 (16%)	42 (33.6%)	36 (28.8%)
*	36%	34.1%	29.5%
Analytical/Critical—149	29 (19.4%)	47 (31.5%)	43 (28.8%)
*	52.7%	38.2%	35.2%

Disadvantages	NDT-55 debaters	CEDA-123 debaters	NPDA-122 debaters
Time—199 responses	31 (15.5%)	65 (32.6%)	62 (31.1%)
*	56%	52.8%	50.8%
Academics—138	23 (16.6%)	47 (34%)	40 (28.9%)
*	41.8%	38.2%	32.7%
Health—69	10 (14.4%)	19 (27.5%)	23 (33.3%)
*	18.1%	15.4%	18.8%
Cost—56	4 (7.1%)	17 (30.3%)	24 (42.8%)
*	7.2%	13.8%	19.6%

Note: * = percentage of responses in that debate organization.

Note: Frequency numbers will be greater on this table than on the total responses chart. If a debater identified himself or herself as competing in two or more formats, the item was recorded in both columns. For example, respondent #125 competed in NPDA and LD and listed "speaking skills" as a benefit to debate participation. The response was recorded in both the NPDA and LD columns.

Over half (54%) of all NPDA debaters who completed the survey listed the public speaking/communication benefit. The percentage of CEDA debaters seeing this benefit dropped by 10%, and there was another 10% drop in the percentage of NDT debaters listing this benefit. The other debate formats had too few respondents to make a meaningful comment about their specific activity with the possible exception of Lincoln-Douglas (L-D) debaters, half of all L-D respondents (14 of 28) identified public speaking/communication skill as an advantage of debate participation. However, no matter what debate format they have experienced, the intercollegiate debaters in this sample regularly insisted that debate develops oral communication competencies.

There were also sufficient responses for the improved analytical/critical thinking benefit to allow some comparison between debate organizations. Over half of all NDT respondents (52.7%) listed analytical/critical thinking as a benefit. The other two organizations with enough respondents for meaningful comparison had noticeably smaller analytical/critical thinking responses (CEDA, 38.2%; NPDA 35.2%) While these two organizations were relatively similar in recognition of the benefit NDT respondents demonstrated the greatest reverence for analytical/critical thinking. No other benefit was cited as frequently by NDT debaters. The next largest benefit for NDT debaters was social benefits with 20 responses or 36% of all NDT respondents. Analytical/critical thinking was the second most frequently noted benefit among CEDA debaters and was noted by 38.2%, 14.5% fewer than the NDT debaters. With the exception of the research skills category, CEDA debaters' responses were more similar to those of CEDA debaters than to NDT debaters, despite the shared CEDA/NDT debate topic.

The social aspects of debate participation were ranked very highly by students in the current survey. It should be noted that social life/meet people was identified more frequently by students completing this survey than most of the benefits that would be considered educational advancement or personal development. It would appear that the current generation has elevated the role that debate plays in their college life. It has moved from an educational supplement to their college experience to a social supplement as well. (The social function of contemporary intercollegiate debate is discussed further in the following pages.)

The development of research skills continues to be a valued element of debate participation. It should not be surprising to those familiar with intercollegiate debate that NDT and CEDA debaters were most likely to indicate research skill acquisition as an advantage to debate participation (see Table 2) with 29% and 31.7% respectively. A high percentage of NEDA debaters (57%) also valued research skills, but the total number of CEDA respondents (seven) was too low to make these responses meaningful in any practical way.

Knowledge/Education is another common benefit of debate participation that appeared in this study. This category comprised responses that indicated the student benefited from general knowledge acquisition or that intercollegiate debate was a positive supplement to their overall college education. These responses were distinguished from those that identified learning about specific issues (e.g., the Supreme Court, feminism). There were eight items that dealt with learning specific issues.

[...]

The responses to the open-ended question seeking benefits to debate participation revealed some predictable responses and some unique insights. Benefits related to education were most numerous, but it also appears that the social benefit of debate may be at an all time high for intercollegiate participation when compared to earlier studies. The responses to Question 23 (disadvantages to debate participation) will also reveal some predictable results, given the previous research, but also potentially disturbing trends.

Disadvantages of Intercollegiate Debate Participation

[...]

Although time concerns did not appear in the Matlon and Keele (1984) study as a disadvantage to intercollegiate debate, it should not be a surprise to find it in the top ten in this study. Brooks (1984) long ago warned "the tune demands on both debaters and coaches are severe" (p. 14). The vast majority of respondents in this study who listed time as a disadvantage recorded this as their first concern. Although students were not asked to rank order their benefits and disadvantages, this would suggest that time was their first, or must obvious, concern.

Reviewing the time disadvantage by differentiating among debate organizations proved to be quite interesting. One might predict that the evidence-oriented debaters would feel the brunt of the time burden, especially in CEDA and NDT. However, the percentage of respondents from each debate format who indicated the time disadvantage was quite similar (see Table 3). Aside from NEDA and IPDA, which had a small number of respondents (seven and ten) but a very high percentage (85.7% and 80%) reporting the time burden, all other percentages ranged from 48.1% (ADA) to 56% (NDT).

Furthermore, NPDA was only two percentage points behind CEDA and 5.2 points behind NDT. This would seem to contradict the commonly held position that NPDA can be a less time-consuming alternative to debate formats requiring the use of expert evidence (Epstein, 1996). These results certainly cannot indicate that an equal amount of time is spent by debaters in each activity,

TABLE 3: DISADVANTAGES OF DEBATE PARTICIPATION

Item	Frequency	% of Total
Time	138	23.7
Hurts academics	104	17.8
Health/sleep/frustration/stress	56	9.6
Affects social life	54	9.2
Financial costs	42	7.2
Travel time	21	3.6
Lack of involvement in other campus activities	19	3.2
Too competitive/win attitude	18	3.0
Loss of work	17	2.9
Workload	12	2.0

but they do suggest that, across the board, intercollegiate debaters believe that the time commitment is a disadvantage to intercollegiate debate. (Of course, participants presumably could offer the same observation about some other extra and co curricular activities.)

[...]

"Hurts academics" and "affects social life" would seem to be results of the time commitment to debate. These two items, second and fourth respectively on the top 10 disadvantages list, also present a seeming contradiction in intercollegiate debaters' perception of the activity. On the benefits question, 46 debates had indicated that debate contributed to their education and helped them acquire knowledge. However, 104 debaters indicated that their participation in debate hurt them academically. This would seem to suggest that there is a muddled view of how debate accentuates a students' education. Many of the benefits are oriented toward education and learning. Yet, at the same time, the students' course work, when not related to debate, is likely to suffer. Several respondents indicated that their academic performance suffered because of missing classes, lack of time to devote to papers and projects, and an inability to attend weekend special events, lectures, or opportunities to study abroad because of debate travel.

A second apparent contradiction arises with the 54 respondents who indicated that debate negatively affected their social life. This would seem to conflict with the 77 who suggested debate benefited their social life. The contradiction begins to clear with a closer look at the negative effects on social life. The respondents included specific examples such as missing dates because of debate, limiting time spent with friends not involved in debate, and missing out on weekend or evening activities because of debate responsibilities. There were 11 respondents who noted that debate did harm to their family life. These 11 were not included in the "affects social life" category, but the cause of the problem might be much the same. In short, it appears that today's intercollegiate debaters value the friendships fostered with others in the activity, but those relationships might come at the cost of relationships held outside debate.

"Financial cost," the fifth most frequently noted disadvantage, can be combined with "loss of work," the ninth disadvantage. These two items combined would constitute 59 responses or 10.1%, of the disadvantages. It is worth noting that NDT debaters recorded a much lower concern over financial cost than CEDA and NPDA participants (see Table 2). Only four of 55 NDT respondents (7.1%) identified cost as a disadvantage. CEDA (13.8%) and NPDA (19.6%) debaters recognized a greater financial burden. One would expect that NPDA would be a less expensive form of debate because of lower photocopying costs and other expenses incurred in evidence acquisition. This finding may suggest that NDT programs are typically better funded than programs sponsoring other types of debate, thus insulating debaters from more of the financial costs of participation. The increased cost of higher education and the prevalence of the working student might contribute to this disadvantage for intercollegiate debaters.

With concerns being expressed about time constraints, academics, social life, and financial strain, the third most prevalent disadvantage seemed inevitable. Concerns over personal health, sleep frustration, and stress were put into one health concern category. Fifty respondents (9.6%) proclaimed that their health was negatively affected by debate participation. The specific responses ranged from having/starting bad habits (e.g., smoking), lack of sleep at tournaments, eating poorly, and tournament/competitive stress.

DISCUSSION

The results of this study suggest several issues worthy of note. The first concern recognizes three conflicting visions that were revealed by thus study. The conflicting visions involve the controversy over speaking skill development and speaking rate, the role of debate in debaters' social lives, and whether the acquisition of knowledge from debate balances the apparent tradeoff of underachievement in debaters' class work. These conflicting visions become problematic when attempting to portray the activity to those possible newcomers or other concerned publics (deans, presidents, employers, etc.).

Forensics literature is replete with concerns about the argument selection and delivery practices in which student advocates engage, and these concerns have been voiced repeatedly for over three decades (e g., Brooks, 1984; Frank, 1993; Horn & Underberg, 1993; Howe, 1981; Howe & Brownlee, 1993; Kruger, 1973; McGee, 1990; Morello, 1979; Olsen, 1971; Rowland & Deatherage, 1988; Simerly, 1991; Swinney, 1968; Towne, 1974; Vasilius & DeStephen, 1979). For example, advocates of public forum debate "fear that the socialization of squads in tournament debating to the exclusion of public forums teaches unsound communication practices" (Simerly & McGee, 1991, p. 6). Despite these concerns over the merits of contemporary pedagogy in intercollegiate debate, especially where communication skills are concerned, students engaged in the activity, whatever the debate format with which they are familiar, seem generally satisfied with what the activity teaches. There were 171 responses for speaking/communication skills as a benefit, and only five debaters listed speaking too fast as a disadvantage. We do not suggest that this is evidence that there should not be a concern over delivery skills in debate. Instead, we suggest that the concern is not shared by a majority of debaters, who perceive debate as fostering communication skills.

More importantly, we believe that this finding highlights the first of three conflicting visions of intercollegiate debate revealed in this study. The disagreement between coaches over the delivery issue is well known, but now the student perspective adds further confusion to the issue. This dilemma creates a conflicting vision of how competitive debate should be presented to prospective student participants and other important publics. Members of these publics, who have limited knowledge of the activity, and our organizations, would be confused over this conflicting vision of how debate does or does not help in the development of speaking skills.

In contrast, the long held claim that debate fosters the development of analytical skills and critical thinking is shared by today's debaters. This claim dates back to Howell (1943) and had been repeated in various forms since (e.g., Allen, Berkowitz, & Louden, 1995; Bradley & Mulvaney, 1964: Beckman, 1955; Brembeck, 1947; Cross, 1971; Colbert, 1987, 1995; Colbert & Biggers, 1985; Jackson, 1961; Murphy & Samosky, 1993; Williams, 1951). Most recently Allen, Berkowitz, Hunt, and Louden (1999) conducted a meta-analysis of previous research and concluded:

> The findings illustrate that participation in public communication skill building exercises consistently improves critical thinking. Participation in forensics demonstrated the largest improvement in critical thinking scores whether considering longitudinal or cross-sectional designs. (p. 27)

Today's student seems not to be concerned with McGlone's (1974) observation that the students drawn to debate may already possess greater critical thinking abilities than their non-debating peers or with Hill's (1993) criticism of studies that have found a link between debate participation and critical thinking abilities. The development of critical thinking skills presents a strong, agreed upon benefit that can be understood by current students, prospective students, and other publics. The desire to teach critical thinking skills is very strong in university settings. This is even reflected in the titles of some texts used in debate classes (i.e., Freeley, 1996; Inch & Warnick, 1998). The development of critical thinking skills should be the primary benefit proposed in efforts to reach out to new students and publics. This has long been perceived as a benefit of participation by program directors, instructors, coaches, and students alike.

The second conflicting vision revealed in this study regards the social life of intercollegiate debaters. In the Matlon and Keele (1984) study, "make friends" was not a frequently cited benefit of participation. Similar categories were largely absent in the studies completed by Hill (1982), Rowland-Morin (1989), and Jones (1994). However, in the present study there is a strong indication that debate develops strong relationships with others in the activity but this comes at the expense of other friendships and family commitments. The amount of time required by the activity would certainly help explain why the relationships are so strong between debaters. It is also possible that the current generation of debaters includes students who are more likely to place increased value on peer-group relationships. The dynamics of gaining friendships through debate while losing other friendships creates the conflicting vision of whether debate has a social benefit. The reports of participants who sacrifice family obligations to participate in debate further complicate the issue, given that some debate tournaments are held during holiday breaks when students presumably would spend time with family and friends.

The third conflicting vision revealed in this study centers around the knowledge versus academic success tradeoff. The time involved in debate and the evidence of critical thinking development suggests that debaters would have a drive to learn and thoroughly investigate issues. These are valued qualities often found in honors students (Jensen & Williams, 1998; Sharp & Johnstone, 1969). These qualities in most students would lead to academic success, and other studies also have found that debaters have above average academic achievement when compared with their non-debating peers (Hunt, Garard, & Simerly, 1997; Jones, 1994). However, the responses to the open-ended questions dearly indicate that many of these students are underachieving in the classroom. The conflicting vision occurs when debaters learn about a topic in extraordinary detail, learn the most sophisticated means of research and analysis, and then receive low grades in coursework. The current results suggest that these cases of academic tradeoff do exist insofar as students are concerned. The vision of debaters being bright, analytically gifted, research oriented students is muddied by such cases of academic underachievement.

Beyond the conflicting visions that make the case for debate's efficacy less than clear-cut, a few other findings require close attention as well. The top three disadvantages to participation (time, academics, health) should be a cause for concern. As discussed at the 1991 CEDA Assessment Conference (Ulrich, 1991), intercollegiate debate has the longest competitive season of any university competitive activity. Most college sports teams, while essentially having year round practice schedules, are limited in competition to one semester. However, debate tournaments run from September to April during the academic year. For those who attend summer camps, the debate season can become a year round activity. While those who are fully committed to the activity may take pleasure in this time commitment, it could and probably does limit the appeal of the activity to newcomers. The connection between time and the second most frequently cited disadvantage, harm to academics, is not difficult to see.

Health is a new concern that did not appear prominently in previous studies, yet was mentioned by several of our respondents. Recent efforts to address wellness issues, by the American Forensic Association for example, would appear to be a move in the right direction. However, many responses indicate that the culture of the activity includes elements inimical to participants' health. Aside from the lack of sleep during tournaments, respondents cited drug and alcohol use as contributing to the deterioration of their health. The important question remains, does the activity foster poor health habits, or would students engage in these unhealthy activities even If they were not in debate? Mundanely, debate participation probably leads to lack of sleep, given the schedule of the typical debate tournament. Some respondents did suggest that the "tournament atmosphere" also led to alcohol and drug abuse.

Finances is another concern that earned some prominence in these responses but is absent from the Matlon and Keele (1984) study. Many of today's debaters are shouldering a significant portion of their educational costs. Individual costs to students will certainly vary from program to program, and some programs dearly do offer debate scholarships. However, these results would suggest that additional scholarship moneys would be useful, as well as measures designed to reduce student costs (e.g., short two day tournaments, free or low-cost food at tournaments). Debate teams that offer financial assistance to students are certainly a move in the right direction. Season length and extended tournament travel are other considerations that put a financial strain on participants. However, we currently have little published data and what is available is badly outdated. Research by Murphy (1992), Rogers, (1991), and Watt (1991) focused solely on CEDA programs. Hunt and Inch (1993) suggest a relationship between scholarships and competitive success. More information is needed to warrant strong conclusions about the financial burdens associated with debate participation.

[...]

Debate texts often cite various ways of improving one's role in society as a reason for studying debate and argumentation. For example, Bartanen and Frank (1994) note argument is a "foundation of a free society" (p. 8) and a "life skill" (p. 10). Freeley (1996) adds that the study of argumentation helps to "protect our rights" and "maintain freedom of speech" (p. 6). Hollihan and Baaske (1994) suggest that we should study argumentation to learn "democratic decision-making" (p. 6). The current study included one response which cored "express beliefs" as a benefit and four responses for "personal growth" as a benefit. Other benefits dealing with one's role in society were absent from the results. There is likely nothing alarming in what was not included in student responses to the open-ended question. The occurrences simply further suggest that today's intercollegiate debaters differ from their predecessors and possibly differ from what might he considered a traditional view of debate as reflected in our texts. Also, what some issues are regularly discussed by coaches and judges today as potential problems in intercollegiate forensics, including sexual harassment (e.g., Simerly, Hunt, Gerard, McGee, & Stepp, 1996) and a lack of diversity among debate participants (e.g., Loge, 1991). These issues apparently were not salient for our respondents, since they were essentially absent from student lists of disadvantages of debate participation.

Finally, a review of the data reported in Table 2 suggests one of the most interesting findings of this study. Despite the Ideological and pedagogical differences that led to the creation of various debate organizations and the resulting fragmentation of the intercollegiate debate community in the 1970s, the students responding to this survey generally listed the same benefits to and disadvantages of debate participation, no matter what their experience with one or more extant debate formats. The only exception to this general tendency involved the development of research skills, since parliamentary debaters are barred from acquiring expert evidence for use in debate rounds. While the small number of CEDA, L-D, and IPDA respondents makes it difficult to compare those debate formats to other formats with any confidence, the comparison of the NDT, CEDA, and NPDA data suggests that the benefits and disadvantages of debate are perceived similarly by student competitors, despite some substantial differences in debate formats, rules governing debate practice, and organizational culture when comparing CEDA/NDT with NPDA. Given this finding, we would caution debate coaches and directors of forensics against overstating the merits of their preferred debate organizations and the drawbacks of competing organizations, since students who have competed in intercollegiate debate appear to believe that these organizations basically deliver the same services to participants. However, the relative emphasis given to those benefits may change from organization to organization.

[...]

This study has reported on the responses to open-ended questions regarding the benefits and disadvantages of debate participation. We hope that these results are of use to individual program directors and to the debate community as a whole. To some degree these results can assess where we are and how that compares to where we have been. Ideally the study can help the community assess where it needs to go in the future in terms of meeting the needs of student participants.

ENDNOTES

1. The oldest version of collegiate debate is associated with the topic and format used by the National Debate Tournament (NDT), which is affiliated with the American Forensic Association (AFA). The American Debate Association (ADA) uses the NDT policy debate topic with slightly different rules for adjudication at its tournaments. The Cross Examination Debate Association (CEDA) was established in the 1970s and offered an alternative debate format for two decades, though it now shares a common national debate topic and format with NDT schools. In the late 1990's other debate-sponsoring organizations formed in the United States including the American Parliamentary Debate Association (APDA) and National Parliamentary Debate Association (NPDA), which currently do not allow the use of expert evidence in debates. Still other formats are offered by the International Public Debate Association (IPDA), the National Education Debate Association (NEDA), and the Lincoln-Douglas debate division offered by the National Forensic Association (NFA).

2. Watt and Van Den Berg (1995) note that response rates "of 20 percent or less for a general mailing are typical" (p. 355). While one popular guideline suggests that a response rate of at least 50% is needed for minimally adequate data analysis (Babbie, 1992), the trend to lower response rates in recent years is particularly obvious in forensic research, where response rates of below 20 percent are fairly common (e.g., Rogers, 1997). The demands on the time of forensic coaches and competitors may account in part for this problem. Also, the present study required directors of forensics to seek out competitors, encourage them to complete the survey, collect the completed questionnaires, and return them to the first author. Ordinarily, a general mailing requires less work of the addressees, who need only complete and return the questionnaires that were mailed to them. As is the case with long questionnaires or complex scales, this additional work on the part of the addressee is likely to lower the response rate. The low response rate is an obvious limitation of this study, as we should be cautious about assuming that these findings are generalizable.

REFERENCES

Allen, M., Berkowitz, S., Hunt, S., and Louden, A. (1999). A Meta-analysis of the Impact of Forensics and Communication Education on Critical Thinking. *Communication Education, 48,* 18–30.

Allen, M., Berkowitz, S., and Louden, A. (1995). A study comparing the impact of communication classes and competitive forensics on critical thinking. *The Forensic, 81,* 1–7.

[...]

Babbie, E.R. (1992). *The Practice of Social Research.* (6th ed.). Belmont, CA: Wadsworth.

Bartanan, M., & Frank, D.A. (1994). *Nonpolicy debate* (2nd ed.). Scottsdale, AZ: Gorsuch Scarisbrick.

Beckman, V. (1955). *An investigation of the contributions to critical thinking made by courses in argumentation and discussion in selected colleges.* Unpublished doctoral dissertation, University of Minnesota, Minneapolis, MN.

Bradley, E.E., and Mulvaney, A. (1964). Logical reasoning and success in speech contests. *The Forensic, 50,* 9–15.

Brembeck, W. (1947). *The effects of a course in argumentation on critical thinking ability.* Unpublished doctoral dissertation, University of Wisconsin, Madison.

Brooks, J. (1984). Current problems in college debate. *Debate Issues 18,* 14–16.

Colbert, K. (1987). The effects of CEDA and NDT debate on critical thinking. *Journal of the American Forensics Association, 23,* 194–201.

Colbert, K.R. (1995). Enhancing critical thinking ability through academic debate. *Contemporary Argumentation and Debate, 16,* 52–72.

Colbert, K., & Biggers, T. (1985). Why should we support debate? *Journal of the American Forensics Association, 21,* 237–240.

Cross, G. (1961). *The effects of belief systems and the amount of debate experience on the acquisition of critical thinking.* Unpublished doctoral dissertation, University of Utah, Salt Lake City, UT.

Epstein, S. (1996). What about research? How to be well-read. *Parliamentary Debate 4,* 3–13.

Frank, D.A. (1993). Debate as rhetorical scholarship: Changing delivery practices in CEDA. In D.A. Thomas & S.C. Wood (Eds.), *CEDA 1991 20th Anniversary Assessment Conference Proceedings* (pp. 75–95). Dubuque, IA: Kendall Hunt.

Freeley, A.J. (1996). *Argumentation and Debate: Critical Thinking for Reasoned Decision Making* (9th ed.). Belmont, CA: Wadsworth.

Herbeck, D. (1990). Debate scholarship: A needs assessment. *National Forensic Journal, 8,* 1–16.

Hill, B. (1982). Intercollegiate debate: Why do students bother? *Southern Speech Communication Journal, 48,* 77–88.

Hill, B., (1993). The value of competitive debate as a vehicle for promoting development of critical thinking ability. *CEDA Yearbook, 14,* 1–23.

Hollihan T.A., & Baaske, K.T. (1994). *Arguments and arguing: The products and process of human decision-making*. Prospect Heights, IL: Waveland.

Horn, G., & Underberg, L. (1993). Educational debate: An unfulfilled promise? In D. A. Thomas & S. C. Wood (Eds.), *CEDA 1991 20th anniversary assessment conference proceedings*, (pp. 37–74). Dubuque, IA: Kendell Hunt.

Howe, J.H. (1981). CEDA's objective: Lest we forget. *CEDA Yearbook, 2*, 1–3.

Howe, J., & Brownlee, D. (1993). The founding principles of CEDA. In D.A. Thomas & S.C. Wood (Eds.), *CEDA 1991 20th Anniversary Assessment Conference Proceedings* (pp. 249–262). Dubuque, IA: Kendall Hunt.

Howell, W. S. (1943). The effects of high school debate on critical thinking. *Speech Monographs*, 10, 96–103.

Hunt, S.B., & Inch, E.S. (1993). *The top 50 forensics programs in the US: A twenty year retrospective*. Paper presented at the annual meeting of the Western Speech Communication Association, Albuquerque.

Hunt, S. K., Garard, D., & Simerly, G. (1997). Reasoning and risk: Debaters as an academically at-risk population. *Contemporary Argumentation and Debate, 18*, 48–56.

[…]

Inch, E.S., & Warnick, B. (1998). *Critical thinking and communication: The use of reason in argument*. Boston: Allyn & Bacon.

Jackson, T. (1961). The effects of intercollegiate debating on critical thinking. *Dissertation Abstracts International, 21*, 35–56.

Jensen, K.K. & Williams, D.E. (1998). Teaching the honors public speaking course. *Basic Communication Course Annual, 10*, 133–156.

Jones, K.T. (1994). Cerebral gymnastics 101: Why do debaters debate? *CEDA Yearbook, 15*, 65–75.

Kruger, A. N. (1973). Are debate coaches becoming misologists? *Journal of the American Forensic Association, 10*, 47–48.

Loge, P. (1991). Black participation in CEDA debate: A quantification and analysis. *CEDA Yearbook, 12*, 79–87.

Matlon, R.J., and Keele, L.M. (1984). A Survey of Participants in the National Debate Tournament, 1947–1980. *Journal of the American Forensic Association* 20, 194–205.

McGee, B.R. (1990). Debate as dialogic communication: Implications of Martin Buber's thematics in communicology for academic debate. Paper presented at the meeting of the Speech Communication Association, Chicago.

McGee, B.R. & Simerly, G. (1994). Intuition, common sense, and judgment. *CEDA Yearbook 15*, 86–97.

McGlone, E. L. (1974). The behavioral effects of forensics participation. *Journal of the American Forensics Association, 104*, 140–146.

McKean, D.D. (1934). Debate or conference? *Quarterly Journal of Speech, 20,* 222–236.

Morello, J.T. (1979). Intercollegiate debate: Ten years of sound and fury signifying nothing. *Speaker and Gavel, 17,* 39–42.

Murphy, S.K., and Samosky, J.A. (1993). "Argumentation and Debate: Learning to Think Critically." *Speaker and Gavel 17,* 39–45.

Murphy, T.I. (1992). A survey of top CEDA programs 1989–1990. *CEDA Yearbook 13,* 44–55.

Olsen, D.O. (1971). A survey of attitudes on the spread. *Speaker and Gavel, 8,* 66–69.

Porter, S. (1990). Forensics research: A call for action. *National Forensic Journal, 8,* 95–103.

Rogers, J. E. (1991). What do they have that I haven't got? Comparison survey data of the resources and support systems of top CEDA programs and directors. *CEDA Yearbook 12,* 95–105.

Rogers, J. E. (1997). A community of unequals; An analysis of dominant and sub-dominant culturally linked perceptions of participation and success within intercollegiate competitive debate. *Contemporary Argumentation and Debate, 18,* 1–22.

Rowland, R. C., & Deatherage, S. (1988). The crisis in policy debate. *Journal of the American Forensic Association, 24,* 246–250.

[…]

Semlak, W.D., and Shields, D.C. (1977). The Effects of Debate Training on Students Participation in the Bicentennial Youth Debates. *Journal of the American Forensic Association 13,* 193–96.

Sharp, H., Jr., & Johnstone, C. (1969). Independent study for undergraduates. *Speech Teacher, 18,* 308–311.

Simerly, G. (1991). *The utility of IE participation for teaching public speaking skills to intercollegiate debaters.* Paper presented at the meeting of the Central States Communication Association, Chicago.

Simerly, G., Hunt, S.K., Gerard, D., McGee, B.R., & Stepp, P. (1996, November). *Sexual harassment in intercollegiate debate II The Nationals survey.* Paper presented at the meeting of the Speech Communication Association, San Diego.

Simerly, G., & McGee, B.R. (1991). A conceptual schema for assessing the educational function of a forensics program. *Speech and Theater Association of Missouri Journal, 27,* 5–14.

Stanfield, S.J. (1993). A response to Frank, Horn and Underberg. In D.A. Thomas & S.C. Wood (Eds.), *CEDA 1991 20th Anniversary Assessment Conference Proceedings* (pp. 97–101). Dubuque, IA: Kendall Hunt.

Steinberg, D.L. (1993). Some thoughts on debate in the 90's. In D.A. Thomas & S.C. Wood (Eds.), *CEDA 1991 20th Anniversary Assessment Conference Proceedings* (pp. 97–101). Dubuque, IA: Kendall Hunt.

Swinney, J.P. (1969). The relative comprehension of contemporary tournament debate speeches. *Journal of the American Forensic Association, 5,* 16–20.

Towne, R. (1974). Rat-a-tat tat. *Speaker and Gavel, 12,* 8–10.

Ulrich, W. (1991). Reflections on the 1991 CEDA Assessment Conference. *CEDA Yearbook, 12,* 106–107.

Vasilius, J.M., & DeStephen, D. (1979). An investigation of the relationship between debate tournament success and rate, evidence, and jargon. *Journal of the American Forensic Association, 15,* 194–204.

Watt, J.H., & Van Den Berg, S.A. (1995). *Research methods for communication science.* Boston: Allyn and Bacon.

Watt, W.M. (1991). Exploring some possible success variables in CEDA debate programs. *The Forensic, 76,* 1–11.

Williams, D. (1951). *The effects of training in college debating on critical thinking ability.* Unpublished Master's Thesis, Purdue University, Lafayette, IN.

Wood, S., & Rowland-Morin, P. (1989). Motivational tension: Winning vs. pedagogy in academic debate. *National Forensics Journal, 7,* 81–97.

---

*David E. Williams is an associate professor of communication at Florida Atlantic University.

Brian R. McGee is a former professor of communication and is currently the senior policy adviser in the Office of the President at the College of Charleston.

David S. Worth is a lecturer in humanities and director of debate at Rice University.

Williams, David E., Brian R. McGee, and David S. Worth. "University Student Perceptions of the Efficacy of Debate Participation: An Empirical Investigation." *Argumentation and Advocacy* 37 (2001): 198–209.

Used by Permission.

PART 3

Debate Teaching

The three articles in this section offer important perspectives on the actual teaching of debate. While focusing on the "debate across the curriculum" movement, Joe Bellon, in "A Research-based Justification for Debate Across the Curriculum," makes the general case that teaching debate to students is so important that it should be taught to as many students as possible. Some educational institutions are even adopting the curriculum to teach debate to all students as a sort of general education requirement. Such a policy may be out of reach for many, but the underlying premise is that teaching debate is extremely valuable for our students—arguments that are compelling for anyone trying to persuade others about the on-balance benefits of debate. In "Competitive Forensics Experience as a Predictor of Teaching Effectiveness," by Sheila L. Hughes, we see that debate participation provides key experiences and skills for future teachers. In essence, debate experience strengthens the ability to teach. The final article in this section, "An Assessment of University Administrators: Do They Value Competitive Debate and Individual Events Programs?" by Robert S. Littlefield, provides a study that discusses the relative merits of debate. What separates the Littlefield article from other studies in this book is that Littlefield concentrates on arguments that emphasize debate's value to educational administrators and potential donors. In other words, these are arguments intended for decision makers and policy-makers.

A Research-based Justification for Debate Across the Curriculum

*by Joe Bellon**

One of the most notable recent developments in the forensics community is a desire to move the activity beyond its traditional boundaries. One manifestation of this trend is the rise of activist and outreach programs sponsored by college debate programs. These efforts are often aimed at bringing more (and more diverse) people into the world of competitive debate, and several such programs are experiencing dramatic success. This desire to expand debate is not limited to bringing others in, however. Increasingly, former debaters in the academic community initiate efforts to move debate outward, encouraging their colleagues to incorporate the skills and practice of debate in a broader range of classroom settings. Ultimately, those of us who have witnessed the power of debate to enhance learning and motivate students are becoming advocates of instituting debate across the entire college curriculum.

Of course, advocates of debate across the curriculum must produce strong evidence demonstrating pedagogical benefits if such initiatives are to succeed. Fortunately, the idea of distributing certain kinds of instructional practices across the college curriculum is no longer considered revolutionary. The effort to incorporate writing into many different subjects has been underway for decades and is now supported by hundreds of studies. As even a cursory search of academic periodicals will demonstrate, many different disciplines have begun to suggest that their practices should exist across the curriculum. Unfortunately, and in part because so few institution-wide debate across the curriculum programs exist, relatively little specific research concerning the benefits of debate across the curriculum has been published. As a new generation of scholars focuses on debate as an appropriate subject for research-and as more debate across the curriculum programs are created—more resources may be devoted to debate assessment.

It would be a mistake, however, to assume that the dearth of direct research on debate across the curriculum renders us incapable of meeting our evidentiary obligation in advocating such initiatives. A considerable tradition of scholarship exists verifying the benefits of engaging in forensics. Furthermore, research conducted by educational psychologists is demonstrating the substantial cognitive gains by students involved in participatory learning activities like debate. My purpose is to review the findings of several scholarly communities and in the process make the case for debate across the curriculum a more compelling one.

[...]

THE BENEFITS OF DEBATE

Competitive debate has a much longer history than the effort to implement CAC. For as long as it is possible to trace the history of democratic societies, testimonial accounts have espoused the benefits of forensic activities for developing an educated and aware citizenry. Although contemporary competitive policy debate achieves its specialized form only in this century, the forensic arts have existed formally at least since ancient Greek civilization. Successive experiments with limited democracy have provided their own examples of forensic importance, ranging from Socrates' advocacy of directed questioning to the traveling debates of Lincoln and Douglas to the arrival of the televised age as evidenced by the Kennedy-Nixon debates. Debate is so fundamentally connected to democratic practice that, for much of our civilization's history, its benefits have been thought nearly self-evident.

As modern scholars began to turn their attention to studying our own society in the middle of this century, however, these assumptions began to be tested by social scientists. Their research has not only confirmed that debate is beneficial for members of democratic societies—it has actually helped explain more effectively how participation in forensic activities improves our lives. Students who participate in competitive debate enjoy a number of positive benefits. The first and most obvious of these is improved communication skills. Where many undergraduates may have, at best, a single classroom experience involving public speaking, debaters spend many hours assembling and practicing hundreds of public speeches on topics of national importance. The questioning skills developed in cross-examination make debaters more capable of eliciting important information from their peers, thereby sharpening their analytical skills. Semlak and Shields (1997), for example, determined that debaters are "significantly better at employing the three communication skills (analysis, delivery, and organization)" than students who have not had debate experience (194). Such superior communication skills do not go unnoticed. Pollock's (1982) study of legislators concludes that "persons with oral communication skills honed by varied forensic events were also regarded highly by their colleagues in group discussion activity" (17). This sort of study supports Colbert & Biggers' (1985) contention that debate training improves interpersonal communication skills as well as public speaking competence.

While it seems intuitive that an activity involving competitive speaking would improve communication skills, debate also facilitates education in other, more subtle ways. Debate experience induces student involvement in important social issues. Every year, debaters study one prominent social issue, researching policy options from multiple perspectives. The knowledge thus gained often far surpasses the typical educational experience of non-debaters. Robinson (1956) describes debate experience as "an introduction to the social sciences" (62). The sheer breadth of topics a debater is likely to encounter, along with the competitive incentive to understand how the political world operates, virtually ensures that students who debate will be well versed in current events and public decision-making dynamics.

Barfield (1989) found that participation in competitive debate among high school students positively correlates with significant gains in cumulative GPA. The most comprehensive study to date of the effects of participation in debate was conducted by the Open Society Institute in 1999. Melinda Fine, the Institute's independent evaluator, investigated the impact of participation in the Urban Debate League on hundreds of high school students in New York City. She concludes that debate "appears to strengthen students' ability to persevere, remain focused, and work toward challenging goals.... Coaches and students agree that debaters have a heightened capacity to hang in and struggle—often in the face of disappointment and defeat" (62).

Academic debate does more than simply inform students—it teaches them how to evaluate the information they receive on a daily basis. Dauber (1989) asserts the unique emancipatory potential of forensics:

> To me, academic debate is primarily valuable in that it is a mechanism for empowerment.... Whatever else academic debate teaches (and I would argue that it teaches a great deal), it empowers our students and ourselves, in that it proves to them they ought not be intimidated by the rhetoric of expertise surrounding questions of policy. They know that they are capable of making and defending informed choices about complex issues outside of their own area of interest because they do so on a daily basis (206).

Indeed, Fine came to much the same conclusion when studying students in New York. She argues that debaters are more likely to speak out because they "feel they have something useful to say, and because they feel more articulate in saying it" (61). These finding closely resemble Corson's conclusion that encouraging students to speak forces them to "confront learners with viewpoints different from their own" and therefore to achieve "an openness to the world and others" (25). Fine also discovered that participating in debate gives student better social skills and causes them to place more value on their social relationships. Debate is thus not only a way to connect students with academic subjects in meaningful ways; it is also a way to re-connect students to public life if they have been overcome by feelings of alienation.

The best documented educational benefit of debating elaborates the connection between forensics and critical thinking. As far back as 1949, Brembeck demonstrated that students with argumentation training "significantly outgained the control students in critical thinking scores" (187). Colbert (1987) reviews the contemporary literature and concludes that both the consensus of the literature and his own experimental findings justify the conclusion that "debaters' critical thinking test scores are significantly higher than those of nondebaters" (199). Barfield also found significant correlation between debate participation and increased critical thinking skills.

The most definitive research in this area has been conducted by Allen, et al. Their first (1995) study explicitly sought to correct the flaws of previous efforts to quantify the connection between debate and critical thinking. In comparing the effects of both forensic participation and formal communication instruction on critical thinking skills, they concluded that, while "both argumentation classes and forensic participation increased the ability in critical thinking ... participation in competitive forensics demonstrates the largest gain in critical thinking skills" (6). Indeed, their study provides support for preferring debate to formal communication instruction. Their results "demonstrate that the gain [in critical thinking] is larger for a semester of competitive forensic participation than a similar time period spent in an argumentation class (and the argumentation class was superior to public speaking or an introduction to interpersonal communication course)" (6). These findings were largely replicated in their more recent (1999) meta-analysis of studies exploring the link between communication skills and critical thinking.

The positive benefits of debate are not limited to the classroom. In fact, much of the current research establishing the value of debate does account for the time students spend preparing for debate tournaments. Competitive tournaments are preceded by substantial cooperative research, argument development, and practice. Policy debate teams consist of two students, but the competitive success of any particular team is made possible only by the combined efforts of an entire school's roster of debaters and coaches. The contrast of cooperative preparation and competitive performance provides debaters with the unique opportunity to experience all the benefits of what Johnson and Johnson (1979) might call constructive controversy. They conclude that, properly managed, "controversy can arouse conceptual conflict, subjective feelings of uncertainty, and epistemic curiosity; increase accuracy of cognitive perspective-taking; promote transitions from one stage of cognitive and moral reasoning to another; increase the quality of problem solving; and increase creativity" (57). For controversy to be managed properly, however, instructors must also promote cooperative learning and intellectual disagreement. Competitive forensics provides opportunities for both modes of learning, and policy debate specifically teaches students to adopt multiple perspectives—which Johnson and Johnson describe as one of the most important problem-solving skills.

Given the positive benefits of debating, it is not surprising that forensic experience helps debaters succeed in the business world as well. Research demonstrates that certain of the professions are more likely to approve of students if they have debate experience. We have already seen how debate improves one's ability to succeed in governmental service (Pollock). Church (1975) surveyed opinion leaders in the legal field, finding that "both college prelegal advisors and law school deans expressed general approval of forensic participation" (52). These findings are certainly in keeping with the astonishing number of former debaters who now earn their living in the law. Schroeder and Schroeder (1995) similarly surveyed educational administrators, many of whom were former debaters. Their respondents "overwhelmingly indicated that debate was the single most important educational activity they engaged in and attributed many of their administrative skills to forensic participation" (19). Colbert and Biggers summarize debate's attraction for those interested in gainful employment:

> In a time when many of our students ask us how educational activities will help them get a job, the answer seems to be unequivocal. Debate experience is highly valued by the business world. The value placed on debate by business is well founded. Former debaters tend to be very successful people (239).

Because debate experience is so effective in helping students achieve positive goals, the preventative value of the activity did not receive a great deal of scholarly attention before the last fifteen years. With the creation of urban debate leagues in Atlanta, New York, Tuscaloosa, and Detroit, the debate community has been flooded with anecdotal reports describing a connection between forensic experience and reduced violence. Many coaches described situations where debate transformed students from gang members and trouble-makers into successful and cooperative students. Increasingly, scholars are proving that these reports represent an underlying and demonstrable relationship between increased debate skills and decreased physical violence.

In 1976, Boone and Montare hypothesized that language skills are related to aggression. In their study, "high language proficiency was associated with low physical aggressive behavior" in minority populations (856). They concluded that "relatively higher levels of language proficiency may function more effectively and efficiently as inhibitors (or perhaps neutralizers) of overt physical aggressive behavior" (856). This relationship is fairly intuitive: when we feel capable of responding to a situation verbally, we are less likely to feel pressured to respond physically. Infante and Wigley (1986) note that this relationship emphasizes the need for those in the communication discipline to act "because [the communication discipline] is particularly able to remedy argumentative skill deficiencies and therefore could be instrumental in reducing the amount of . . . violence in society" (62). There is also reason to believe that debate develops the specific argumentation skills needed to prevent violence. Neer (1994) describes "a consensus . . . among many argument theorists regarding the value of argument within an interpersonal relationship" (17). His recommendation for ideal argumentative style reads like a description of debate practice:

> [F]lexible arguers will actively seek alternative points of view on an issue, hold multiple opinions on an issue, and examine viewpoints to which they are either unfamiliar or opposed when arguing the content of an issue (19).

Because competitive debaters must alternately argue both "sides" of the topic in any given tournament, there is a powerful incentive for them to become flexible arguers. In any given debate round, students may be called on to affirm or negate a particular political perspective. Above all, debate teaches students to understand how others think—even those others with whom they strongly disagree.

The key to understanding how debate helps prevent violence involves the distinction between argumentativeness (or assertiveness) and verbal aggression. This distinction was described by Infante and Wigley:

> The locus of attack may be used for distinguishing argument from verbal aggression (Infante and Rancer, 1982). Argument involves presenting and defending positions on controversial issues while attacking the positions taken by others on the issues. Verbal aggression, on the other hand, denotes attacking the self-concept of another person instead of, or in addition to, the person's position on a topic of communication (61).

While argumentativeness can have many positive benefits, there is broad agreement among scholars that verbal aggression is inherently damaging. Furthermore, verbal aggression tends to create more verbal aggression and, ultimately, physical violence. Infante, et al. (1984)

specifically studied the relationship between argumentation skills and verbal aggression among students. Their research provides an excellent description of the communication-violence dynamic:

> The individuals in an argument realize that they need to attack and defend positions. After an argument begins, the person who lacks skill in arguing is unable to refute the opponent's position. That person then satisfies the need to attack by attacking verbally the object closest to the opponent's position, the opponent. The need to defend is similarly corrupted. Since the unskillful arguer is unable to defend his or her position but still wishes to, he or she sets up a defense around the closest thing to the position, self. The opponent's attacks on position are then perceived as personal attacks and the individual feels justified responding in kind (76).

Thus, improved argument skills can prevent verbal aggression not only by preventing students from being verbally aggressive, but also by preventing them from responding to verbal aggression in kind—creating a positive feedback loop that can impact the entire school community.

Targeted research demonstrates that debate experience tends to increase beneficial argumentativeness while reducing verbal aggression. Colbert (1993) concludes that policy debate training can enhance argumentativeness without increasing verbal aggression and that debating values can actually reduce verbal aggression without decreasing argumentativeness. These findings were substantially replicated in 1994, when Colbert concluded a follow-up study by demonstrating that debate increases argumentativeness in participants without an increase in aggression. Furthermore, Colbert (1994) notes that "debating may be an effective method of assertiveness training," especially for women (7). Four separate studies now support the claim that debating increases argumentativeness and reject the claim that it increases verbal aggression. It is also worth noting that the value-oriented debate Colbert (1993) highlights as reducing aggression has been substantially incorporated into competitive debate. Indeed, students are now more likely to purse value-based perspectives on policy issues than ever before.

Fine makes the connection between debate participation and violence reduction explicit. She concludes that debate gives students greater self esteem and that debaters "appear to assign higher value to resolving their conflicts through dialogue rather than force" (64). The students in her study provide extensive descriptions of their new ability to "stand back, reflect on their arguments, frame them more powerfully, and communicate without conveying an aggressive energy that might inhibit productive exchange" (64).

[...]

Conclusion

The existing academic literature makes a powerful case for debate across the curriculum. Debate training improves communication competence and critical thinking, and the existing research in educational psychology gives us every reason to expect that these benefits will only increase as debate pedagogy is implemented across the curriculum. Properly formulated, DAC [Debate Across the Curriculum] programs incorporate the best aspects of communication across the curriculum and critical thinking across the curriculum. DAC thus answers the challenge that has been issued by regional higher education accreditation agencies, many of whom have asked undergraduate institutions to implement oral guidelines. Debate gives students an opportunity to develop skills they will need in the real world—an opportunity that contributes to their academic success while simultaneously improving their social skills. With the recent national focus on violence in schools, we should work hard to help students find non-violent ways to resolve their conflicts. Debate-intensive instruction has the potential to improve human relationships in the larger community and in the classroom. It is our job to see that potential fulfilled.

REFERENCES

[…]

Allen, M., Berkowitz, S., & Louden, A. 1995 (Fall). A study comparing the impact of communication classes and competitive forensic experience on critical thinking improvement. The Forensic of Pi Kappa Delta, 1–8.

Allen, M., Berkowitz, S., Hunt, S. & Louden, A. 1999. A meta-analysis of the impact of forensics and communication education on critical thinking. Communication Education, 48 (1), 18–30.

[…]

Barfield, K. D. 1989. A study of the relationship between active participation in interscholastic debating and the development of critical thinking skills with implications for school administrators and instructional leaders. Dissertation Abstracts International, 50-09A: 2714.

Boone, S. & Montare, A. 1976. Test of the language-aggression hypothesis. Psychological Reports, 39 (#3, part 1), 851–857.

[…]

Church, R. 1975. The educational value of oral communication courses and intercollegiate forensics: An opinion survey of college prelegal advisors and law school deans. The Journal of the American Forensic Association, 12, 49–53.

Colbert, K. 1987. The effects of CEDA and NDT debate training on critical thinking ability. Journal of the American Forensic Association, 23, 194–201.

Colbert, K. 1993. The effects of debate participation on argumentativeness and verbal aggression. Communication Education, 42 (3), 206–214.

Colbert, K. 1994 (Spring). Replicating the effects of debate participation on argumentativeness and verbal aggression. The Forensic of Pi Kappa Delta, 1–13.

Colbert, K. & Biggers, T. 1985. Why should we support debate? Journal of the American Forensic Association, 21, 237–240.

[…]

Dauber, C. 1989. Debate as empowerment. Journal of the American Forensic Association, 25, 205–207.

[…]

Fine, M. F. 1999 (June). "My friends say, 'Debater girl! Why are you always debating with me?'": A study of the New York Urban Debate League. Unpublished research report prepared for the Open Society Institute (400 West 59th Street, New York, NY 10019).

Infante, D., Trebing, J. Shepherd, P. & Seeds, D. 1984. The relationship of argumentativeness to verbal aggression. The Southern Speech Communication Journal 50 (1), 67–77.

Infante, D. & Wigley, C. 1986. Verbal aggressiveness: An interpersonal model and measure. Communication Monographs, 53 (1), 61–69.

Johnson, D. & Johnson, R. 1979. Conflict in the classroom: Controversy and learning. Review of Educational Research, 49 (1), 51–70.

[…]

Neer, M. 1994. Argumentative flexibility as a factor influencing message response style to argumentative and aggressive arguers. Argumentation and Advocacy, 31 (1), 17–33.

[…]

Pollock, A. 1982. The relationship of a background in scholastic forensics to effective communication in the legislative assembly. Speaker and Gavel 19, 17.

[…]

Robinson, J. 1956. A recent graduate examines his forensic experience. The Gavel 38, 62.

Schroeder, A. & Schroeder, P. 1995 (Summer). Education objectives and forensics: An administration perception. The Forensic of Pi Kappa Delta, 13–21.

Semlak, W. D. & Shields, D. 1977. The effect of debate training on students participation in the bicentennial youth debates. Journal of the American Forensic Association, 13, 194–196.

[…]

---

*Joe Bellon** is a senior lecturer of communication and director of debate at Georgia State University.

Bellon, Joe. "A Research-based Justification for Debate Across the Curriculum." *Argumentation and Advocacy* 36 (2000): 161–175.

Used by Permission.

Competitive Forensics Experience as a Predictor of Teaching Effectiveness

*by Sheila L. Hughes**

For years forensics activity has been developing and expanding within the educational system. In 1974, the National Development Conference on Forensics defined the activity as "an educational activity primarily concerned with using an argumentative perspective in examining problems and communicating with people" (p. 11). The conference offered the premises that forensics allowed competitors opportunities to cultivate and experiment with a variety of skills, which would then allow them to develop their own "abilities and styles of arguments" (McBath, 1984, p. 10).

McBath (1984) suggested further the abilities that competitors may develop: "Forensics serves as a curricular and co-curricular laboratory for improving students' abilities in research, analysis and oral communication. This perspective organizes scholarship, stimulating research and creative activity to promote an understanding of personal and public issues through argument" (p. 9).

It has long been known that forensics activity allows its competitors to enhance their public speaking skills. While contest speaking is, indeed, rare beyond forensics, it can benefit students in job interviews, classroom discussions, business presentations or politics (Dean, 1987). Indeed, participation in forensics activity provides a competitor with skills that can be extremely beneficial in nearly any career choice a student may make (Colbert, 1987; Colbert and Biggers, 1985: Dance, 1980; Dean, 1987; Faules, Rieke & Rhodes, 1976; Lalor, 1987; Matlon and Keele, 1984; McBath, 1984; McGlone, 1974; Ross, 1979; Semlak and Shields, 1977; Weitzel, 1987). McBath (1984) suggested that forensics activity "offers a dependable foundation for careers in such areas as law, communication, public affairs, education, business, and politics" (p. 10). Colbert and Biggers (1985) said that forensics experience provided a competitor with "excellent pre-professional preparation" (p. 237).

But it is disappointing to note that few people realize the value of the activity in any forum outside of the forensics weekend. Thomas (1983) noted that "as long as forensics events am seen simply as competitive events, we should not expect the forensics community to advance towards establishing a practice" (p. 17). It is important, therefore, that we continue to delve into the usefulness of forensics activities, focusing on the merits of the student's educational experience.

Yet, little systematic work has empirically demonstrated measurable benefits or explicated the conceptual underpinnings that presumably produce such desired effects. The purpose of this research was to test the assumptions of forensics participation's beneficial effects by examining perhaps the most direct link between careers, content, and skills: the teaching of Oral Communication. Simply stated, the benefits associated with forensics participation ought to be observed and measurable in a class that focuses on issues inherent to forensics experience: Oral Communication. Teachers with a forensics background ought to provide several advantages to their students as compared to instructors without such background. One might even argue that the conceptual and practical benefits of forensics participation are consistent with models of effective teaching generally, so the value of forensics training ought not be limited to teaching of particular content or within a particular discipline.

The arguments to support the impact of forensics participation on instructional effectiveness are ordered as follows: first, the conceptual/theoretical foundations of forensics will be described and linked to such foundations of instructional effectiveness. From this synthesis, a general hypothesis will be deduced. Second, the "activity" dimension of forensics will be explored and linked to classroom teacher behaviors associated with effective pedagogy. From this analysis, specific hypotheses emerge discriminating the instructor with forensics experience from the instructor without.

CONCEPTUAL AND THEORETICAL FOUNDATIONS
[...]

Instructors
Instructors play a vital role since they have responsibility to students, parents and society. As educating the masses in this day and age is no easy task, the skills that instructors bring with them into the classroom may very well be predictors of how well they carry out that responsibility. It appears that the most important skill that an instructor can possess is effective communication (Bedwell, Hunt, Touzel, and Wiseman, 1984; Chermesh and Tzelgov, 1979; McCroskey, 1982; Nussbaum and Scott, 1979; Rubin and Feezel, 1985; Stanton-Spicer and Marty-White, 1981). According to Stanton-Spicer and Marty-White (1981), "the salience of the teachers to the instructional communication process cannot be overemphasized, given that the essence of teaching is communication" (p. 354). Indeed, Bloom (1976) suggested that quality of communication in the classroom may account for 25% of the variance in student achievement.

[...]

The goals of forensics model those skills necessary for the enhancement of effective teaching. It would seem apparent, therefore, that instructors with forensics training would be at an advantage compared with their non-forensics counterparts when called upon to teach oral communication. However, there is little empirical data on the matter.

Some of the requirements for good teaching include skills such as instructor motivation (Ericksen, 1984; Rubin and Feezel, 1986), enthusiasm (Dimitroff and Torres, 1987; Ericksen, 1984), subject knowledge (Kearney and McCroskey, 1980; McDonald, 1978), organization (Ericksen, 1984; Nuthall, 1987), delivery (Beebe, 1974; McBath and Cripe, 1965), and feedback (Gorham, 1988; Scott and Wheeless, 1977). These can all be acquired from and refined through forensics participation. These factors should produce high student evaluations for instructors with forensics experience when compared with those instructors without such a background. Therefore the following general hypothesis was posited:

H1: *Oral Communication instructors with forensics experience will be evaluated by their students more positively than those instructors without forensics experience.*

While forensics experience may enhance overall teaching effectiveness, it would follow also that specific skills resulting from forensics participation should produce an increase in specific dimensions of teacher effectiveness. Therefore, a number of independent hypotheses surrounding competitive forensics activity and teaching effectiveness were deduced. For purposes of condensing this article, only two will be discussed.

Subject Knowledge

Before a forensics competitor can present a speech in competition s/he must be sufficiently informed on the issue. McBath (1984) argued that competitors must acquire a great deal of subject knowledge in a variety of areas pertaining to the events in which they are involved. Debate, limited preparation and prepared events demand students remain up to date on current issues.

Obviously, an instructor must have command of the subject that is being taught. Rubin and Feezel (1986) reported Boyer's (1984) definition of such knowledge as "an understanding of the curriculum (subject matter and how knowledge of it is assessed)" (p. 254). Moreover, McDonald (1978) suggested that "the major areas of competence to be evaluated are the substantive knowledge about the content of curricula" (p. 10).

[...]

In regard to a public speaking course, a forensics competitor will have more practical *experience* with issues such as persuasive and informative speaking (two major components of instruction in the typical Oral Communication course) than a non-forensics instructor because of the opportunities provided them in competition. In addition, the breadth of experience obtained through debate and prepared events aids in instructing and evaluating these events and creates a greater storehouse of examples for presentation in lectures and discussions. This expertise should become apparent to students and enhance perceptions of instructor competence. Therefore:

H2: *Oral communication instructors with forensics experience will be perceived by their students as possessing more knowledge pertaining to oral communication issues than those instructors without forensics experience.*

Delivery

One major benefit of forensics activity is the cultivation of delivery skills (Colbert, 1987; Lalor, 1987; Lewis et al., 1984; McBath, 1984). Competition in any of the event categories allows a competitor to develop and/or enhance delivery skills. Since, throughout the course of a competition weekend, a competitor delivers a speech a minimum of three times, and usually competes with more than one speech, the experience offers the participant more speaking experience than an entire semester of a public speaking course.

[...]

Studies have shown that instructors who possessed good delivery skills have been perceived as being more credible (Beebe, 1974), more competent (McDonald, 1978; Rubin and Feezel, 1986; Rubin & Henzl, 1984), have more of an ability to motivate (Ericksen, 1984), and create a more positive learning environment (Vohs, 1964).

Good delivery, therefore, has the ability to create desire in one's audience, be it judge or student, to want to listen and has the potential to motivate those listeners to obtain more information regarding the issues. Forensics competitors enhance their delivery skill through the number of opportunities provided them at each tournament to deliver a speech as well as the opportunities to provide coaching, Although a general education Oral Communication course or other performance classes allow a prospective Oral Communication instructor speaking opportunities, they in no way provide the number of opportunities received by a forensics competitor, nor are they as likely to provide the invaluable tutorial assistance to enhance performance. Therefore, the following can he deduced: *H3: Oral Communication instructors with forensics experience will be perceived by their students as more effective in their delivery styles than those instructors without forensics experience.*

METHODOLOGY
[...]

Subjects were 47 Graduate Teaching Assistants at a major university. Twenty-four instructors possessed a background in competitive forensics activity and 23 did not. Response on teacher evaluation forms were gathered from 5,724 students over a five year period; 2,723 for teaching assistants with a forensics background and 3,001 for teaching assistants without. The evaluation forms were completed by students at the end of each semester and categorized in this study by experience level of the instructor (i.e., first semester, second semester, etc.).

[...]

DISCUSSION
All hypotheses in the study were supported. Instructors with forensics experience were evaluated more highly than instructors without, and differences were more pronounced in the first semester. During the third semester there was an unexpected drop in the mean score, possibly resulting from increased confidence in the non-forensics instructor. During the fourth semester, however, the

mean score decreased for the non-forensics instructor, perhaps due to added pressure or responsibilities of school. A possible reason as to why the forensics scores did not decrease may be due to the instructor's previous experience with pressure situations during forensics weekends.

Effect size in this study was small due to the subjectivity of the assessments and the myriad of internal and external factors that comprise assessment. Although the variance accounted for was low in the overall hypotheses (less than 1%), contributing factors to this finding could be that after two semesters the non-forensics group had become more comfortable in the classroom and/or error in the measuring instrument.

As with any study there were limitations. These would include the use of student evaluations as a controversial issue as there is a variety of reasons an instructor may receive high ratings (Coogan, 1987; Henderson, 1984; Kovacs and Kapel, 1976; Morton, 1987). It has also been suggested that students are not in a position to evaluate the content of a course nor the knowledge/effectiveness of an instructor (Braskamp, Branderberg and Ory, 1984; Morton, 1987).

The reliability and validity of student evaluation instruments is something that has been controversial in the past. Howell (1978) argued that student evaluations "are too often presumed to have an ability they don't possess" (p. 616). And while Morrow (1977) found that student evaluations can be reliable, he did not find validity *coefficients* sufficient to support their use. *However,* other studies have confirmed the reliability and validity of such evaluations (Costin, Greenough, and Menges, 1971; Ware and Williamson, 1977). Specific questions utilized on the evaluation form should be more closely examined, in addition to examination of wording.

CONCLUSION

The implications of this study are significant. Competitors, coaches and directors of forensics programs have long been extolling the benefits of the activity, and this provides empirical evidence for such claims. It demonstrates that forensics activity can be a powerful influence on teaching effectiveness. Thus, it can be logically presumed that it would also have an effect on nearly any other profession which requires effective communication.

Further avenues in this area of research may include examination of which forensics events, if any, may provide stronger communication skills. The amount of time an instructor was involved with forensics could also be investigated, and whether or not the instructor had both competitive and coaching experience. It would be interesting to discover if there are any differences in instructors with forensics experience versus instructors without in other communication courses (i.e., Nonverbal, Organizational, or Intercultural Communication courses), as well as courses in other disciplines. Faculty evaluations could be more closely examined, as well as investigation in regard to the status of the graduate teaching assistant.

It is apparent from this study that there area great many benefits to be gained from intercollegiate forensics, and the skills that competitors learn are skills that can be applied in situations outside of the activity. After examining the requirements for effective instruction and how such requirements parallel the skills cultivated through forensics, *those who wish* to become instructors of any subject should be encouraged to participate in the activity for their benefit, as well as for the benefit of their students.

REFERENCES

Bedwell, LE., Hunt, G.H., Touzel, T.J., & Wiseman, D.G. (1984). Effective teaching: Preparation and implementation. Springfield, IL: Charles C. Thomas.

Beebe, S.A. (1974). Eye contact: A nonverbal determinant of speaker credibility. Speech Teacher, 23, 22–25.

Bloom, B.S. (1976). Human characteristics and school learning. New York: McGraw-Hill Book Co.

Braskamp, L., Brandenburg, D.C., & Ory, J.C. (1984). Evaluating teaching effectiveness: A Practical Guide. Beverly Hills: Sage.

[...]

Chermesh, R., & Tzelgov, J. (1979). The college instructor as a leader: Some theoretical derivations from a generalization of a causal model of students' evaluations of their instructors. Journal of Education Research, 72, 109–115.

Colbert, K.R. (1987). The effects of CEDA and NDT debate training on critical thinking ability. Journal of the American Forensic Association, 23, 194–201.

Colbert, K.R., & Biggers, T. (1985). Why should we support debate? Journal of the American Forensic Association, 21, 237–239.

Coogan, D.A. (1987). The relation between student grade and student evaluation of faculty: A meta-analysis of empirical studies. Unpublished master's thesis, San Diego State University, CA.

Costin, F., Greenough, W.E., & Menges, R. J. (1971). Student ratings of college teaching: Reliability, validity and usefulness. Review of Educational Research, 41, 511–535.

Dance, F.E.X. (1980). Speech communication as a liberal discipline. Communication Education, 29, 328–331.

Dean, K. W. (1987). Time well spent: Preparation for impromptu speaking. Journal of the American Forensic Association, 23, 210–219.

Dimitroff, S., & Torres, R. (1987). Undergraduate students' viewpoint on recognizing excellence in teaching. Agricultural Education Magazine, 60, 4–18.

Ericksen, S.C. (1984). The essence of good teaching. San Francisco: Jossey-Bass.

Gorham, J. (1988). The relationship between verbal teacher immediacy behaviors and student learning. Communication Education, 37, 40–53.

Hays, R.D. (1963). Statistics. New York: Holt.

Henderson, A.E. (1984). Validity of student ratings of faculty: A review of the empirical studies. Unpublished master's thesis. San Diego State University, CA.

Kearney, F., & McCroskey, J.C. (1980). Relationships among teacher communication style trait and state communication apprehension and teacher effectiveness. In D. Nimmo, (Ed.), Communication yearbook 4 (pp. 33–551). New Brunswick, NJ: Transaction Books.

Lalor, S.G. (1987). A re-evaluation of forensic competition. Unpublished raw data.

Lewis, T.J., Williams, D.A., Keaveney, M.M., & Leigh, M.G. (1984). Evaluating oral interpretation events: A contest and festival perspective symposium. National Forensic Journal, 2, 19–32.

Matlon, R.J., & Keele, L.M. (1984). A survey of participants in the National Debate Tournament, 1947–1980. Journal of the American Forensic Association, 20, 194–205.

McBath, J.H. (1984). Rationale for forensics. In D.W. Parson (Ed.), American Forensics in perspective (pp. 5–12). Annandale, VA: Speech Communication Association.

McBath, J.H., & Cripe, N.M. (1965). Delivery: Rhetoric's rustic canon. Journal of the American Forensic Association, 1, 1–6.

McCroskey, J. C. (1982). Communication competence and performance: A research and pedagogical perspective. Communication Education, 31, 1–7.

McDonald, F.J. (1978). Evaluating preservice teacher competence. Journal of Teacher Education, 29, 9–13.

McGlone, E.L. (1974). The behavioral effects of forensics participation. Journal of the American Forensic Association, 10, 140–146.

Morrow, J.R. (1977). Some statistics regarding the reliability and validity of student ratings of teachers. Research Quarterly, 48, 372–375.

Morton, P.G. (1987). Student evaluation of teaching: Potential and limitations. Nursing Outlook, 35, 86–88.

Nussbaum, J.F., & Scott, M. D. (1979). Instructor communication behaviors and their relationship to classroom learning. In D. Nimmo (Ed.), Communication yearbook 3 (pp. 561–583). New Brunswick, NH: Transaction Books.

Nuthall, G. (1987). Reviewing and recapitulating. In M.D. Dunkin (Ed.), The international encyclopedia of teaching and teacher education (pp 424–427). New York: Pergamon Press.

Ross, D.L. (1979). A "values" approach to impromptu speaking as a contest event. Speaker & Gavel, 16, 50–54.

Rubin, R.B., and Feezel, J.D. (1985). Teacher communication competence: Essential skills and assessment procedures. Central States Speech Journal, 36, 4–13.

Rubin, R.B., & Feezel, J.D. (1986). Elements of teacher communication competence. Communication Education, 35, 254–268.

Rubin, R.D., & Henzl, S.A. (1984). Cognitive complexity, communication competence, and verbal ability. Communication Quarterly, 32, 263–270.

Scott, M.D., & Wheeless, L.R. (1977). Instructional communication theory and research: An overview. In B.D. Ruben (Ed.), Communication yearbook 1 (pp. 496–511). New Brunswick, NJ: Transaction Books.

Semlak, W.D., & Shields, D.C. (1977). The effects of debate training on students participating in the Bicentennial Youth Debates. Journal of the American Forensic Association, 13, 192–196.

Stanton-Spicer, A.Q., & Marty-White, C.R. (1981). A framework for instructional communication theory: The relationship between teacher communication concerns and classroom behavior. Communication Education, 30, 354–366.

Thomas, D.A. (1983). The ethics of proof in speech events: A survey of standards used by contestants and judges. National Forensic Journal, 1, 1–17.

Vohs, J.L. (1964). An empirical approach to the concept of attention. Speech Monographs, 31, 255–260.

Ware, J.E., Jr., & Williams, R.G. (1977). Discriminate analysis of student ratings as a means for identifying lecturers who differ in enthusiastic of information-giving. Educational Psychological Measurement, 37, 627–639.

Weitzel, A. (1987). Careers for Speech Communication graduates. Salem: Sheffield.

[…]

---

*Sheila L. Hughes is the director of forensics at Macon College.

Hughes, Sheila L. "Competitive Forensics Experience as a Predictor of Teaching Effectiveness." *Phi Rho Pi* (1994). http://www.phirhopi.org/phi-rho-pi/spts/ spkrpts01.1/hughes.html (accessed March 7, 2011).

Used by Permission.

An Assessment of University Administrators: Do They Value Competitive Debate and Individual Events Programs?

*by Robert S. Littlefield**

Although the First and Second Developmental Conferences on Forensics identified the cultivation of administrative support for forensic programs as an important dimension of the forensic director's job, little published research exists to measure the levels of administrative support for such programs. In fact, beyond the survey commissioned by the First Developmental Conference (Pearce, 1974) "to determine what forensics was thought of by groups in the speech communication profession" (p. 134), no study has explored the attitudes of collegiate administrators regarding the values associated with the existence of competitive forensics as a dimension of the college or university's overall academic program.

At the Developmental Conference on Individual Events in 1988, strategies were introduced to build administrative support for competitive forensics. Greenstreet (1988) suggested that a rationale for individual events should be consistent with the mission statement for each institution and steps should be taken to encourage more administrative support. Harris (1988) recommended the creation of annual reports to enable forensic directors to publicize and review their activities in relation to administrative priorities and their own effectiveness in reaching their objectives. Underberg (1988) urged "the collection and dissemination of information about funding levels, activity levels, and instructional demands in forensics" (p. ii). With this information, directors of forensics might be able to better secure support for their forensic programs. Others actually called for a survey of administrative attitudes and institutional support for forensic programs (Littlefield, 1988).

The assumption underlying these suggestions seemingly questions the organizational support for forensic programs among administrators. Discovering some of the prevailing attitudes of administrators regarding the value of forensic programs provides insight into reasons why programs have continued to exist on some campuses while not on others. The present study identifies and interprets some of the attitudes and levels of support that exist on college campuses regarding the value of competitive speech and debate activities.

PROCEDURE

The procedure used in this study consisted of mailing the questionnaire to the chief administrative officer (CEO) at every institution identified in the Speech Communication's 1988 Directory. The survey sought to obtain demographic information about the institution, the status of forensic activities on the campus, and the levels of support for forensic programs.

[...]

Subjects

[...]

Table 1 identifies the number of respondents, their administrative levels, and the size of their institutions. The respondents reflected a rather wide distribution. However, the greatest percentage of the total number of responding administrators came from institutions with enrollments under 2,000 students.

Instrument

A questionnaire using both closed and open-ended questions was developed which asked for the following information: The level of the "chief administrative officer" who completed the survey; demographic information about the institution (student enrollment); status of debate and individual events programs at the institution; levels of personal and institutional support for forensic programs;

Size of Institution	Administrative Level									Total	
	1	2	3	4	5	6	7	8	9		
0–1999	31	25	5	7	33	8	1	1	4	115	34%
2000–3999	17	11	3	2	16	3	1	0	2	55	16%
4000–5999	11	8	0	1	9	6	1	0	1	37	11%
6000–7999	7	7	0	4	1	3	1	1	3	27	8%
8000–9999	8	5	2	1	8	5	1	0	1	31	9%
10000–plus	12	7	9	7	11	21	4	0	3	74	22%
Totals	86	63	19	22	78	46	9	2	14	339	
	25%	19%	6%	6%	23%	14%	3%	1%	3%	100%	

*Administrative Level

1 = Presidents, provosts, chancellors

2 = Vice presidents, vice chancellors

3 = Administrative Assistants to Categories 1 and 2

4 = Directors of college/university offices

5 = Deans

6 = Chairs

7 = Directors of forensics

8 = Faculty members asked to respond

9 = No response

and limited data on levels of budgetary and faculty allocations made during the 1987-88 academic year. The questionnaire was reviewed by several administrators at an upper midwestern university. Following the suggestions of these individuals, minor modifications were made prior to the mailing of the survey.

RESULTS

Status of Forensic Programs

To secure information regarding current and past funding of forensic programs, the survey inquired as to whether or not the institution had ever funded a debate or individual events team and whether or not the institution currently funded either or both of these dimensions of a forensic program. Table 2 identifies the frequency of the responses for debate and individual events programs.

The data suggest that the number of debate programs at the responding institutions had declined by 76 (from 225 to 149); while the number of individual events programs had been reduced by 57 (from 189 to 132).

Barriers Precluding Institutional Support

For those institutions not currently funding a debate or individual events program, four barriers were offered from which administrators were asked to prioritize with a "1" reflecting the greatest barrier, "2" next greatest barrier, through "4." If the administrators wished to offer a barrier of their own, the option was provided and then the prioritization could include a rank of "5." The four barriers identified by several independent, university-level administrators when the survey instrument was developed, included lack of monetary resources to sustain a program, lack of student interest in debate or IE programs, lack of faculty/coach interest in debate or IE programs, and lack of an institutional priority.

The data revealed that a lack of monetary resources was the greatest barrier to the continuation of speech and debate programs.

TABLE 2: INDICATION OF PAST AND CURRENT
FUNDING FOR DEBATE AND INDIVIDUAL EVENTS
PROGRAMS AT RESPONDING INSTITUTIONS

	Debate		Individual Events	
	Past	Current	Past	Current
Yes	225	149	189	132
No	55	149	83	165
Unsure	26	6	37	8
No Response	33	35	30	34
Total		339		339

Benefits Perceived from Forensic Programs

For those administrators from institutions currently funding debate and/or individual events programs, four benefits were offered from which respondents were asked to prioritize using a "1" to reflect the greatest benefit, "2" for the next greatest benefit, through "4." If the administrators provided an additional benefit not listed, the ranking would include a "5." The benefits identified by several independent, university-level administrators when the survey instrument was developed, and generally reflective of the recognized values held by members of the forensic community (Parson, 1984), included that debate and individual events programs enhanced the recruitment of students to the institution, the recruitment of faculty, the attraction of scholarship contributions, and enhanced the education of students.

The data suggest that enhancing a student's education and recruiting students were the greatest benefits to be gained from having debate or individual events programs.

Personal Assessment of Value of Forensic Experience

Aside from institutional support or lack thereof, administrators were asked to provide their personal assessment of a debate or individual events team as an activity for students at their institutions. Using a Likert Scale (5 to 1) with "5" indicating that the administrator valued the team(s) as very important, "3" indicating moderate importance, and "1" as very unimportant, the following results were compiled in Table 5.

Sixty-five percent of those responding valued the forensic experience as "very important" or "important" as an activity for students.

Institutional Support of Debate and IE Teams

To gather some limited data on levels of institutional support, in terms of coaching staff, administrators were asked to use 1987-88 figures and indicate the number of full-time, tenure track and full-time, non-tenure track positions. If they were unsure, they were

TABLE 3: PERCEIVED BARRIERS TO INSTITUTIONAL SUPPORT RESULTING IN THE DISCONTINUATION OF DEBATE AND INDIVIDUAL EVENTS PROGRAMS AT RESPONDING SCHOOLS

Level of Barrier	Barriers				
	1	2	3	4	5
Greatest Barrier (% of Total by Barrier)	34 (30%)	30 (28%)	21 (21%)	17 (19%)	2 a
2nd	21	22	27	14	1 b
3rd	21	17	22	14	2 c
4th	11	13	8	13	1 d
5th	0	0	0	2	1 e
Barrier (Unranked)	25	24	22	23	4 f
Total by Barrier	112	106	100	86	11
No Response	227	233	239	253	328

Barriers

1 = Lack of monetary resources to sustain program

2 = Lack of student interest in debate/IE program

3 = Lack of faculty/coach interest in debate/IE program

4 = Not an institutional priority

5 = Other, as specified:
   a = Speech course only; 100% commuter institution
   b = We live in Alaska
   c = Student on/off pattern; too many competing extracurricular activities
   d = Nature of student body, commuter school
   e = Speech not required for graduation
   f = Not popular at 2-year colleges; no opponents because only university on an island; we decided programs do not help students to improve communication skills; need to use faculty for other assignments

to leave the blanks unfilled. The number of part-time faculty and graduate assistants used as coaches for debate and IE teams was also solicited.

Funding levels, as well as from where the funds used to support the programs were drawn, were requested. While some programs had separate funds to support team and coaching staff travel, other

Table 4: Perceived Benefits to Institutions Having Debate and/or Individual Events Programs

Level of Benefit	Benefits				
	1	2	3	4	5
Greatest Benefit (% of Total by Benefit)	18 (10%)	2 (2%)	0 (0%)	101 (49%)	3 a
2nd	74	3	9	17	12 b
3rd	19	34	29	3	7 c
4th	4	27	35	3	2 d
5th	1	8	3	0	2 e
Benefit (Unranked)	54	11	14	82	13 f
Total by Benefit	170	85	90	206	39
No Response	169	254	249	133	300

Benefits

1 = Enhances recruitment of students

2 = Enhances recruitment of faculty

3 = Attracts scholarship contributions

4 = Enhances education of students

institutions allocated funds for general use by both team and coaching staff. Table Seven identifies levels of funding for the 1987–88 academic year.

The source of the funding for the team travel and coaching staff travel was also requested from the administrators. Respondents were asked to provide the name of the source of the funding.

In brief, the results of the survey provided data corresponding to past and current funding of debate and IE teams, barriers precluding institutional support for forensic programs, benefits of debate and IE teams, personal assessments regarding the value of these teams, and limited data regarding 1987–88 levels of support for debate and IE teams in terms of coaching positions and funding levels.

5 = Other, as specified:
  a = Enhances public image; provides opportunity for student performance and recognition; application of theory brings together the value of a liberal arts
  b = Institutional recognition and visibility; improves retention and student satisfaction; provides major interest activity for these students who wish this sort of student participation; alumni involvement; increases their understanding of significant issues, both national and international; enhances ethos of institution (2); enhances school/community relations; helps maintain an academic campus atmosphere; PR (2)
  c = Institutional visibility (3); enhances institution's reputation (2); encourages nonuniversity attendance at international debates; excellent for job hunting
  d = Gives program visibility with administration and public; enhances university image
  e = Enhances image of college; concentrates attention on a rigorous *academically*-oriented program
  f = Favorable publicity (5); we have an outstanding coach who has earned support; adds a dimension of educational quality and opportunity; improves communication skills of students; aids in building networks; assists with public image of institution through news media and service projects; integral part of communication studies department curriculum; enhances academic reputation; supplementary experience; institutional prestige

DISCUSSION

For the institutions responding, the data suggest that over the years, the number of debate and individual events programs dropped. The data explaining this decline indicate that a lack of monetary resources to sustain the programs, followed by a lack of student interest, a lack of faculty/coach interest, and the absence of an institutional priority all affected the programs no longer in existence.

Despite the reduction in debate and IE programs, for those institutions with forensic teams, the vast majority indicated that the greatest benefit to institutions was the enhanced education of their students. This was followed by the enhanced recruitment of students for their institutions. By and large, administrators personally valued having debate and individual events teams as an activity for students

TABLE 5: PERSONAL ASSESSMENTS OF A DEBATE OR INDIVIDUAL EVENTS TEAM AS AN ACTIVITY FOR STUDENTS

Level of Importance	Administrative Level*									Total
	1	2	3	4	5	6	7	8	9	
Very Important	27	17	5	8	23	22	7	1	3	113 (34%)
4	27	21	9	5	28	10	0	1	3	104 (31%)
3	23	18	2	5	23	7	1	0	3	82 (25%)
2	7	6	2	3	3	3	1	0	0	25 (8%)
Very Unimportant	1	1	0	0		3	0	0	1	8 (2%)
No Response	1	0	1	1	0	1	0	0	3	7

*Administrative Level

1 = President, provosts, chancellors

2 = Vice presidents, vice chancellor

3 = Administrative assistants to categories 1 and 2

4 = Directors of college/university officers

5 = Deans

6 = Chairs

7 = Directors of forensics

8 = Faculty members

9 = No response

at their institutions. Sixty-five percent considered the presence of these teams as either very important or important compared with 10 percent who valued debate and individual events as unimportant or very unimportant. The fact that 97 percent of those responding to the survey answered this particular question, reflects the relatively high level of support found among administrators for debate and individual events activities. In Table Five, four groups of administrators at different levels of budgetary control (presidents, provosts, chancellors, vice presidents, vice chancellors, deans, and department chairs) indicated the high value they placed on debate and IE as activities for students. Seventy-eight percent of the 113 respondents who ranked debated and IE teams as very important fell into these categories.

Institutional support varied. Eighty-one percent of the

Table 6: Selected 1987–88 Number of Coaching Positions for Debate and IE Teams at Responding Institutions

Type of Positions	Number of Positions							No Response
	1	2	3	4	5+	Total		
Full-time, tenure track	76	17	1	–	–	91	26%	248
Full-time, nontenure	17	7	–	–	–	24	7%	215
Part-time faculty	52	12	3	–	–	67	19%	272
Graduate assistants	16	9	4	4	2	35	10%	304

responding administrators with one full-time faculty forensic coach indicated that the position was a tenure track. For the most part, administrators responding had either one or two coaches at their institutions. Levels of funding for debate and IE teams would suggest that the most common budget range was between $3,000 and $5,999 during the 1987-88 academic year. A majority of the programs reviewed (78 percent) included funds to support the coaching staff within the team's travel budget. Based upon the data, the reliance upon institutional budgets was greater than reliance upon student government funds or departmental/institutional budgets.

Table 7: Selected 1987–88 Levels of Travel Support for Team and Coaching Staff

Level of Funding	Team Travel		Coaching Staff Travel
$0–2999	32	18%	33
$3999–5999	40	23%	6
$6000–8999	25	14%	*
$9000–11999	22	13%	*
$12000–14999	12	7%	*
$15000–above	38	22%	1
			*Included with team (101)
No response	170	50%	198

TABLE 8: SOURCES OF FUNDING FOR TEAM TRAVEL AT RESPONDING SCHOOLS

Source of Funding	Team Travel		Coaching Staff Travel
College Academic Dean's Budget	20	12%	9
General University Fund	63	38%	16
Student Government	36	22%	3
Departmental General Budget	10	6%	9
Departmental Instructional Budget	6	3%	1
Combination of Above	23	14%	2
Fundraising	3	1%	–
Private Sources	1	1%	–
Included with Team	1	1%	102
No Response	177		197

The many "no responses" in Tables Six, Seven, and Eight also reflect the values or attitudes of the administrators who answered the survey. Clearly, many respondents were able and willing to share their attitudes on value questions in the survey. However, when asked for more specific information about budgets and institutional support, there may have been some reluctance, or at least an indifference to finding out this information and providing it to the researcher. Organizationally, if the survey were passed along to individuals without specific knowledge of the programs involved, this might reflect the general attitude of the highest administrator toward this project or its area of focus. Despite the no response rates, the information collected provides insight into some programs on a national level.

CONCLUSIONS AND DIRECTIONS FOR FUTURE RESEARCH

The assumption underlying this study questioned the levels of support for forensic programs among administrators who tend to control the funding for these programs. Despite the identification of benefits for those institutions having debate and IE teams, the data suggest that there are fewer programs in the responding schools now than in the past. Although a majority of the administrators personally viewed having forensic teams as very important or important, the data are not conclusive as to whether these personal "feelings of value" translate into faculty positions or funding.

The large "no response" rate for the questions requesting information about faculty positions and budget sources and levels makes the development of generalizable conclusions in this area difficult. However, there is a value in exploring attitudes and levels of support at various institutions. While this study cannot claim to provide reasons why some programs continue to exist while others cease, the collection of the kinds of information included here is useful for the forensic director seeking to provide information about other programs to local administrators. Administrators may find this study interesting as they compare their levels of support for debate and IE Programs with the others across the country. Simply being aware that travel funds can be acquired from varying sources may spark an administrator to review her or his method of supporting forensic programs.

Comparing the level of institutional commitment, in the form of tenure track/tenured faculty versus part-time faculty, may also suggest variations in terms of funding options that are available. If a forensic director at one school can justify to local administrators that other schools have already made tenure-track commitments to their debate and IE programs, an argument may be made to increase funding or positions at his or her home institution.

If members of the forensic community are going to continue to seek support for their speech and debate programs, an understanding of how some administrators view forensics may prove useful. The more information that is available on levels of support and reasons why programs were discontinued, the more able forensic directors will be to shape their arguments in the justification of their programs.

WORKS CITED

Greenstreet, R. W. (1988). "Earning support for individual events programs." Paper presented at First Developmental Conference on Individual Events, Denver, CO.

Harris, E. J., Jr. (1988). "Strategies to enhance university support for individual events programs." Paper presented at First Developmental Conference on Individual Events, Denver, CO.

Littlefield, R. S. (1988). "The cultivation of administrative and general support for individual events programs: Some practical suggestions." Paper presented at First Developmental Conference on Individual Events, Denver, CO.

[...]

Parson, D. (1984). *American forensics in perspective.* Annandale, VA: SCA.

Pearce, W. B. (Winter, 1974). Attitudes toward forensics. *Journal of the American Forensic Association.* 10(3), 134–139.

Underberg, L. (1988). "Recommendations on administrative support and publicity for individual events programs." Paper presented at First Developmental Conference on Individual Events, Denver, CO.

*Robert S. Littlefield is a professor of communication and the interim dean of the College of Humanities and Social Sciences at North Dakota State University.

Littlefield, Robert S. "An Assessment of University Administrators: Do They Value Competitive Debate and Individual Events Programs?" *National Forensic Journal* 9 (1991): 87–96.

Used by Permission.

PART 4

Debate and Advocacy

Of course, debate is about making arguments and advancing positions, generally covering issues of social controversy. To this end, we would expect that debate should foster valuable advocacy skills. The two articles in this section report precisely on this point. In "Pedagogical Possibilities for Argumentative Agency in Academic Debate," Gordon R. Mitchell offers a variety of reasons for how debate trains future advocates. The chapter also details how debate participation does this. Joseph P. Zompetti, in "The Role of Advocacy in Civil Society," suggests that debate training and experience are crucial for developing advocacy skills—skills that are also vital for a vibrant civil society. Along the lines of Susan Herbst's argument from the main introduction of this book, the Zompetti chapter makes the case that debate training is an important component for sustaining participatory democracy.

Pedagogical Possibilities for Argumentative Agency in Academic Debate

*by Gordon R. Mitchell**

[...]

> *Our principle is the power of individuals to participate with others in shaping their world through the human capacity of language;*
>
> *Our commitment to argument expresses our faith in reason-giving as a key to that power; Our commitment to advocacy expresses our faith in oral expression as a means to empower people in situations of their lives;*
>
> *Our research studies the place of argument and advocacy in these situations of empowerment;*
>
> *Our teaching seeks to expand students' appreciation for the place of argument and advocacy in shaping their world, and to prepare students through classrooms, forums, and competition for participation in their world through the power of expression; and Our public involvement seeks to empower through argument and advocacy.*
>
> —AMERICAN FORENSIC ASSOCIATION CREDO

The lofty goals enumerated in the American Forensic Association's Credo have long served as beacons that steer pedagogical practice in argumentation and debate. The Credo's expression of faith in "reason giving," "oral expression" and critical thinking as formulas for student "empowerment" is reflected in the many textbooks that have been written to guide the academic study of argumentation. "The relevance of skill in argumentation seems self-evident to anyone living in a democratic society," write George W. Ziegelmueller and Jack Kay in *Argumentation: Inquiry and Advocacy*; "The notion of full and free public debate on the vital issues facing society is deeply rooted in the documents and ideas comprising the American conscience" (1997, p. 6). Making a similar point in the introduction to their textbook *Argumentation and Critical Decision Making*, Richard D. Rieke and Malcolm O. Sillars suggest that "the ability to participate effectively in reasoned discourse leading to critical decision making is required in virtually every aspect of life in a democracy" (1997, p. xvii), "We need debate not only in the legislature and the courtroom but in every other area of society as well." echoes Austin J. Freeley in *Argumentation and Debate*, "since most of our rights are directly dependent on debate" (1996, p. 5).

For those schooled in the tradition of argumentation and debate, faith in the tensile strength of critical thinking and oral expression as pillars of democratic decision-making Is almost second nature, a natural outgrowth of disciplinary training. This faith, inscribed in the American Forensic Association's Credo, reproduced in scores of argumentation textbooks, and rehearsed over and over again in introductory argumentation courses, grounds the act of argumentation pedagogy in a progressive political vision that swells the enthusiasm of teachers and students alike, while ostensibly locating the study of argumentation in a zone of relevance that lends a distinctive sense of meaning and significance to academic work in this area.

Demographic surveys of debaters suggest that indeed, the practice of debate has significant value for participants. Some studies confirm debate's potential as a tool to develop critical thinking and communication skills. For example, Semlak and Shields find that "students with debate experience were significantly better at employing the three communication skills (analysis, delivery, and organization) utilized in this study than students without the experience" (1977, p. 194). In a similar vein, Colbert and Biggers write that "the conclusion seems fairly simple, debate training is an excellent way of improving many communication skills (1935, p. 237). Finally, Keefe, Harte and Norton provide strong corroboration for these observations with their assessment that "many researchers over the past four decades have come to the same general conclusions. Critical thinking ability is significantly improved by courses in argumentation and debate and by debate experience" (1982, pp. 33–34; see also Snider 1993).

Other studies document the professional success of debaters after graduation. For example, 15% of persons in Keele and Malton's survey of former debaters went on to become "top-ranking executives" (Keele and Matlon 1984). This finding is consistent with the results of Center's survey, which suggests that participation in forensics is an employee attribute desired strongly by businesses, especially law firms (Center 1982, p. 5). While these survey data bode well for debate students preparing to test the waters of the corporate job market, such data shed little light on the degree to which argumentation skills learned in debate actually translate into practical tools of democratic empowerment. Regardless of whether or not survey data is ever generated to definitively answer this question, it is likely that faith in debate as an inherently democratic craft will persist.

Committed to affirming and stoking the progressive energies produced by this faith in argumentation, but also interested in problematizing the assumptions that undergird prevailing approaches to argumentation pedagogy for heuristic purposes, in this essay I make a double gesture. On the one hand, I underscore the importance of grounding the practice of academic argumentation to notions of democratic empowerment. On the other hand, I challenge the notion that such a grounding maneuver can be accomplished with faith alone. Moving beyond the characterization of argumentative acumen as a skill to be acquired exclusively through classroom or tournament training, I propose a notion of argumentative agency that brings questions of purpose to the center of pedagogical practice: For what purpose are argumentation skills used? Where can they be employed most powerfully (for better or worse)? What can be learned from efforts to bring argumentation skills to bear in concrete rhetorical situations outside of tournament contest rounds? [...] I advance an analysis that contextualizes these questions and proposes reflective ideas that invite response in the ongoing conversation about the meaning and purpose of contemporary academic debate. [...]

[...]

ARGUMENTATIVE AGENCY

In basic terms the notion of argumentative agency involves the capacity to contextualize and employ the skills and strategies of argumentative discourse in fields of social action, especially wider spheres of public deliberation. Pursuit of argumentative agency charges academic work with democratic energy by linking teachers and students with civic organizations, social movements, citizens and other actors engaged in live public controversies beyond the schoolyard walls. As a bridging concept, argumentative agency links decontextualized argumentation skills such as research, listening, analysis, refutation and presentation to the broader political telos of democratic empowerment. Argumentative agency fills gaps left in purely simulation-based models of argumentation by focusing pedagogical energies on strategies for utilizing argumentation as a driver of progressive social change. Moving beyond an exclusively skill-oriented curriculum, teachers and students pursuing argumentative agency seek to put argumentative tools to the test by employing them in situations beyond the space of the classroom. This approach draws from the work of Kincheloe (1991), who suggests that through "critical constructivist action research," students and teachers cultivate their own senses of agency and work to transform the world around them.

The sense of argumentative agency produced through action research is different in kind from those skills that are honed through academic simulation exercises such as policy debate tournaments. Encounters with broader public spheres beyond the realm of the academy can deliver unique pedagogical possibilities and opportunities. By anchoring their work in public spaces, students and teachers can use their talents to change the trajectory of events, while events are still unfolding. These experiences have the potential to trigger significant shifts in political awareness on the part of participants. Academic debaters nourished on an exclusive diet of competitive contest round experience often come to see politics like a picturesque landscape whirring by through the window of a speeding train. They study this political landscape in great detail, rarely (if ever) entertaining the idea of stopping the train and exiting to alter the course of unfolding events. The resulting spectator mentality deflects attention away from roads that could carry their arguments to wider spheres of public argumentation. However, on the occasions when students and teachers set aside this spectator mentality by directly engaging broader public audiences, key aspects of the political landscape change, because the point of reference for experiencing the landscape shifts fundamentally.

[...]

The notion of argumentative agency is not only important for the task of lending weight to projects in debate oriented toward the telos of democratic empowerment. The pursuit of action research carries intrinsic transformative benefits in the form of concrete political change. Building on Felski's argument that "it is not tenable to assume that hermetically sealed forums for discussion and debate can function as truly oppositional spaces of discourse" (1989, p. 171), Giroux points to Foucault and Gramsci as scholars who have made engagement with broader public spheres a matter of academic responsibility.

Academics can no longer retreat into their careers, classrooms, or symposiums as if they were the only public spheres available for engaging the power of ideas and the relations of power. Foucault's (1977) notion of the specific intellectual taking up struggles connected to particular issues and contexts must be combined with Gramsci's (1971) notion of the engaged intellectual who connects his or her work to broader social concerns that deeply affect how people live, work, and survive (Giroux 1991, p. 57; see also Giroux 1988, p. 35).

Within the limited horizon of zero-sum competition in the contest round framework for academic debate, questions of purpose, strategy, and practice tend to collapse into formulaic axioms for competitive success under the crushing weight of tournament pressure. The purpose of debate becomes unrelenting pursuit of victory at a zero-sum game. Strategies are developed to gain competitive edges that translate into contest round success. Debate practice involves debaters "spewing" a highly technical, specialized discourse at expert judges trained to understand enough of the speeches to render decisions. Even in "kritik rounds," where the political status and meaning of the participants' own discourse is up for grabs. (see Shanahan 1993) the contest round framework tends to freeze the discussion into bipolar, zero-sum terms that highlight competitive payoffs at the expense of opportunities for co-operative "rethinking."

When the cultivation of argumentative agency is pursued as a central pedagogical goal in academic debate, questions of purpose, strategy, and practice take on much broader meanings. The purpose of participating in debate gets extended beyond just winning contest rounds (although that purpose does not need to be abandoned completely), as debaters intervene in public affairs directly to affect social change, and in the process, bolster their own senses of political agency. In this approach, debate strategy begins to bear a resemblance to social movement strategizing, with questions of timing, coalition-building, and publicity taking on increasing importance. Finally, debate practice itself becomes dynamic as debaters invent new forms of argumentative expression tailored specifically to support particular projects of political intervention into fields of social action.

CLEARING SPACES FOR ARGUMENTATIVE AGENCY

Up to this point, I have been describing argumentative agency in general terms, striving to locate the notion in a wider frame of reference. In this final section, I distill more specific ideas that serve as provisional answers to the questions that initially drove the study: How can argumentation skills be used? Where can they be most powerfully employed? What can be learned from efforts to apply argumentation skiffs in concrete rhetorical situations? Ultimately, the dimensions and dynamics of argumentative agency are properties that emerge organically out of situated pedagogical milieux. The idiosyncratic interests and talents of particular students and teachers shape the manner in which skills of argumentation receive expression as tools of democratic empowerment. Attempting to theorize the proper, precise nature of these expressions would inappropriately pre-empt creative efforts to invent modes of action tailored to fit local situations. A more heuristically valuable theoretical task would involve an exploration of historical attempts to pursue argumentative agency in debate practice. [. . .]

Primary Research

Possibilities for argumentative agency are obscured when debate scholarship is approached from a purely spectator-oriented perspective, an activity to be conducted on the sidelines of "actual" public policy discussion. Insofar as the act of research is configured as a one-way transaction in which debaters gather and assimilate information passively through impersonal channels. This spectator orientation gains currency and becomes an acquired habit. Within this pedagogical horizon, possible options for action that move beyond traditional library research and contest round advocacy become more difficult to visualize. However, when debaters reconfigure themselves as producers of knowledge, rather than passive consumers of it, it becomes easier to cultivate senses of personal agency. One very basic way that academic debaters can reverse this equation is by turning more to primary research as a tool of debate preparation.

Primary research involves debaters generating evidence "from scratch," by contacting sources directly and engaging them in conversation. If the resulting dialogue is illuminating, and the conversation partner(s) agree, the transcripts of such conversations can be published, and subsequently quoted as evidence in contest rounds. For example, Loyola (LA) debater Madison Laird once authored a high school debate handbook that contained traditional and expected evidence on the 1987/88 high school topic, but also included transcripts of interviews conducted by laird with Loyola University political science professors. Laird produced extremely powerful, legitimately published evidence by qualified sources merely by asking provocative questions to such sources and then distributing the document throughout the debate community. The resulting exchange yielded an illuminating stream of newly-generated knowledge, especially since Laird pitched questions to the professors in a manner that highlighted anticipated stasis points of contest round debate. Interlocutors engaged by students in this manner have responded enthusiastically and reciprocated by asking questions about the nature of the debate activity itself as well as the specific features of projects pursued by argumentation scholars.

[...]

Primary research is commonplace in most academic circles; sources often contact each other directly and then reference these conversations in public texts, and multitudes of published interviews can be found in scholarly books and journals. While primary research has not taken root as a widespread practice in academic debate, some fear that if primary research gains in popularity, authors, experts, and other published writers will be deluged by a torrent of annoying correspondence from insolent academic debaters. Apart from this fact that this concern reflects a fundamentally low opinion of high school debaters' senses of civic responsibility, this scenario would be most likely to occur if debaters pursued primary research projects from an exclusively competitive perspective, asking questions purely to elicit answers that might contain valuable contest round evidence. However, if debaters grasp that primary research methodology carries with it the political responsibilities of public engagement, it will be easier for them to see that primary research projects not only generate evidence for academic debates; such projects also feed new information and ideas into discussions taking place in wider public spheres of deliberation.

Public Debate

Once students begin to conceive of research areas as fields of action, it becomes easier to invent strategies for intervention. One such strategy involves the extension and adaptation of the debate process beyond the immediate peer audience. For example, familiarity with debate affords students the expertise and wherewithal to organize, execute and amplify public debates. By creating forums where salient and pressing contemporary Issues can be debated and discussed in a robust, wide-open fashion, students can lend vibrancy to the public sphere. Public debates represent sites of social learning where the spirit of civic engagement can flourish, ideas can be shared, and the momentum of social movements can be stoked. Unlike top-down communication engineered by mass media news outlets and public opinion polling, the interaction that occurs in public debates is a unique form of dialectical communication. Dynamic, back-and-forth exchange among audience and advocates pushes issues beyond shallow lines of sound-bite development. The drama of debate draws in interested audiences, creating the possibility that dialogue wilt spill outward beyond the immediate debate venue and into communities, schools, universities and other civic groups. It is through this process that the fabrics of multiple public spheres are spun and woven together to form the variegated patterns of "social knowledge," or shared understandings and expectations that "govern subsequent discourse" (see Farrell 1916; Goodnight 1992).

[...]

Many actors outside the debate community find the debate process very attractive, and this makes it easier to organize and promote public debates. But the political effects of debate are not automatically emancipatory or progressive. The debater's instinct, culled from the democratic faith inscribed in argumentation texts, is that more discussion is always good. This is a tidy principle, but when it comes to on-the-ground social change, it depends on [the] type of discussion that debate enables. Institutions often use debate as a legitimating tool. They can point to their participation in debates as evidence demonstrating their "commitment to the community," i.e., proof of their democratic pedigree. If one's goal is to use debate as a tool to challenge corrupt or regressive institutions, the possibility exists that such efforts can and up making the institutions stronger and less responsive to public concerns.

One way around this pitfall is to embrace the notion that an essential part of the debate process involves citizens empowering themselves to invent. clarify, and amplify their viewpoints in public forums. For example, in evaluating a recent EPA grant proposal for a series of national public debates on the topic of environmental justice in brownfields redevelopment policy, Charles Lee of the United Church of Christ endorsed the idea of public debates on the grounds that such debates can generate "social capital" for previously excluded stakeholders to assert their voices in policy discussions. "The production of social capital, a form of which is the ability to conduct public discourse," Lee explained, "is critical to solving complex problems and achieving healthy and sustainable communities" (1996).

In order to maximize the potential of the debate medium as a generator of citizen empowerment, however, debate resources need to be put toward projects such as citizen advocacy training and community action research that are designed to build community capacity for public discussion. Public debate organizing is partly a logistical endeavor, involving such tasks as securing debate venues, interacting with media, and planning on-site set management. While these efforts can yield new spaces for public discussion, if academically sterile, irrelevant, or one-sided discussion dominates such spaces, prevailing patterns of alienating public discourse will be mirrored and reproduced in such events. Such an unfortunate outcome would only galvanize the rocks barring traditionally excluded segments of the population from public discussion. Thus, it is imperative that "[m]embers of impacted and disadvantaged communities must be part of the interactive process of planning and developing this concept [of public debate]" (Lee 1996). What does "interaction" mean in this context? On a basic level, an interactive planning process would seem to require shared decision-making power regarding determination of formats, dates, venues, and topics of public debates, with each stakeholder having a say in negotiating these matters. But on a more fundamental level, interaction must occur that enables academic debaters to learn from people living in impacted communities; "[T]here is also the need for students and universities to learn from and be trained by community residents regarding the history, aspiration, concerns, assets, wisdom, culture, knowledge, genius, and vision resident in that community" (Lee 1996). Ultimately, the power of public debate as a medium of democratic empowerment for disadvantaged and impacted communities may depend on the extent to which academic scholars and debaters push for "a deeper examination of the word 'interactive'" (Lee 1996) when it comes time to forge partnerships between academic institutions and community groups.

[...]

Public Advocacy

It is possible to go beyond thinking of debate as a remedial tool to redress educational inequities and to start seeing debate as a political activity that has the potential to empower students and teachers to change the underlying conditions that cause Inequities among schools and communities in the first place. In this task, the public advocacy skills learned by debaters can be extremely efficacious.

The ability to present ideas forcefully and persuasively in public is powerful tool, one that becomes even more dynamic when coupled with the research and critical thinking acumen that comes with intensive debate preparation. A crucial element of this transformative pedagogy is public advocacy, making debate practice directly relevant to actors who are studied during research, and making the topics researched relevant to the lives of students and teachers.

[...]

The skills honed during preparation for and participation in academic debate can be utilized as powerful toots in this regard. Using sophisticated research, critical thinking, and concise argument presentation, argumentation scholars can become formidable actors in the public realm, advocating on behalf of a particular issue, agenda, or viewpoint. For competitive academic debaters, this sort of advocacy can become an important extension of a long research project culminating in a strong personal judgment regarding a given policy issue and a concrete plan to intervene politically in pursuit of those beliefs.

For example, on the 1992–93 intercollegiate policy debate topic dealing with U.S. development assistance policy, the University of Texas team ran an extraordinarily successful affirmative case that called for the United States to terminate its support for the Flood Action Plan, a disaster-management program proposed to equip the people of Bangladesh to deal with the consequences of flooding. During the course of their research, Texas debaters developed close working links with the International Rivers Network, a Berkeley-based social movement devoted to stopping the Flood Action Plan. These links not only created a fruitful research channel of primary information to the Texas team; they helped Texas debaters organize sympathetic members of the debate community to support efforts by the International Rivers Network to block the Flood Action Plan.

The University of Texas team capped off an extraordinary year of contest round success arguing for a ban on the Flood Action Plan with an activist project in which team members supplemented contest round advocacy with other modes of political organizing. Specifically, Texas debaters circulated a petition calling for suspension of the Flood Action Plan, organized channels of debater input to "pressure points" such as the World Bank and U.S. Congress, and solicited capital donations for the International Rivers Network. In a letter circulated publicly to multiple audiences inside and outside the debate community, Texas assistant coach Ryan Goodman linked the arguments of the debate community to wider public audiences by explaining the enormous competitive success of the ban Flood Action Plan affirmative on the intercollegiate tournament circuit. The debate activity, Goodman wrote, "brings a unique aspect to the marketplace of ideas. Ideas most often gain success not through politics, the persons who support them, or through forcing out other voices through sheer economic power, but rather on their own merit" (1993). To emphasize the point that this competitive success should be treated as an important factor in public policy-making, Goodman compared the level of rigor and intensity of debate research and preparation over the course of a year to the work involved in completion of masters' thesis.

A recent article in the Chronicle of Higher Education estimated that the level and extent of research required of the average college debater for each topic is equivalent to the amount of research required for a Master's Thesis. If you multiplied the number of active college debaters (approximately 1,000) by that many research hours the mass work effort spent on exploring, comprehending, and formulating positions around relevant public policy issues is obviously astounding (Goodman 1993).

[...]

A more recent example of public advocacy work in debate took place at the National High School Institute. a summer debate workshop hosted by Northwestern University in 1998. At this workshop, a group of high school students researched an affirmative case calling for an end to the U.S. ballistic missile defense (BMD) program. Following up on a week of intensive traditional debate research that yielded a highly successful affirmative case, the students generated a short text designed as a vehicle to take the arguments of the affirmative to wider public audiences. This text was published as an online E-print on the noted Federation of American Scientists website (see Cherub Study Group 1998). In this process of translating debate arguments into a public text, care was taken to shear prose of unnecessary debate jargon, metaphors were employed liberally to render the arguments in more accessible terms, and references to popular culture were included as devices to ground the ban-BMD argument in everyday knowledge.

Some may express reservations about the prospect of debaters settling on particular viewpoints and defending them in public, given that the tradition of switch-side policy debating has tended to tie effective critical thinking with the notion of suspended judgment. However, it is possible to maintain a critical posture, even while taking an active, interventionist stance vis-a-vis political affairs. "Generally speaking, action researchers see the process of gaining knowledge and changing society as interlinked, even inseparable," explains Martin, "Intervention to change society produces understanding—including new perspectives of fundamental theoretical significance—which in turn can be used to develop more effective intervention" (p. 264; see also Sholle 1994). "Research and activism should operate in tandem," Milan Rai writes in a discussion on Noam Chomsky, "you need to Interact with others in order to develop ideas" (Rai 1995, p. 59).

A critical and transformative method of action research requires constant reflection to ensure that all aspects of the research enterprise (e.g., purpose, normative assumptions, methodological tools, and tentative conclusions) are problematized and revised throughout the endeavor as part of an ongoing learning process. The notions of constant change and unlearning on the part of the researcher and continuous rearticulation of knowledge (understanding) throughout the research act draw from the field of critical (transformative) pedagogy and cultural studies. As Kincheloe explains, "[t]he critical core of critical action research involves its participatory and communally discursive structure and tile cycle of action and reflection it initiates" (1993, p. 183). Woolgar has characterized the synergistic interplay among dimensions of inquiry as the "dynamic of iterative reconceptualization," a process whereby "practitioners from time to time recognize the defects of their position as an occasion for revising its basic assumptions" (1991, p. 382). According to Woolgar, what sets this dynamic in motion is the practitioner's embrace of "reflexivity"; i.e., affirmative problematization of scholars' own conceptions of themselves as critical agents in light of continually shifting theoretical assumptions.

[...]

By assuming a reflexive stance that relentlessly destabilizes and interrogates the assumptions undergirding particular public advocacy projects, debaters can add a crucial element of reflection to their practice. Such reflection can highlight the potential dangers of political engagement and generate strategies to negotiate these pitfalls through shared discussion. Coverstone's fear that the radical heterogeneity of political opinions found in the debate community "means that mass political action is doomed to fail" (1995, p. 9) is accurate as a diagnosis of the utopian prospects for a monolithic and ideologically consistent social movement to spring forth from the ranks of activist debate participants. However, Coverstone overlooks the emancipatory potential of smaller groups within the debate community to organize with like-minded colleagues. While the radical heterogeneity of political orientation in the debate community likely blocks the formation of a homogenous mass political movement, the same diversity also has the potential to support a panoply of ideologically diverse (and even contradictory) micromovements. Although participants in these smaller movements may be advocating different causes and pursuing distinct strategies of intervention, the common thread linking their projects together is a quest to develop argumentation skills as tools to impact events unfolding in fields of social action.

CONCLUSION

The continuing desertification of the public sphere is a phenomenon that serves as an urgent invitation for argumentation scholars to develop remedial responses. As the Credo of the American Forensic Association trumpets, members of the forensics community in this nation are well positioned to make such responses, given the community's commitment to debate and argumentation as tools of democratic empowerment. In this essay, I have argued that faith alone is insufficient to bring about the translation of argumentation skills into tools of democratic empowerment. Instead, such a successful translation requires affirmative efforts to clear spaces that free scholars to exercise and develop senses of argumentative agency. With greater room to maneuver for inventing strategies for action, taking risks, making mistakes and affecting change, scholars can begin to envision how to do things with arguments not only in the cozy confines of contest round competition, but in the world beyond as well.

Evolution of the idea of argumentative agency, in both theory and practice, is driven by the idiosyncratic and often eccentric personal sentiments and political allegiances held by students and teachers of argumentation. Those interested in seeing debate skills become tools for democratic empowerment have the ability to cultivate argumentative agency in their respective pedagogical and political milieux. This might involve supporting and encouraging efforts of students to engage in primary research, organize and perform public debates, undertake public advocacy projects, and/or share the energy of debate with traditionally underserved and excluded student populations through outreach efforts. Much has already been done in this regard, but there are also many new challenges on the horizon. Methodologies and philosophies of primary debate research are in need of ongoing refinement; research and reflection on innovative public debate formats are necessary to extend the democratic potential of such events; emaciated public spheres everywhere are waiting for spirited public advocacy projects to energize forums for citizen discussion, and new strategies for debate outreach are essential to stoke the momentum already building in urban debate leagues across the nation.

[...]

At a recent dinner held in his honor, Brent Farrand (Debate Coach of Newark High School of Science) gave a brilliant and moving speech that touched on many of the themes discussed in this essay. Looking back on his own career, Farrand offer a poignant charge for the future. "Perhaps the time has come for each of us to consider choosing a road that travels to other places than just between practice rounds and tournament sites," Farrand reflected; "Through some admittedly dark times when each of us felt like voices in the wilderness, we cradled, protected, refined and polished this gem of education. It is time now to carry it out into the world and share it" (Farrand 1997).

REFERENCES

[...]

Center, D. "Debate and the Job Market." Debate Issues 15 (1982): 5.

Cherub Study Group. "Return of the Death Star?" Internet E-print. Federation of American Scientists website. July 31, 1998. Online at http://www.fas.org/spp/eprint/.

Colbert, Kent and Thompson Biggers, "Why Should We Support Debate?" Journal of the American Forensic Association 21 (Spring 1985): 237–240.

Coverstone, Alan. "An Inward Glance: A Response to Mitchell's Outward Activist Turn." In Roger Salt, Ed. United States Foreign Policy: China Cards. Winston-Salem, NC: Wake Forest University, 1995: 7–10.

Farrand, Brent. Emory Key Coach Address. 1 February 1997. Transcript printed in Gordon Mitchell, Ed. Proceedings of the First Diversity Recruitment and Retention Ideafest. Pittsburgh: University of Pittsburgh, 1998.

Farrell, Thomas B. "Knowledge, Consensus, and Rhetorical Theory." Quarterly Journal of Speech 62 (February 1976): 1–14.

Felski. Rita. Beyond Feminist Aesthetics. Cambridge: Harvard University Press, 1989.

Foucault, Michel. Discipline and Punish. New York: Vintage, 1977

Freeley, Austin J. Argumentation and Debate. 9th Ed. New York: Wadsworth, 1996.

[…]

Giroux, Henry. Postmodernism, Feminism, and Cultural Politics. Albany: State University of New York Press, 1991.

_____. Schooling and the Struggle for Public Life. Minneapolis: University of Minnesota Press, 1988.

Goodman, Ryan. Letter circulated at 1993 National Debate Tournament. October 29, 1993. Copy on file with the author.

Goodnight, G. Thomas. "Controversy." In Donn Parson, Ed. Argument in Controversy: Proceedings of the Seventh SCA/AFA Conference on Argumentation. Annandale, VA: Speech Communication Association, 1992: 1–13.

Gramsci, Antonio. Selections from the Prison Notebooks. New York: International Publishers, 1971.

[…]

Keefe, L, T. Harte and L. Norton. Introduction to Debate. New York: Macmillan, 1982.

Keele, Lucy and Ronald Matlon. "A Survey of Participants in the National Debate Tournament 1947–1980." Journal of the American Forensics Association 20 (1984): 194–205.

Kincheloe. Joe L. Toward a Critical Politics of Teacher Thinking. Westport: Bergin and Garvey, 1993.

_____. Teachers as Researchers: Qualitative Inquiry as a Path to Empowerment. London: Falmer Press, 1991.

[…]

Lee, Charles. Letter to Gordon Mitchell and John Dellcath. October 12, 1996. Copy on file with the author.

[…]

Martin, Brian. "Sticking a Needle into Science: The Case of Polio Vaccines and the Origin of AIDS." Social Studies of Science 26 (1996): 245–76.

[…]

Rai, Milan. Chomsky's Politics. London: Verso, 1995.

Rieke, Richard D. and Malcolm O. Sillars. *Argumentation and Critical Decision Making*, 4th Ed. New York: Addison Wesley Longman, 1997.

Semlak, W. and D. Shields. "The Effect of Debate Training on Students Participation in the Bicentennial Youth Debates." *Journal of the American Forensic Association* 13 (1977): 194.

Shanahan, William. "Kritik of Thinking." In Roger E. Salt and Ross K. Smith, Eds., *Health Care Policy: Debating Coverage Cures*. Winston-Salem, NC: Wake Forest University, 1993: 3–8.

Sholle, David. "The Theory of Critical Media Pedagogy." *Journal of Communication Inquiry* 18 (Summer 1994): 8–29.

[...]

Snider, Alfred. "Speech Communication Must Be Emphasized in American High Schools: A Survey of Empirical Findings." *The Rostrum* (January 1993).

[...]

Woolgar, Steve. "The Very Idea of Social Epistemology: What Prospects for a Truly Radical 'Radically Naturalized Epistemology'?" *Inquiry* 34 (September 1991): 377–89.

Ziegeimueller, George W. and Jack Kay. *Argumentation: Inquiry and Advocacy*, 3rd Ed. Needham Heights, MA: Allyn and Bacon, 1997.

[...]

---

*Gordon R. Mitchell** is associate professor of communication and director of debate at the University of Pittsburgh.

Mitchell, Gordon R. "Pedagogical Possibilities for Argumentative Agency in Academic Debate." *Argumentation and Advocacy* 35 (1998): 41–60.

Used by Permission.

The Role of Advocacy in Civil Society

*by Joseph P. Zompetti**

1. INTRODUCTION

The 1960s witnessed renewed vibrancy in American civil society when gains in civil rights occurred, citizens engaged in sustained activism, and public discourse about the state of affairs was rich and lively. In the 1990s, post-Communist countries in Eastern Europe began actively pursuing non-Communist versions of contemporary civil society with the hope of ushering in meaningful participatory democracy (Seligman, 1992, p. 4; Bryant, 1993, p. 397; Kumar, 1993, p. 375). Despite its recent popularity, the concept of civil society is still ambiguous, unmanageable, complicated, and even in some ways unreachable. Given its varied history and ambiguous meanings, recent scholars have suggested that civil society is under-theorized and lacks, as it currently stands, a cohesive framework for sustainability (Lenzen, 2002; Katz, 2002). Yet, most Americans believe that civil society is an important component to democracy. In fact, with voter registration drives, reports from national commissions, increasing levels of volunteerism, and higher political contributions from average citizens (Ladd, 1996; Schudson, 1996), one would think that civil society is not only a mainstay of American society, but flourishing.

However, we also know that there is growing political apathy, declining membership in civic organizations, and a burgeoning, albeit elaborate, network of market and government forces that largely influence major societal decisions (Council on Civil Society, 1998; National Commission on Civic Renewal, 1998; Putnam, 1995, 1996; Skocpol and Fiorina, 1999; Brint and Levy, 1999). While activists and leaders in government, business and education have been clamoring for a renewed civil society since the 1960s, very little has been done to achieve a more vibrant sense of public space and discourse. In short, cynicism, apathy, lack of access, seduction of television, economic inequality and other social pressures have caused deterioration in American civil society. Even in areas of the United States where civil society seems to be thriving, we would do well to notice how it is sustained, improved, and perhaps how it can be emulated elsewhere.

In this paper I acknowledge the reformist ideas to reinvigorate civil society. However, an essential component of many strategies to sustain civil society appears lacking. What is missing is a strategy for training or encouraging citizens to participate more fully in civil society. Given this, I propose that skills of advocacy can, at least in part, help renew civic activism. Thus, the role of advocacy will be explored as a potential way to resuscitate civil society. In what follows, I sketch the different ideas and definition of civil society, some criticisms of civil society, and then the value of civil society itself. While my main argument centers on the role of advocacy, the modest discussion about civil society is vitally important, and a determination about its value must be addressed before we even consider the significance of advocacy. After discussing the concepts of civil society, I will trace the concept of advocacy and discuss what role, if any, it has in shaping contemporary civil society.

[...]

3. THE IMPORTANCE OF CIVIL SOCIETY

Over the centuries, civil society has morphed into different concepts, but the underlying principle of a *societas civilis* has generally been considered worth the struggle. Of course, criticisms of civil society separate from the objections posed about particular versions of civil society that have already been discussed, exist as rejections of the concept *in toto*. One criticism argues that civil society excludes women. A main advocate of this position is Carole Pateman (1988) who posits that civil society merely transfers patriarchal oppression from one sphere of society to another, especially since men control the access of power which defines the positions of women to begin with. Another criticism attacks civil society as being imperialistic (Noumoff, 2000), especially when American civil society is used as a model or to influence other societies. Most recently, this position relates to the budding democracies of Eastern Europe, and critics such as Encarnacion (2000) argue that the Western model of the U.S. fails to consider the unique experience and positioning of other countries. In a related way, some scholars also argue that civil society does little by itself to advance democracy since other mechanisms such as the protection of liberties are necessary, and civil society allows counter-democratic movements to prosper (Foley and Edwards, 1996; Encarnacion, 2000; Scholte, 2002). In addition, civil society may be seen as unnecessary, especially given the vulnerabilities for intolerant and counter-democratic groups to emerge. Kumar (1993, 1994), for example, argues that other concepts such as "constitutionalism, citizenship, and democracy" sufficiently provide a sphere for civic engagement without the risks of civil society (1993, p. 391). Kumar (1994) also suggests that civil society is nothing more than Habermas's "public sphere" in disguise, indicating that civil society is not a new concept, and not a necessary element to society (p. 128). Many have refuted the public sphere analogy by stating that civil society overcomes the exclusionary nature of the public sphere, civil society allows for more activism, and civil society encourages more citizen activism instead of the public spheres reliance on open communication (Calhoun, 2002; Cohen and Arato, 1992; Dean, 2001). Still others argue that even if civil society holds on to the promise of progressivism, elites who are in positions of power will preclude any gains made from civil society (Gellner, 1994, p. 64; Skocpol, 1999, pp. 503, 505; Ehrenberg, 1999, p. 238). Finally, many scholars suggest that no matter how influential civil society becomes, it simply cannot overcome capitalism. Market forces and the seduction of consumerism will always overdetermine civic engagement, or at the very least, make it look unattractive (Cohen and Arato, 1992, p. viii; Ehrenberg, 1999, pp. 244–245).

These criticisms notwithstanding, civil society is not only a valuable concept to discuss the roles of participating citizens as they relate to the state, the market, or other societal domains, but civil society is also an important ideal for us to construct, maintain, and preserve. As Ehrenberg declares:

> Civil society's dense networks of associations increase citizens' political influence on the state, make them less vulnerable to mass demagoguery, and reduce the importance of politics by spreading interests over a wide public space ... Civil society makes possible the sort of moderate political activity that reconciles Tocquevillean localism with the large institutions of contemporary political life (1999, p. 205).

And, Gouldner suggests: "No emancipation is possible in the modern world ... without a strong civil society that can strengthen the public sphere and can provide a haven from and a center of resistance to the Behemoth state" (1980, p. 371). Of course, Antonio Gramsci, the Italian communist–philosopher who was imprisoned by Mussolini, argued the merits of civil society, perhaps before anyone else in the 20th century. According to Gramsci, "... one might say that State = political society + civil society, in other words hegemony protected by the armour of coercion.... It is possible to imagine the coercive element of the State withering away by degrees, as ever-more conspicuous elements of regulated society (or ethical State or civil society) makes their appearance" (1971, p. 263). In these ways, civil society is an important check against excessive political and economic power.

Of course, if we take a more contemporary definition of civil society as the "realm of society, lying outside the institutionalized political and administrative mechanisms of the state and the state-regulated part of the economy, where people carry on their publicly oriented social and economic activities" (Ehrenberg, 1999, p. 197), then we can begin to see the transformative potential of civil society. Indeed, what all of the critiques of civil society have in common is a pessimism of the will, or a reliance on a flawed conception of what civil society entails. Both themes can be addressed if citizens become more engaged in civic affairs—what I will argue is the meaning of advocacy. And, according to Price (2003), there are empirical examples of successful pressure from civil society on both the state and the market to change. Or, if the criticisms are correct, then there is very little hope for deliberative democracy in general. In either case, reinvigorating civil society seems to be the better course to take. Indeed, as Bryant (1993) declares, "civil society...refers to a cluster of phenomena of contemporary social and political significance more sensitively than any of the familiar components of liberal democratic theory" (p. 399). In short, civil society is our only hope of fostering citizen activism and preserving liberties.

4. THE IMPORTANCE OF ADVOCACY

It is rather common knowledge that American civil society has waned (Putnam, 1995, 1996; Council on Civil Society, 1998; National Commission on Civic Renewal, 1998; Skocpol and Fiorina, 1999; Brint and Levy, 1999). When we look at some of the reasons why American civil society has waned, we realize they are premised on the possibility that Americans simply don't know how to be engaged in a civil society (Putnam, 1995). Richard Putnam (1995; Dewey, 2003) adamantly proposes that the popularity of television is directly proportional to the decline of civil society. But, John Ehrenberg (1999) convincingly argues, that television is not enough to explain this social phenomenon. Instead, Ehrenberg declares, civil society is constructed and threatened by a number of factors, including political, cultural, economic and social forces. What we need, then, is a concept that helps transcend the different factors to enable us to revive and sustain civil society.

One possible element that transcends the different problems

plaguing civil society is advocacy, since the skills associated with advocacy help foster critical thinking and provide opportunities for civic voice against larger cultural trends. It is not surprising that previous scholars have not picked-up on the importance of advocacy in its relation to civil society, since, as Cairns (1998) declares advocacy "has never been a subject for scholarly consideration" (p. 445). Americans, in general, do not know how to discuss, much less research, items of importance concerning contemporary America (Dewey, 2003). What we see, then, is a correlative relationship between the inability to advocate and the collapse of civil society. I am not so naive as to suggest that this relationship is causal or that advocacy is the only factor involved in the very complex civil society phenomenon. Nevertheless, the *role* of advocacy could play an important part in resuscitating American civil society.

4.1. A Brief Sketch on the History of Advocacy

It is perhaps no coincidence that advocacy, as a concept, has similar origins as does civil society. Both concepts related to the *polis* as well as to the *res publica*. The ancient Greeks and Romans were fond of discussing advocacy as a means of speaking on someone else's behalf (Dunne, 1999; Grace, 2001; Whalen, 2003). There were two types of advocates: the *advocatus*, the advocate for civic engagement and improvement of society, and the *jurisconsult*, or the advocate for someone else (Cohen, 2000). The role of *advocatus* was highly respected; it was seen as a special gift and eventually became a frequently sought-after profession, particularly with the development of Roman law. The *jurisconsult* was precisely that—a counsel to the court. The *jurisconsult* was less respectable than the *advocatus*, since the *jurisconsult* was an "advocate for hire" and lacked the passion to change society for the better, as opposed to the *advocatus*.

With Cicero (1949), we have the five canons that are key to advocacy as it primarily pertains to the *advocatus*—Invention, Arrangement, Style, Memory, and Delivery. In fact, it is with Cicero that we see the importance of civic engagement *qua* advocacy, as opposed to simple legal persuasion with the *jurisconsults* (Cicero, 1949; Hanrahan, 2003). Accordingly, Cicero emphasized the value of "expressing civic virtue and political stability as well as providing intellectual structure," in order to advance the cause of a "good society" (Hanrahan, 2003, pp. 313–314). Of course, it is Quintilian, after Cicero, who emphasized the ethical and moral element to advocacy. By highlighting that the "good person speaking well" is the keystone of a good society, Quintilian was advancing his conception of the valuable society. What's more, Quintilian offered the idea that the "good man" [sic] who speaks well was a model for society, and that their speech should reflect their own personal advocacy (Scallen and Wiethoff, 1998, p. 1143).

While we often think of the Roman *advocatus* as the origin of advocacy, we should not forget the importance of Aristotle. For Aristotle, the advocate was more about civic improvement than it was about individual improvement or financial gain. Aristotle, in *The Politics* (1968), described the *polis* as an entity of civic associations. In fact, Aristotle referred to the *polis* as the "association of associations" (Hodgkinson and Foley, 2003, p. ix). It was in the *polis* that individual citizens could interact and discuss matters, including those central to politics and law. Regarding legal matters, Aristotle was careful to explain the role of the orator, as they studied the *logos, pathos* and *ethos* of their advocacy. In *The Rhetoric*, Aristotle advanced that "the speaker," when discussing legal affairs, "must appeal to the universal law, and to the principles of equity as representing a higher order of justice" (1932, p. 80). Advocacy, then, for Aristotle, was premised on an ethical–political notion of justice. We might say that an Aristotelian advocacy is geared toward an ethical civic engagement.

After Aristotle, Cicero and Quintilian, very little is written that discusses advocacy. We know that during the Medieval and Renaissance eras disputes were settled through means of advocacy, which followed the traditions of the ancient Romans and Greeks. One may even chart the word "advocate" to 14th century France to mean the "pleading for or supporting" (Grace, 2001, p. 154). The lack of material describing advocacy since Greece and Rome is telling of the durability of the concept. Advocacy, simply put, is the passionate plea for a particular position. What's more, the concept of "advocacy" has essentially meant this for over 2000 years.

4.2. The Skills of Advocacy

Contemporary training in advocacy directly corresponds to the ancient teachings of Aristotle, Quintilian and Cicero (Jamail, 1995). David S. Coale, a former law clerk in the Fifth Circuit of the U.S. Court of Appeals and currently a private attorney in Dallas, convincingly argues that Aristotle's formula for effective advocacy —ethos, pathos and logos—is the key to successful legal advocacy today (2001, p. 734). Additionally, James S. Gifford, who is an attorney in Hawaii, defends Aristotle's description of advocacy is laying the groundwork for modern American constitutional law (1999, p. 490).

Aristotle, as we know, was not the only one to expound about the nature of advocacy in the ancient period. In Rome, Quintilian and Cicero borrowed the Greek idea that advocacy was persuasion. As far as that would go, Cicero, in particular, was not satisfied. For him, specific elements such as style, arrangement, delivery, and so on, were vital for effective speeches, especially oratory concerning legal or political affairs. Like Aristotle, we know that the Ciceronian "canon"—particularly of delivery, style, and memory—is vital for contemporary lessons of advocacy (Hanrahan, 2003). In fact, Hanrahan helps explain that Cicero's "five canons" are used "to appeal to a jury's sense of ethos, pathos, and logos," thereby bridging the contributions of both Aristotle and Cicero (2003, p. 308).

Finally, at its core, advocacy requires persuasion. Aristotle includes advocacy as a form of rhetoric, which he defines as "discovering in the particular case what are the available means of persuasion" (1932, p. 7). More contemporary argument and persuasion scholars also view advocacy as tied to persuasion:

It is the advocate's job to persuade others as to the seriousness of a problem, i.e., to get others to recognize the existence of a problem, as well as persuade others that the advocate's solution to the problem is a wise and workable one which should be adopted. The advocate, accordingly, is concerned with influence and power: he [sic] wants to be effective, to be able to influence person A to accept solution X when otherwise A might accept solution Y or no solution at all (Windes and Hastings, 1965, p. 24).

We may say that persuasion is to convince someone else of some item or belief. Advocacy, however, demands unique forms of persuasion. Aside from arguing a problem and a solution, as Windes and Hastings differentiate, advocacy includes special persuasive skill sets by attempting to avoid coercion. According to current legal scholars (Jamail, 1995; Hanrahan, 2003), advocacy is the impassioned making of one's case. Its delivery and content are prepared and presented in ways that are integrally tied to the advocate's identity, ensuring that the onus is on the advocate, not the audience. This form of rhetoric minimizes the degree of coercion since the advocacy is, by definition, offered, rather than forced upon its listeners. This does not eliminate the coercive impulse of persuasive exchanges, but it does provide a rhetorical situation where the advocate has a degree of control over the content of their persuasive message.

In addition, the persuasive role of advocacy could be seen as a *gravitas placitum*—a plea of severity. In short, the advocate has something serious at stake in the communicative exchange; the nature of advocacy requires it, otherwise the rhetor would be engaged in simple deliberative speaking, and not the involved as an *advocatus*. To advocate, as we have already clarified, suggests a higher duty for our rhetor than simply speaking on someone's behalf or articulating a certain position. The advocate, armed with sharpened oratorical and reasoning skills, must persuade others —and were mainly talking about audiences lodged within civil society—about an issue of extreme importance. The cause for the advocate, then, is not a simple rhetorical situation, but rather is of enormous significance, such as the future of the society, the appropriate methods of rule, to wage war or not, to put another to death for some crime, etc. In essence, the gravity of the advocates cause creates a persuasive situation distinct from other persuasive episodes.

The skills of advocacy, then, relate to the ability to persuade, including the skills of *ethos*, *pathos*, *logos*, and the Ciceronian five canons. We may specify this by saying that advocacy also relates to persuasion by means other than coercion. In other words, the advocacy is premised on the advocate's passion for the content. While the goal of persuading the audience is always evident, the actual meaning underlying the content of advocacy is centered on the advocate's subjectivity, not the audiences. Finally, we can say that advocacy relates to a problem and a solution, as described by Windes and Hastings (1965). This emphasis requires us to learn basic skills of research, argument composition and construction, delivery, style, and evidentiary proof. Of course, if the advocacy generates discussion, particularly in the public realm, then skills of refutation must also be acquired (Windes and Hastings, 1965).

4.3. Advocacy's Role for Civil Society

In the spirit of de Tocqueville, Thomas Jefferson referred to the new American democracy as a "free marketplace," not as capitalism run amuck, but rather as a free-flow of open possibilities for citizens to discuss political affairs (Windes and Hastings, 1965, p. 9). This "freedom" occurs on two levels, both inquiry and advocacy, where inquiry refers to the ability of individuals to make rational judgments and advocacy as a form of persuasion. Indeed, as Windes and Hastings suggest, the freedom of "advocacy" develops as "people attempt to influence the belief of others *through* advocacy and are, in turn, influenced *by* advocacy, by the forceful presentation of the beliefs of other citizens" (1965, p. 11). In essence, advocacy enables citizens to perform their roles as a citizens *qua* citizens.

Fundamentally, if civil society is meant to provide a space of civic engagement separate from political or economic interference, then discussions should emerge about political and economic affairs that avoid the coercive, albeit hegemonic, influence of both the state and the market. What does advocacy bring to the table? By definition, a citizenry trained in the skills of advocacy would do the following:

1. Learn to recognize and avoid arguments of coercion (Quintilian),
2. Learn to research and reflect on civic issues of importance (Cicero),
3. Learn to be impassioned by means of reason to issues at hand (Cicero and Aristotle),
4. Learn to prepare and deliver effective arguments about the issue (Cicero and Aristotle),
5. Learn to refute oppositional claims and sustain credibility (Cicero and Aristotle).

Skills, not just ideals, can help propel citizens to become better citizens. Some of the greatest philosophers of all time (Aristotle, Rousseau, Marx, Tocqueville, Jefferson, Gramsci, etc.) have clamored for individual subjects to take a more active role in areas of governance that affect them personally. Advocacy skills can reinvigorate civic participation and deliberative democracy (Jewell, 1998; Hanrahan, 2003). Learning how to engage in advocacy can also help citizens understand the importance of civic engagement, thereby curtailing some of the distracting societal forces that have to date discouraged civic participation (Putnam 1995, 1996; Ehrenberg, 1999). These skills must be taught; unlike rights, they are not self-evident (Hanrahan, 2003). Elementary and middle school classes in citizenship and civic participation are a good start. Somewhere along the line, however, we have forgotten that civic engagement is a process; a process that requires sustained influence, especially when considering the number of distractions and impediments to participating in civil society (Putnam, 1995).

Educating the public about their responsibilities and duties to civic engagement is also a start (Dewey, 2003). Where Dewey and others fall short, however, is their neglect of advocacy as an important process to give value to civil society. Advocacy, while not a cure-all, can help jumpstart the civil society process in many areas of the country. Where civil society is already taking root, the ability to advocate salient public issues can galvanize additional support and help maintain the spirit of civic engagement that is so critical to a functioning democracy (Hauser and Benoit-Barne, 2002, p. 271). Again, advocacy will not necessarily usher in a utopia, particularly in societies with traditions of dictatorship, or even democracies with entrenched party politics. Nevertheless, with a renewed and vibrant civil society, these countries can begin a path of social transformation which may create opportunities for important political and cultural change.

Perhaps the most important question to ask is: How can advocacy help civil society? The skills associated with advocacy should already appear significant when drawing a connection between advocacy and civil society. In addition, there are a number of events and opportunities that can use advocacy skills to maintain or construct notions of civil society. Besides training students and citizens about the skills of advocacy, public forums and/or public debates could help with reviving civil society. Gordon Mitchell (1998, 2000) has already argued that public debates can help foster a sense of community and inclusion. The idea here is that we can utilize the infrastructure that already exists within collegiate debate and speech programs to facilitate planned public debates about issues regarding our communities. Aimed at encouraging student and citizen participation, these debates could help foster additional discussions and possibly even generate additional public *fora* where deliberative, civic discussions take place.

Venues for a civil society can all be improved through the process of advocacy. Universities are a natural fit with this conception since advocacy skills can be easily disseminated in course curricula and student organizations. A university scene can also play an important part in the development and maintenance of civil society since, according to Gerard Delanty, "[t]he university is an institution of the public sphere; it is not above civil society but a part of its cultural tradition, in particular it is a part of the public sphere and its tradition of debate and reflection" (1988, p. 22). Universities can simultaneously instruct students in advocacy skills while also offering community outreach programs and public discussions about issues pertaining to civil society.

Finally, I have touched on the importance of civil society for deliberative democracy. Many scholars point to civil society's contribution to democracy, some even arguing that civil society is the *sine qua non* for democracy (Cohen and Arato, 1992; Bryant, 1993; Ehrenberg, 1999; Hodgkinson and Foley, 2003). But what is the role of advocacy in securing a functioning and prospering democracy? Advocacy is the lynchpin for preparing and delivering arguments. For a functioning democracy, public discussions about the merits and disadvantages of different courses of action are vital. Only through thorough research and development of arguments can this occur. Advocacy, then, is essential for both civil society and democracy. Skocpol, borrowing from de Tocqueville, argues that "[u]nderstanding the causes and consequences of civic Americas recent transition from membership to advocacy is vital if we are to reflect wisely on prospects for our democracy" (1999, p. 462). In a society where cynicism and apathy run rampant, learning how to advocate might just be the anecdote for a disease of despair.

5. Conclusion

Civil society for contemporary society should embrace the concept of the *third space*, as discussed by Bryant (1993), Cohen and Arato (1992), and Hauser and Benoit-Barne (2002). The third space envisions civil society as an autonomous sphere, separate from governmental or economic influence. The third space minimizes the amount of undue influence that can emanate from the state or the market. As Cohen and Arato suggest, "the insistence that without public spaces for the active participation of the citizenry in ruling and being ruled, without a decisive narrowing of the gap between rulers and ruled, to the point of its abolition, politics are democratic in name only" (1992, p. 7). Venues for a civil society conceived as a third space, such as churches, synagogues, unions, voluntary organizations, schools, women's groups and other arenas can all be improved through the process of advocacy. These groups and organizations, according to Skocpol, are "sites where citizens learn—and practice—the 'knowledge of how to combine' so vital to democracy" (1999, p. 462). As we have seen, advocacy skills are important for citizens not only to appreciate their role in civil society, but also to advance and refute positions regarding civic involvement and efforts at improving society. As I have discussed, incorporating advocacy into civil society, one can hope, will foster more meaningful discussion, less coercion, and more productive civic engagement.

I have wrestled with the concept of civil society—what does it mean, how does it function, is it important? Civil society is not without its flaws, one of which is it is not sustainable on its own. Something else must also be present for civil society to flourish. Its existence may depend on multiple factors, but one that seems most evident is a citizenry who is capable of using the skills of advocacy. Quite simply, this relationship between civil society and advocacy seems particularly salient to me since civil society requires civil engagement and advocacy generates the ability and skill sets necessary to engage in discussions affecting the populace. Again, I am not suggesting that advocacy is a panacea. Civil society is struggling over other factors as well, such as the distraction of sports and television, the collusion between politicians and their constituents, economic demands preventing civic participation, and so on. However, assuming there are enough citizens who have the ability and willingness to engage in civil society, how could their participation be improved? How could civil society be more influential in its relationship to the state and market? How can citizens feel more secure and enthusiastic about their participation? I believe that the skills of advocacy can help answer these questions.

Some of the greatest thinkers in history have discussed civil society. Most agree that it is a concept worth keeping. Indeed, if democracy intends on listening to the voice of the people, then the people need to have a voice. Civil society serves as a tool for citizens to engage each other as well as the affairs of society. Only through a process of civic discourse, respect, and argument can this discourse serve any purpose. The ancient principles of advocacy are a reminder of how each individual has a part to play in civic engagement. Advocacy, not acrimony, can improve and resuscitate our civil society. And, in turn, perhaps it can improve our democracy.

REFERENCES

Aristotle: 1932, *The Rhetoric of Aristotle* (Lane Cooper, Trans.), Prentice-Hall, Englewood Cliffs, NJ.

Aristotle: 1968, *The Politics* (Steven Emerson, Ed.), Cambridge University Press, Cambridge, UK.

Brint, S. and Levy C. S.: 1999, 'Professions and Civic Engagement: Trends in Rhetoric and Practice, 1875–1995', in Skocpol T. and M. P. Fiorina (eds.), *Civic Engagement in American Democracy*, pp. 163–210. Brookings Institute Press, Washington D.C.

Bryant, C. G. A.: 1993, Social Self-Organisation, Civility and Sociology: A Comment on Kumar's 'Civil Society', *The British Journal of Sociology* **44**, 397–401.

Cairns, D. J. A.: 1998, *Advocacy and the Making of the Adversarial Criminal Trial 1800–1865*, Oxford, Clarendon Press.

Calhoun, C.: 2002, Imagining Solidarity: Cosmopolitanism, Constitutional Patriotism, and the Public Sphere, *Public Culture* **14**, 147–171.

Cicero, M. T.: 1949, *De inventione; De optimo genere oratorum* (In H.M. Hubbell, Trans.). Harvard University Press, Cambridge, MA.

Coale, D. S.: 2001, Developments and Practice Notes: Classical Citation, *The Journal of Appellate Practice and Process* **3**, 733–742.

Cohen, J. A.: 2000, Lawyer role, Agency Law, and the Characterization 'Officer of the Court', *Buffalo Law Review* **48**. Available: Lexis-Nexis.

Cohen, J. L. and A. Arato: 1992, *Civil Society and Political Theory*, MIT Press, Cambridge, MA.

Council on Civil Society: 1998, *Why Democracy Needs Moral Truths*, Council on Civil Society, New York.

[...]

Dean, J.: 2001, Cybersalons and Civil Society: Rethinking the Public Sphere in Transnational Technoculture, *Public Culture* 13, 243–265.

Delanty, G.: 1988, The Idea of the University in the Global Era: From Knowledge as an End to the End of Knowledge?, *Social Epistemology* 12, 3–25.

Dewey, J.: 2003, The Public and Its Problems (Reprinted in), in V. A. Hodgkinson and M. W. Foley (eds.), *The Civil Society Reader*, pp. 133–153, Tufts University Press Hanover, NH.

Dunne, P. J.: 1999, July, 'The Origins of Advocacy', Historical Perspectives. Bar Association of Metropolitan St. Louis Web page. Accessed January 22:2004. Available online: http://www.bamsl.org/stlawyer/archive/99/July99/Dunne.html.

Ehrenberg, J.: 1999, *Civil Society: The Critical History of an Idea*, New York University Press, New York.

Encarnacion, O. G.: 2000, Tocqueville's Missionaries: Civil Society Advocacy and the Promotion of Democracy, *World Policy Journal* 17, 9–18.

Foley, M. W. and B. Edwards: 1996, The Paradox of Civil Society, *Journal of Democracy* 7, 38–52.

Gellner, E.: 1994, *Conditions of Liberty: Civil Society and Its Rivals*, Allen Lane, New York.

Gifford, J. S.: 1999, Jus Cogens and Fourteenth Amendment Privileges or Immunities, *Arizona Journal of International and Comparative Law* 16, 481–498.

Gouldner, A.: 1980, *The Two Marxisms*, Macmillan, London.

Grace, P. J.: 2001, Professional Advocacy: Widening the Scope of Accountability, *Nursing Philosophy* 2, 151–163.

Gramsci, A.: 1971, *Selections From the Prison Notebooks* (Quintin Hoare & Geoffrey Nowell Smith, Eds. and Trans.), International Publishers, New York.

Hanrahan, J. K.: 2003, Truth in Action: Revitalizing Classical Rhetoric as a Tool for Teaching Oral Advocacy in American Law Schools, *Brigham Young University Education and Law Journal* 2003, 299–338.

Hauser, G. A. and C. Benoit-Barne: 2002, Reflections on Rhetoric, Deliberative Democracy, Civil Society, and Trust, *Rhetoric & Public Affairs* 5, 261–275.

[...]

Hodgkinson, V. A. and M. W. Foley (eds.): 2003, *The Civil Society Reader*. Tufts University Press, Hanover, NH.

[...]

Jamail, J. D.: 1995, Advocacy and Lawyers and Their Role, *Baylor Law Review* **47**, 1157–1158.

Jewell, E. A.: 1998, 'Exploring the Role of Advocacy in the Arts Community', Thesis Abstract for Ohio State University. Accessed March 8, 2004. Available online: http://arts.osu.edu/ArtEducation/APA/abstracts/jewell.html.

Katz, S. N.: 2002, Constitutionalism, Contestation, and Civil Society, *Common Knowledge* **8**, 287–303.

Kumar, K.: 1993, Civil Society: An Inquiry Into the Usefulness of an Historical Term, *The British Journal of Sociology* **44**, 375–395.

Kumar, K.: 1994, Civil Society Again: A Reply to Christopher Bryant's 'Social Self-Organization, Civility and Sociology', *The British Journal of Sociology* **45**, 127–131.

Ladd, E. C.: 1996, Civic Participation and American Democracy: The Data Just Don't Show Erosion of Americas Social Capital, *The Public Perspective* **7**, 1 & 5–6.

Lenzen, M. H.: 2002, The Use and Abuse of 'Civil Society' in Development, *Transnational Associations* **3**, 170–187.

Mitchell, G.: 1998, Pedagogical Possibilities for Argumentative Agency in Academic Debate, *Argumentation & Advocacy* **35**, 41–61.

Mitchell, G.: 2000, Simulated Public Argument As a Pedagogical Play on Worlds, *Argumentation & Advocacy* **36**, 134–151.

National Commission on Civic Renewal: 1998, *Americas* Civic and Moral Beliefs, University of Maryland Press, College Park, MD.

[…]

Noumoff, S. J.: 2000, September 21, 'Civil Society: Does It Have Meaning?' Paper Presented at Development: The Need for Reflection, Centre for Developing Area Studies, McGill University, Montreal, Quebec. Accessed January 27, 2004. Available online: ww2.mcgill.ca/cdas/conf2000e/noumoff.pdf.

Pateman, C.: 1988, *The Sexual Contract*, Polity, Cambridge, MA.

Price, R.: 2003, Transnational Civil Society and Advocacy in World Politics, *World Politics* **55**, 579–606.

Putnam, R. D.: 1995, Bowling Alone: Americas Declining Social Capital, *Journal of Democracy* **6**, 65–78.

Putnam R. D.: 1996, 'The Strange Disappearance of Civic America', *The American Prospect* **7**, 34–48.

Scallen, E. A. and W. E. Wiethoff: 1998, April, 'The Ethos of Expert Witnesses: Confusing the Admissibility, Sufficiency and Credibility of Expert Testimony', *Hastings Law Journal* **49**. Available: Lexis-Nexis.

Scholte, J. A.: 2002, Civil Society and Democracy in Global Governance, *Global Governance* **8**, 281–304.

Schudson, M.: 1996, What if Civic Life Didn't Die?, *The American Prospect* 7, 17–20.

Seligman, A. B.: 1992, *The Idea of Civil Society*, The Free Press, New York.

Skocpol, T.: 1999, 'Advocates Without Members: Recent Transformations of Civic Life', in T Skocpol and M. P. Fiorina (eds.), *Civic Engagement in American Democracy*, pp. 461–510, Brookings Institute Press, Washington D.C.

Skocpol, T. and M. P. Fiorina: 1999, 'Making Sense of the Civic Engagement Debate', in T. Skocpol and M. P. Fiorina (eds. *Civic Engagement in American Democracy*, pp. 1–24, Brookings Institute Press Washington D.C.

[...]

Whalen, W. W.: 2003, February, 'The Lawyer That Was Rome', *The American Lawyer*. Available: Lexis-Nexis.

Windes, R. and A. Hastings: 1965, *Argumentation and Advocacy*, New York, Random House.

---

*Joseph P. Zompetti is an associate professor in the School of Communication and former director of forensics at Illinois State University.

Zompetti, Joseph P. "The Role of Advocacy in Civil Society." *Argumentation* 20 (2006): 167–183. Published with kind permission from Springer Science + Business Media B.V.

PART 5

Debate and Career Training

In our final section, we present articles that discuss the relationship between debate participation and training for future careers. In "High School Student Perceptions of the Efficacy of Debate Participation," Robert S. Littlefield discusses the perceptions of students on how debate trained them for their current careers. Similarly, "Graduate School, Professional, and Life Choices: An Outcome Assessment Confirmation Study Measuring Positive Student Outcomes beyond Student Experiences for Participants in Competitive Intercollegiate Forensics," by Jack E. Rogers, describes how skills in debate prepare participants for their career preparation. Finally, "The Impact of Prior Experience in Intercollegiate Debate upon a Postsecondary Educator's Skill-set," by Doyle Srader, concerns a study that asked professionals how debate training helped them in their professions. These articles examine the specific ways debate training impacts the skills necessary for effective professional careers. Of course, one of the flaws of these studies is that they rely on self-reporting; however, it is important to keep in mind that these reports also provide insight from the perspective of the people who directly benefit from their debate experience.

High School Student Perceptions of the Efficacy of Debate Participation

*by Robert S. Littlefield**

Over the past twenty years, the nature and benefits of inter-scholastic debate have come under scrutiny from administrators and others who question whether the investment of time, effort, and resources is justified. While some argue that debate improves a student's ability to communicate with an audience, conduct research, think quickly and critically, construct persuasive arguments, and successfully transfer these skills to other settings (Bellon, 2000), the question of whether or not debaters perceive the debate activity as enabling them to accomplish these objectives has received limited attention.

Williams et al. (2001) sought to ascertain the perceptions of collegiate debaters regarding the benefits and disadvantages of participating in competitive debate at a time characterized by the emergence of a variety of debate-sponsoring organizations.[1] They concluded that debaters, across all formats, perceived participation in collegiate debate to produce the same benefits and disadvantages as those found by debaters in earlier studies before the expansion of formats.[2] However, missing from their discussion of perceived benefits and disadvantages of debate was the inclusion of perceptions from high school debaters. In fact, very few manuscripts dealing with high school debate have been published in academic journals.

The absence of much recent scholarship pertaining to the high school debate community is perplexing, given the fact that similarities and relationships between high school and collegiate debate exist.[3] However, the limited scholarship about high school debate during the last twenty years should not suggest that the high school debate community was not of interest to earlier scholars in the field of speech communication and/or forensics. While not excessive, early communication scholars investigated the nature of high school debate (Konigsberg, 1935; Turner, 1941; Larson, 1952; Barber, 1954, and Simonson & Strange, 1961), the characteristics of high school debaters (Thompson, 1931; Hargis, 1934; Hetlinger & Hildreth, 1961; Patton, 1962; Semlak and Shields, 1977; and Anderson & Matlon, 1974), relationships between high school and collegiate debate environments (Lewis, 1942; Hettinger & Hildreth, 1961; Tucker, Koehler, & Mlady, 1967; King & Phifer, 1968; Stewart & Merchant, 1969; and Schug, 1954), and perceptions of high school debaters about the activity (Fine, 2000; and Fine, 1999).

Only two studies provided a methodology surveying high school debaters about their perceptions toward debate. Thomas (1965) surveyed coaches in selected Michigan high schools, and 70 debaters at the Michigan State University Forensic Institute, regarding their perceptions about participation in debate, the amount of time spent working alone or with a coach, and specific practice-related issues. The second study used a population of students participating in a summer debate institute at the University of Georgia (Pruett, 1972). Both sets of respondents inferred that experience at debate institutes contributed to their positive educational development and self-enhancement. While these two studies established a model for further exploration of the perceptions of high school debaters, no subsequent investigations resulted. In the absence of comparative studies considering the similarities and differences between the perceptions of high school and collegiate debaters about debate, this examination is timely and useful.

METHOD

The current study assessed high school student perceptions of debate and compared these perceptions with those generated at the collegiate level. The survey instrument modeled the one described by Williams et al. (2001) and included 15 items requesting demographic data and prior speech experience, experience in policy and Lincoln Douglas formats, perceptions of collegiate debate, and perceived advantages and disadvantages of debate.[4]

High school students in the National Forensic League were identified as a source of data since the NFL is a national high school organization with a significant number of debaters included among its members and the NFL has been a source of data for several earlier studies (Klopf & Rivers, 1965; Hensley, 1972; Anderson & Mallon, 1974; G. A. Fine, 2000). Following approval from the National Forensic League to collect data at its National Tournament held June 10–15, 2001, at the University of Oklahoma, surveys were made available to any high school student who met the requirements of the study.[5]

The population from which the sample was drawn included the 400 policy debaters and 229 Lincoln Douglas participants registered for competition at the 2001 NFL National Tournament.

[...]

In summary, seven of the disadvantages cited by the respondents in this study were similar to those cited in the Williams et al. (2001) study (Takes Time/Trade-off, Significant Time Commitment, Causes Stress/Tension, Fosters Unhealthy Habits, No Social Life/Isolation, Costly/Expensive, and Competition/Politics/Judging Issues). Three disadvantages cited by the high school respondents that were not included among the top ten on the collegiate study reflected the negative stigma associated with debate, negative criticism of self and other debaters, and negative criticism of the debate activity. Essentially, based upon the responses from high school debaters, three themes can be identified: Debate takes a significant amount of time; debate negatively affects debaters psychologically, physically, socially, and economically; and debaters experience negative stigma coming from themselves, other debaters, and their peers outside of the debate activity.

Discussion

The most obvious finding of this study is that the perceptions of high school debaters about the benefits and disadvantages of debate are very similar to those of collegiate debaters. The results of the present study reinforce the first conclusion drawn by Williams et al. (2001) that debaters across all levels and debate formats believe their communication skills are being enhanced through participation in debate. However, the data are not conclusive from high school debaters regarding what they perceive good communication skills to be.

The present study also contributes to a better understanding of how debaters construct a social culture that is conducive to their well-being. Williams et al. (2001) concluded that college debaters today were more concerned about social lives than debaters in the past. This may be because college debaters are not viewed as positively today as they were in the past (Tucker, Koehler, & Mlady, 1967), fueled by the popular press and film industry casting debaters as "pocket-protector 'geeks'" (Hutchins, 1998, 18). Williams et al. (2001) concluded that one of the reasons why debaters have such strong social bonds with other debaters stems from the time they spend together. The data from the present study furthers this claim by suggesting that a social culture for debaters develops due to the positive self-concept that is inherent in the nature of debaters.

The third conflicting vision identified by Williams et al. (2001) reflected the "knowledge versus academic success tradeoff" (205). College debaters claimed that debate hurt their academic performance; high school debaters did not. Among the factors cited as having a negative impact on the academic success of collegiate debaters were: The flexible collegiate schedule; the absence of mandatory class attendance at the university-level; and the impact of being away from home or more self-reliant. As college debaters devote more of their time to debate, something must suffer; in this case, their academic performance. High school debaters, while able to miss school for tournaments, attend classes on a regular basis in order to remain academically eligible. The high school debaters reflected their sense that they had more knowledge than their peers and were better at reading, writing, and speaking. The existence of a social system, away from the academic environment, further motivated the high school debater to remain eligible to travel and interact with friends on a regular basis.

Clearly, the findings from this study support and further explain those identified by Williams et al. (2001). Additionally, seven of the benefit categories and seven of the disadvantage categories listed by high school and collegiate debaters were included within the top ten for each group.[13] Within these common perceptions of debate, additional insight may be gained by comparing how the categories of benefits and disadvantages were ranked by the two groups.

[...]

Comparison of the Perceived Benefits

In the benefit categories, the high school and collegiate ranks of Knowledge/Education and Critical/Analytical Skills were reversed. Knowledge/Education was ranked second by high school debaters and fifth by collegiate debaters. Critical/Analytical Skills was ranked sixth by high school debaters and second by collegiate debaters. This reversal of rankings offers an explanation for the stages of the learning experienced by debaters.

As students advance in school, they find themselves being exposed to greater and greater amounts of information. While in high school, students receive a broad sampling of a wide range of subject areas which contributes to their overall knowledge base. At the university level, while students are still exposed to unfamiliar topics, the emphasis often shifts to learning how to analyze, synthesize, and use information. This is consistent with the decision-making process where knowledge of a topic or new idea comes first, followed by the formation of a favorable or unfavorable attitude toward the idea, and activities leading to the adoption or rejection of the idea (Rogers, 1995, 20). Debaters at the high school level learn a great deal about the topics that are selected for use during a particular school year. For a four-year high school debater, the overlap between the topic areas is minimal and each year represents a significant amount of knowledge about a topic. For collegiate debaters, some of whom with multiple years of high school debate, there may be more back files and the overlapping of arguments. Hence, critically assessing the available information may be perceived as a more valuable skill than simply gaining knowledge about the topic. Also, at the high school level, knowledge about the topic often provides the basis for settling disputes about whether or not claims are true or false. However, at the collegiate level, more advanced levels of argumentation result in debaters challenging the theoretical premises upon which the debate activity is based. The reliance on analytical arguments over fact-based claims also could contribute to the higher rank for critical/analytical thinking among collegiate debaters.

[...]

Comparison of the Perceived Disadvantages

For the disadvantage categories, the high school and collegiate debaters were similar in their rankings. However, the inclusion of three categories in the high school survey that were not in the top ten categories of the Williams et al. (2001) study deserves discussion.

High school debaters included comments about the negative stigma debaters feel from others, perceptions and criticisms of themselves and other debaters by high school debaters, and comments reflecting criticisms of the debate activity itself. These three categories reflect a state of mind among high school debaters that is clearly in an evaluative mode.[14] The majority of the respondents liked debating and knew the benefits derived *from* the activity, but they were concerned about their identity, the way others saw them, and how the activity was perceived by those outside of the debate community. Studies in adolescent growth and development are consistent in their findings that how children see themselves, and how children believe they are seen by their peers, can have a significant effect on the creation of their self-identity. Gergen (1991) found that "...relationships make possible the concept of self...we are manifestations of relatedness" (170). The awareness and concern about how high school debaters are perceived by others reflected this trait. When debaters perceive themselves to be separated from their peers by negative stereotypes, their sense of self is affected. Self-deprecation is a by-product of the negative stereotyping. If debaters perceive themselves in a negative way, based upon how they think that others see them, they tend to criticize themselves. Some of the high school responses were distinctly negative: "I'm a loser" and "I hate my life." Similarly, just as high school debaters question whether the stereotyping about them is accurate, it would not be unreasonable to question whether the activity in which they invested so much time was worth the effort. The comments reflected such observations as: "Debate forces you to prostitute your views" and "debate gives you a warped sense of morality."

For the high school debaters in this study, concern about how debaters and the debate activity are perceived may have been the reason why, when asked if they intended to debate in college, 57 said yes, 66 responded no, and 70 were unsure. It should be noted that 89 of the 193 respondents had a favorable or very favorable attitude toward college debate, as opposed to 41 respondents had an unfavorable or very unfavorable impression of collegiate debate. Sixty-two respondents were unsure of how they felt about collegiate debate.

Comparison of Perceived Benefits and Disadvantages

Two additional areas for further discussion emerged from a comparison of the perceived benefits and disadvantages identified by the high school and collegiate debaters: First, the contrast between the educational benefits of debate versus the time commitment portrays a struggle between enhancing the mind at the expense of the body; and second, the feeling of isolation versus the creation of a social life revolving around the debate community demonstrates the ability of high school debaters to create a culture in which they can thrive.

Initially, the most frequently cited perceived advantages reflected an emphasis on improved speaking skills, education and knowledge acquisition, research skills, and critical/analytical abilities. The infrequent mention of the disadvantage of harming or negatively affecting academic growth confirmed a consistency level among the respondents that debate provided them with educational benefits. Conflicting with the perception of these benefits were the overwhelming number of responses identifying Significant Time Requirement and Takes Time/Trade-Off, along with the increased stress, tension, and unhealthy habits. In other words, high school debaters felt that their participation in debate was beneficial, contributing to their academic skills and performance; but the benefits were coming with a significant cost in terms of lost time, added stress, and unhealthy habits.

A second aspect of the findings focused on the conflicting responses over having or not having a social life. Some of those citing isolation from family, friends, and school-related activities as a disadvantage suggested that they felt left out and lonely. The negative responses about being labeled a "nerd," or being stereotyped by those outside of the debate community, also suggested a sense of isolation that was not welcomed. However, a sizable number of responses cited participation in debate as a benefit because debaters meet people and make friends with students from other schools and other areas of the country. This reflected a cosmopolitan trait that Rogers (1995) perceived to be a positive personal characteristic (27).

One theory relating perceived ability to self-concept, developed by Hamachek (1995) and others (Hansford & Hattie, 1982; Byrne, 1974; Marsh, 1990; and Marsh, Byrne, & Shavelson, 1988), contributed insight to the initial discussion of debate's academic benefit versus personal and physical harms. These studies concluded that positive student perceptions of their abilities contributed to positive self-concepts, which in turn, increased academic performance. By citing the acquisition of skills to help them to be more successful thinkers, researchers, intelligent, and persuasive speakers, the high school debaters demonstrated positive perceptions of their abilities. If Hamachek's claim is true, this positive perception should contribute to a positive self-concept.

In his Informal Self-Concept Assessment Inventory, Hamachek (1995) provided fourteen inventory items comparing students with a positive versus a negative self-concept.[15] An examination of these items supports the underlying conclusion that high school debaters have a positive self-concept which sustains them through the difficulties they experience in the activity. Based upon the responses from debaters in this study, the respondents tended not to be self-disparaging. They liked meeting new people and making friends at tournaments. Despite the time commitment, they perceived themselves as benefiting from debate by learning research skills, argument construction, and acquiring broader knowledge than their peers on a wide range of topics. The debaters preferred to win their rounds, making success in competition a goal; and their persistence in debating was reflected in the fact that 161 out of 193 claimed three or more years of debate experience, doing significant amounts of work alone, with their coach, and in the off-season at debate institutes, often attending more than one.[16] Many respondents planned to continue debating in college and viewed themselves as successful or good at debating. Respondents also indicated their self-confidence and interest in trying other forensic events.[17] Clearly, the data suggest that the high school debaters in this study had positive self-concepts. This enabled them to weigh the benefits against the negative factors of debate and to decide that their continued involvement in debate was advantageous.

This positive self-concept also was related to the second factor of having or not having a social life as a consequence of participation in debate. Researchers claim that people gain their sense of self primarily through their social interactions and the roles they play in various social contexts (Mead, 1934; Gecas, 1982). Erikson (1968) further suggested that adolescents spend a significant amount of time creating their "identity construct," or a set of values, belief systems, goals, and attitudes that provide them with a sense of coherence and continuity in their lives. High school debaters who spend considerable time away from their homes, family, friends, classes, and school activities can feel isolated and alone. However, the inherent, positive self-concept that debaters possess may provide the means by which they channel their efforts to create a social system or culture of their own.

In a study exploring the impact of culture on the individual, Markus and Kitayama (1991) noted that the independent self remained separate from others in a cultural context; while the interdependent self sought connections to others within the social system. While the independent self was perceived to be "unitary and stable" and focused on "private and internal psychological states;" the interdependent self was "flexible... varied, and employed 'an external locus of attention with more public expression'" (on-line). For the high school students in this study, the interdependent nature of debate created a flexible and varied culture in which their interconnected self functioned and allowed itself to be governed by audiences interested in what it had to say. Further, Cushman (1995) suggested that the self "is a product of specific cultural values." The labeling and stereotyping cited by the respondents contributed to the cohesiveness of the social system that debaters created for themselves. Termed "embeddedness"—the "interdependence between individuals and their psychological, social, historical, and cultural contexts" (Blustein, 1994; Josselson, 1988; Lerner, Skinner & Sorrel, 1980; and Vondracek et al., 1986)—debaters created for themselves an image of them as bright, persuasive, and scholarship material for colleges and universities with national debate programs. The embedded identity enabled debaters to draw upon their common experiences and perceptions stemming from the debate activity itself. Within this culture, debaters demonstrate and practice all of the social skills they perceive their peers to be experiencing. They meet new people, make friends, and develop positive relationships with their teammates, coaches, and judges.

DIRECTIONS FOR FUTURE RESEARCH

This study yields significant insight into how high school debaters perceive their involvement in debate. As one of the very few studies that has surveyed the opinions of senior-level high school policy and Lincoln-Douglas debaters, the data should contribute to a better understanding of high school debaters and how they view this time consuming activity. As the only comparative study of the similarities and differences between the perceptions of high school and collegiate debaters, this data should be useful to debate teachers and coaches called upon to justify their programs to supervisors and administrators since both groups identified many aspects of debate contributing to their education. The quality of this sample was high and the data corresponded with the collegiate study conducted by Williams et al. (2001), further adding to its reliability.

Another conclusion supported by this study suggests that knowledge acquisition and critical thinking in debate follows a linear process. High school debaters valued debate because it exposed them to a wide range of topics, giving them more knowledge of subject areas than their non-debate classmates. However, collegiate debaters viewed debate as providing them with a means by which they could demonstrate their critical thinking skills through the analysis and synthesis of ideas and theories. These related perspectives illustrate the difficulty some debaters may experience when they have an understanding of the topic but make little sense of complicated theory arguments. Future studies should pursue this aspect to more clearly identify the differences between knowledge acquisition and critical thinking for debaters.

The fact that high school debaters are more concerned than college debaters about the negative stigma some have associated with the debate persona and the debate activity itself should not be taken lightly by collegiate debate teachers and coaches. The image of collegiate debaters, as reflected by college coaches and the college debaters who return to the high school circuit as judges, may need to portray a more positive picture of the activity if college debate programs are going to continue to attract bright students who view debate as a positive dimension to their activity, but who do not want to be themselves cast in a negative light.

While contributing to conclusions similar to those drawn by Williams et al. (2001), the nature of the comments from the high school debaters in this study reflected their state of mind as participants in the National Forensic League's National Tournament. These debaters had considerable expertise and familiarity with the activity and their comments supported the conclusion that they had positive self-concepts and had created their own social culture in which they functioned to meet people and make friends. Future studies should explore the perceptions of debaters from different segments of the debate community. For example, those who do not qualify to compete at the national tournament or students in their first year of debate should be surveyed or interviewed to determine if the level of self-confidence experienced by those at the National Tournament was present at the local, state, or regional levels. Despite the restrictions on particular survey methodologies due to the age of the high school subjects, scholars should continue to explore different ways to get in touch with this important group of young debaters.

Finally, the role of the coaches and teachers in the lives of debaters should be more thoroughly explored. The positive self-concepts of the debaters in this study enabled them to deal with the negative stigma of debaters as "nerds," to manage the negative comments of other debaters about debaters, and to remain in an activity with its own set of drawbacks. However, the role debate coaches and teachers played in helping high school debaters to deal with these issues may be considerable. Longitudinal studies pertaining to the influence of high school coaches and forensic educators on the self-concept and subsequent lives of their students may provide rich data for analysis.

ENDNOTES

1. The debate organizations cited by Williams et al. (2001) included the following: National Debate Tournament sponsored by the American Forensic Association, Cross Examination Debate Association, National Educational Debate Association, American Debate Association, International Public Debate Association, National Parliamentary Debate Association, and National Forensic Association. For a brief description of the different formats advocated by these organizations, see Williams, McGee, and Worth (2001).

2. Benefits cited by Williams et al. included: Speaking Skills/Communication Skills; Analytical/Critical Skills; Social Life/Meet People; Research Skills; Knowledge/Education; Self-Esteem/Confidence; Argumentation; Travel; Learn about Issues; Organizational Skills; and Thinking fast. Disadvantages cited included: Time; Hurts Academics; Health/sleep/frustration/stress; Affects Social Life; Financial Costs; Travel Time; Lack of Involvement in Other Campus Activities; Too competitive/Win Attitude; Loss of Work; and Workload.

3. For example, both high school and college debate tournaments follow similar formats and many collegiate debaters and coaches got their start in the high school debate environment. The high school debate community has often mirrored the practices of the collegiate community; as high school debaters adopt the practices, norms, and arguments of their collegiate counterparts. Many college students, who were former high school debaters, migrate back to the high school debate community as mentors and coaches. Further, in the public policy arena, as Fine (2000) suggested, "the fact that numerous public policy analysts, lawyers and politicians began as high school debaters suggests that . . . such training serves them well."

4. After its initial construction, the instrument was field-tested with former and current forensic coaches. Following the addition and clarification of several items, the instrument was field-tested with a group of high school debaters with varying levels of experience. Any item prompting a question for clarification from the students was further refined. Once the clarity of the items was assured, the instrument's validity was accepted.

5. Participants were asked the following questions: "Are you 18 years of age?" "If so, were you a debater during the 2000–2001 school year?" "What state are you from?" "What is the name of your school?"

[…]

13. When categories in the collegiate study included responses that would have fit into the high school categories, notes were provided to show the intended relationships.

14. It is useful to note that for those who indicated they had been in debate the longest, particularly for five or six years, none listed any disadvantages in the categories: Negative Stigma by Others; Perceptions/Criticism of Self/Other Debaters; or Criticism of Nature of Debate Activity.

15. Hamachek suggested that students with a positive self concept reflected the following traits: Their behaviors are more upbeat than self-disparaging; they tend to be popular and have better interpersonal relationships; they are motivated and interested in engaging in difficult tasks; they attribute their success to ability and effort rather than luck; they are more likely to establish reachable goals; they are more assertive and confident in their interpersonal communication skills; they have more success than failure experiences; they are more task-persistent and willing to invest whatever time and effort necessary to successfully complete difficult tasks; they believe they were more capable than their classmates and capable of working harder; they are more able to work with minimal supervision; they possess the desire to master difficult and complex tasks; they tend to prefer work that is challenging and mind-stretching; they believe they are more cognitively competent, thus intrinsically motivated to do well; the presence of parents or role-models to provide support makes them more likely to succeed.

16. Of 193 respondents, when asked how much time they worked each week alone or with a partner, 61 spent 5–10 hours and 78 spent more than 10 hours. When asked how much time they worked each week with their coach(es), 94 spent 0-5 hours, 66 spent 5–10 hours, and 29 spent more than 10 hours. When asked how much time they worked each week during the off-season, 125 indicated 0–5 hours, 36 spent 5–10 hours, and 25 answered more than 10 hours.

17. Of the 193 respondents, the following percentages reflect the number of debaters who had competed in other forensic events for at least one year: 79.27% competed in Student Congress; 72.54% competed in Public Address events; 39.90% competed in Oral Interpretation events; and 76.17% were in Limited Prep events.

REFERENCES

Anderson, B., & Matlon, I. (1974). A description of high school forensic programs: Report on a national survey. *Journal of the American Forensic Association, 10,* 121–126.

Barber, G. B. (1954). An analysis and evaluation of forensic contests as conducted in the secondary schools within the area of the North Central Association. *The Speech Teacher, 3,* 20–22.

Bellon, J. (2000). A research-based justification for debate across the curriculum. *Argumentation and Advocacy, 36,* 161–176.

Blustein, D. L. (1994). "Who am I?": The question of self and identity in career development. In M. L. Savickas & R. W. Lent (Eds.), *Convergence in career development theories* (pp. 139–154). Palo Alto, CA: Consulting Psychologists.

Byrne, B. M. (1974). The general/academic self-concept nomological network: A review of the construct validation research. *Review of Educational Research, 54,* 427–456.

Cushman, P. (1995). Constructing *the self, constructing America: A cultural history of psychotherapy.* Reading, MA: Addison-Wesley.

Erikson, E. H. (1968). *Identity. Youth and crisis.* New York: Norton.

Fine, G. A. (2000). Games and truths: Learning to construct social problems in high school debate. *Sociological Quarterly, 41,* 103–124.

Fine, M. F. (1999). *My friends say, "debater girl! Why are you always debating with me?": A study of the New York Urban Debate League.* (Available from the Open Society Institute, 400 West 59th Street, New York, NY 10019).

Gecas, V. (1982). The self-concept. *Annual Review of Sociology, 8,* 1–33.

Gergen, K.J. (1991). *The saturated self: Dilemma of identity in contemporary life.* New York: Basic.

Hamachek, D. (1995). Self-concept and school achievement: Interaction dynamics and a tool for assessing the self-concept. *Journal of Counseling and Development, 73*(4), 419–425.

Hansford, B. C., & Hattie, J. A. (1982). The relationship between self and achievement/performance measures. *Review of Educational Research, 52,* 123–142.

Hargis, D. E. (1934). A note on championship debaters. *Quarterly Journal of Speech, 24,* 57–58.

Hensley, W. (1972). A profile of the NFL high school forensic director. *Journal of the American Forensic Association, 9,* 282–287.

Hetlinger, D. F., & Hildreth, R. A. (1961). Personality characteristics of debaters. *Quarterly Journal of Speech, 47,* 398–401.

Hutchins, G. B. (1998). Times, they are a changin'. *IIE Solutions, 30,* 18.

Josselson, R. (1988). The embedded self. I and thou revisited. In D. K Lapsley & F. C. Clark (Eds.), *Self, ego, and identity: Integrative approaches* (pp. 91–106). New York: Springer-Verlag.

King, T. R., & Phifer, G. (1968). The college debater as seen by himself and by his peers. *Journal of the American Forensic Association, 5,* 48–52.

Klopf, D., & Rivers, S. (1965). Characteristics of high school and collegiate forensic directors. *Journal of the American Forensic Association, 2,* 33–37.

Konigsberg, L. (1935). What should be our objective in high school debating. *Quarterly Journal of Speech, 21,* 392–396.

Larson, P. M. (1952). Some suggestions for high school forensics. *The Spud Teacher, 1,* 52–54.

Lerner, R. M., Skinner, L. A., & Sorrel, G. T. (1980). Methodological implications of contextual/dialectic theories of development. *Human Development, 23,* 225–235.

Lewis, L. (1942). The effect of high school debating on college speech training. *Quarterly Journal of Speech, 28,* 27–30.

Markus, H. & Kitayama, S. (1991). Cultural variations in the self-concept. In J. Strauss & G. R. Goethals (Eds.), *The self: Interdisciplinary approaches* (pp. 188). New York: Springer-Verlag.

Marsh, H. W. (1990). A multidimensional, hierarchical, model of self-concept: Theoretical and empirical justification. *Educational Psychology Review, 2,* 77–172.

Marsh, H. W., Byrne, B. M., & Shavelson, R. J. (1988). A multifaceted academic self-concept Its hierarchical structure and its relation to academic achievement. *Journal of Educational Psychology 80,* 366–380.

Mead, G. H. (1934). *Mind, self, and society.* Chicago, IL: University of Chicago.

Patton, B. R. (1962). A descriptive analysis of successful high school debaters in Kansas. *The Register, 10,* 10–13.

Pruett, R. (1972). The student's perception of the effects of a summer high school debate institute. *Journal of the American Forensic Association, 9,* 279–281.

Rogers, E. M. (1995). *Diffusion of innovations* (4th ed.). New York: Free Press.

Schug, C. H. (1954). A study of attitude change toward debate propositions among high school and college debaters. *The Speech Teacher, 3,* 15–19.

Semlak, W. D., & Shields, D. A. (1977). The effect of debate training on students participating in the Bicentennial Youth Debates. *Journal of the American Forensic Association, 13,* 192–196.

Simonson, W. I., & Strange, B. (1961). An analysis of high school debate programs in the southeast United States. *Southern Speech Journal, 26,* 235–240.

Stewart, J. R., & Merchant, J. J. (1969). Perceived differences between debaters and non-debaters. *Journal of the American Forensic Association, 6,* 67–72.

Thomas, G. (1965). A survey of debate practices in Michigan high schools. *Central States Speech Journal, 16,* 129–135.

Thompson, R. N. (1931). The intelligence of high school debaters. *Quarterly Journal of Speech 17,* 403–405.

Tucker, R. K., Koehler, J. W., & Mlady, L. (1967). The image of the college debater. *Journal of the American Forensic Association, 4,* 1–9.

Turner, R. G. (1941). Whither high school forensics? *Quarterly Journal of Speech, 27,* 550–554.

Vondracek, F. W., Lerner, R. M., & Schulenberg, J. E. (1986). *Career development: A life-span developmental model.* Hillsdale, NJ: Erlbaum.

Williams, D. E., McGee, B. R., & Worth, D. S. (2001). University student perceptions of the efficacy of debate participation: An empirical investigation. *Argumentation and Advocacy, 37,* 198–209.

---

*Robert S. Littlefield is a professor of communication and the interim dean of the College of Humanities and Social Sciences at North Dakota State University.

Littlefield, Robert S. "High School Student Perceptions of the Efficacy of Debate Participation." *Argumentation and Advocacy* 38 (2001): 83–97.

Used by Permission.

Graduate School, Professional, and Life Choices: An Outcome Assessment Confirmation Study Measuring Positive Student Outcomes beyond Student Experiences for Participants in Competitive Intercollegiate Forensics

by Jack E. Rogers*

Participation in competitive, intercollegiate forensics is a unique educational opportunity that teaches direct and indirect skills with educational and societal implications. Hundreds of studies over the past nine decades have attempted to examine exactly what competitive debate is, what it should teach and to whom, and what benefits, if any, our student competitors should look forward to as they graduate and exit the competitive experience. In a meta-analysis conducted by Rogers (2002) of 682 forensic articles, books, conference proceedings, and organizational reports, 657 credited debate participation with having positive outcomes consistent with a wide variety of educational, social and behavioral goals.

According to a representative sample of these studies, competitive debate is credited with increasing critical thinking skills (Beckman, 1957; Brembeck, 1949; Colbert, 1987; Cross, 1961; Gruner, Huseman & Luck, 1971; Hill, 1993; Horn & Underberg, 1993; Howell, 1943; Huseman, Ware & Gruner, 1972; Jackson, 1961; Rowland, 1995; Williams, 1951; Williams et al., 2001), increasing public presentational skills (Colbert & Biggers, 1985; Millsap, 1998; Stenger, 1999; Williams et al., 2001); teaching public advocacy and social responsibility (Bartanen, 1998; Brand 2000; Brownlee, 1978;

Derryberry, 1998; Williams et al., 2001) and offering excellent professional training (Colbert & Biggers, 1985; Hill, 1983; Schneider, 1984; Spangle & Knapp, 1996). It also increases knowledge, self confidence, poise, and a wide range of skills necessary for academic success (Bartanen, 1998; Colbert & Biggers, 1985; Derryberry, 1998; Hill, 1983; Jones, 1994; Williams et al., 2001).

In addition, forensic educators argue that debate teaches social responsibility and advocacy (Bartanen & Frank, 1994; Freeley, 1996; Hollihan & Baaske, 1994: Jones, 1994; Rowland, 1995) and enhances a student's academic and professional abilities (Carleton, 1949; Colbert & Biggers, 1985; Derryberry, 1998; Hill, 1983; Jones, 1994; Level, 1957; Pratt, 1990; Schneider, 1984; Spangle & Knapp, 1996; Stenger, 1999; Walker, 1971; Williams, et al. 2001). Researchers (Bartanen, 1998; Derryberry, 1998; Millsap, 1998) have concluded that debate teaches important leadership skills. As Bartanen (1998) concludes: "debate fosters leadership skills of reflection, connectedness and advocacy. Forensics programs are valuable models of learner-centered pedagogy and are underutilized resources for diversity education on the liberal arts campus" (pp. 12–13). Susan Millsap (1998) goes so far as to say that a forensics education alone has the ability to be pedagogically effective across the liberal arts curriculum.

These are bold claims, to be sure, but claims that the majority of the readership of this article would probably support for the majority of their forensics students. However, the literature offers little in terms of quantitative evidence to support the positive outcomes for participation that it claims. The majority of the research to date offers random "snapshots" of performance based largely upon anecdotal evidence that fails to offer valid comparisons to non-debate control groups. More than thirty years ago, Anderson argued that "[I]n an age of educational accountability, the forensic community is and will increasingly be called upon to tell what it seeks to do, how well it accomplishes its goals, and what other effects it has. Surprisingly, there seems little interest in such research at this time" (1974,

p. 155). Little has changed in the literature to address Anderson's concerns over the past three decades.

What is needed for administrators, fellow academicians, and parents is quantitatively based assessment data that tracks, evaluates, and assesses populations of both *debate* and *non-debate* students highlighting significant differences between the two populations as they matriculate through their college careers and into the post-graduation world. Differences in outcomes at various junctures in the longitudinal study period could be directly attributed to the differences in the study populations.

The purpose of the original study published in 2002, hereafter referred to as *Study One*, and this follow up study, referred to as *Study Two*, was and is to provide quantitative support for the conclusion that participation in competitive, intercollegiate forensics is directly correlated with positive educational, social, and behavioral outcomes as compared to outcomes for non-debate students. A summary of *Study One* is helpful to understand fully the background and scope of *Study Two*.

STUDY ONE

During the Summer of 1997, twenty-eight Directors of Forensics were asked to identify incoming first-year students who had been recruited to participate on their forensics teams and twenty non-debate, first-year student volunteers recruited from their basic teaching load. A basic intake survey was distributed to a total of 760 first-year students (563 non-debate and 197 debate). The survey was designed to minimize demographic, academic, extracurricular and social differences between the two groups. 100 *debate* and 100 *non-debate* students were eventually selected for inclusion in the four-year study. For a complete discussion of the methodology of the selection criteria and process see Rogers (2002).

[...]

The conclusion reached by *Study One* was clear: in almost

every case, in almost every area examined, participation in debate engendered significant positive outcomes for the *debate* group as compared to those respondents from the *non-debate* group. Therefore, for an undergraduate population, participation in intercollegiate competitive debate had educational, social and behavioral benefits that were not experienced by the non-debate comparison group. The question is whether these benefits extend beyond the undergraduate experience. Rogers (2002) suggested that "it would be interesting to follow the populations 'post graduation' to see if the positive outcomes reported were long lasting or dissipated over time. Do the outcomes of debate participation have life-long results that continue to engender overall success?" (p. 23). To follow up on the previous research, *Study Two* was launched in Summer 2001. The intent of *Study Two* was to extend the original research to answer

RQ1: Will significant positive differences in the five critical areas of: academic success; social responsibility; psychological multipliers; cultural tolerance and understanding; and moral/ethical issues as reported in Study One continue for the debate study population in their post-graduation experiences?

In addition to investigating the continued validity of positive differences in the five critical outcomes, an additional research question is advanced. Because many of the subjects from both respondents pools, *debate* and *non-debate*, were moving into their first job after graduation,

RQ2: Are there differences in performance between debate and non-debate groups in their career paths post-graduation?

Study Two

Subjects
Upon completion of the final 2001 survey and graduation at the close of the Spring and Summer terms of 2001, all respondents

were provided with a self-addressed, stamped contact information card and asked to keep in touch with the research team. In early Fall 2001, the respondents were asked to continue their participation in the study for an additional four years. Attrition from the respondent pool resulted in a final N of 119 for the four-year, post-graduation comparisons (68-*debate*; 51-*non-debate*). Roughly 60% (.595%) of the original 200 respondents completed the full eight-year study. As in *Study One* all data from mid-study dropouts was excluded from the final comparison analysis.

[...]

RESULTS AND DISCUSSION

As in *Study One*, the responses of each respondent group for each of the five critical outcomes were examined using Pearson correlations. *Study One* concluded that in almost every case, in almost every area and sub-grouping compared, participation in debate had significant positive outcomes for the respondent population as compared to their *non-debate* peers. This study compares entry into and success within graduate school programs, law and professional schools, first career moves and promotions, continued social responsibility and participation, and whether the positive outcomes identified in *Study One* continue to be supported in the former *debate* respondent pool.

Critical Outcome 1—*Social Responsibility*

Study One reported that the *debate* respondents experienced much higher positive outcomes than their *non-debate* peers in all four areas of comparison during their undergraduate years. The results from this study are even more dramatic. During the four years following graduation, the positive outcome gap in *social responsibility* between the *debate* participants and their *non-debate* peers became even more pronounced. All comparisons were statistically significant.

[...]

Former *debate* participants were much more likely than their *non-debate* peers to consistently vote in political elections. Voter participation for both *debate* and *non-debate* respondents increased after graduation. However, the increase for former debate participants was much higher; in effect, widening the gap between groups. The *debate* respondents increased their participation in *social volunteerism* and reported slight decreases in both *political volunteerism* and participation in *social activism*. During the same four-year period, *non-debate* respondents reported a modest decrease in *social volunteerism*, but dramatic reductions in both *political volunteerism* and *social activism*.

In summary of the outcome *social responsibility*, former *debate* participants reported increased correlations to positive outcomes in behavior when compared to their *non-debate* peers. In the four years after graduation, the *debate* group was much more likely than their *non-debate* peers to continue to act in a way that reflected the acceptance of social responsibility through voting, to volunteer their time to participate in social and political campaigns, and to use their skills to advocate social change.

Critical Outcome 2—*Cultural Understanding and Tolerance*

In *Study One*, two comparisons emerged as statistically significant. *Debate* respondents were slightly more likely to enroll in cross-cultural coursework and were much more likely to reject classical definitions of social norming. No significant differences were noted in either group's propensity to maintain intercultural relationships or to be involved in cross-cultural organizations.

[...]

During the four-year follow-up period, former *debate* respondents reported significant differences in behavior, once again widening the positive outcome gap between themselves and their *non-debate* peers. Of those students enrolled in graduate programs (N=66), the *debate* group was much more likely to enroll in cross-cultural coursework. The *debate* group's positive correlation with the sub-assessments of *cross-cultural relationships* and *membership in cross-cultural organizations* strengthened during the four-year follow-up period. During the same period, the *non-debate* group's correlations registered slight declines in both areas. Thus, what was not reported as a significant difference between the groups during their undergraduate years emerged as significant differences in behavior postgraduation. Both groups reported weaker positive correlations with the tendency to *reject social norming*. However, the difference between groups is still significant.

In summary of the examination of critical outcome 2: *cultural tolerance and understanding*, in each of the four sub-assessment scales, former *debate* participants reported increased correlations to positive outcomes in behavior when compared to their *non-debate* peers. In the four years after graduation, the *debate* group was much more likely than their *non-debate* peers to continue to act in a way that reflected social tolerance and understanding of cultural identities other than their own through the maintenance of intercultural relationships, membership in intercultural organizations, enrollment in cross-cultural course-work, and the rejection of social norming.

Critical Outcome 3—*Academic Success*
Study One reported that the *debate* grouping held a slight edge in maintaining a GPA of 3.5 or better than their *non-debate* peers. No statistically significant differences were found in terms of *matriculating* on time or *changing majors* between study groups. However, debate respondents were much more likely to participate in professional internships related to their majors, to be accepted into graduate school, and to have a job offer upon graduation than their *non-debate* peers. In the following comparisons for *Study Two*, only those respondents enrolled in a professional or graduate school are included.

[...]

Of the 58 *debate* subjects accepted into a graduate or professional school at the close of *Study One* (2001), 53 expressed an intention to continue. This study began with 51 of those respondents. Twenty-nine were accepted into Master's degree programs. Eighteen were accepted in law school. Four were accepted into professional schools. This study ended with 46 subjects successfully completing their post-graduation academic career with the awarding of 26 Master's degrees, sixteen successfully passed B.A.R. examinations, and four completed professional schools (certified accountants, computer programmers, military officer's training). As of May 2005, the remaining 5 *debate* respondents had either dropped out (2) or were not finished but still enrolled (3).

Of the 28 *non-debate* subjects accepted into a graduate or professional school at the close of *Study One*, this study began with 26. Twenty had been accepted in graduate schools with the remaining 6 being split between law school (4) and medical school (2). This study concluded with 20 *non-debate* subjects successfully completing their post-graduation academic careers: 15 Master's degrees, four passing the B.A.R., and one M.D. Of the remaining six *non-debate* subjects, three had dropped out, two were still enrolled but not finished, and one was deceased.

The successful academic completion rates are 90.2% for the *debate* grouping and 76.92% for the *non-debate* group. A cursory examination of this study group would seem to indicate that the *debate* group was somewhat more successful in terms of completing their graduate programs than their *non-debate* peers. In addition, the *debate* group reported higher scores on the LSAT and GRE than their *non-debate* peers. The LSAT (Law School Admission Test) contains two logical reasoning sections with between 24 and 26 questions that analyze statements for errors in logic. In addition, there is an analytical section made up of 24 questions that seek to measure the respondents' ability to solve complex deductive puzzles. The *debate* group scored an average of 5.5 points higher on the two logical reasoning sections and 3 points higher on the analytical section for an increase, on average, of 8.5 points on the LSAT over their *non-debate* peers (debate: 168; non-debate: 159).

The *debate* group also outperformed their *non-debate* peers on the GRE (Graduate Record Examination). The GRE is comprised of three sections: verbal, quantitative, and analytic writing. The verbal section is designed to test the respondents' ability to understand and analyze written material. The verbal section is worth between 200 and 800 points. The *debate* group averaged a score of 687 on the verbal section while the non-debate group's averaged a score of 630. Quantitative scores were similar: *debate* 583; *non-debate* 574. However, on the final section, analytic writing, designed to test the respondents' ability to examine claims and accompanying evidence and to support ideas with relevant reasons and examples, the *debate* group averaged a 5.1 (scores range from 0–6) dramatically outperforming the *non-debate* peers who averaged a score of 3.7.

In summary of the examination of the critical factor of *academic success*, the *debate* group was much more likely to maintain a GPA above a 3.5 while enrolled in their graduate or professional studies. Although there was no statistical difference in either group to matriculate on time as undergraduates, graduate *debate* subjects were much more likely to finish their graduate studies on time. Finally, the *debate* respondents had a much higher *job offer at graduate* rate than their *non-debate* peers. The authors are pleased to report that eight new forensic coaches were graduated from the ranks of the *debate* respondents.

Hopefully, these results will help to somewhat mitigate the concerns of Wood and Rowland-Morin (1989), Jones (1994), Hunt et al. (1997), and Williams, McGee, and Worth (2001) who warn of the pedagogic and personal tradeoffs when competition becomes the prime motivator for continued participation. At least for this study population, the *debate* subjects did no worse—and, in some cases—significantly better than their *non-debate* peers in the arena of academic success.

Critical Outcome 4—*Moral/Ethical Issues*

In *Study One,* no significant differences were reported between the subject groups in the areas of *propensity to distort the truth or a belief in situational ethics. Study One* did report that debate students were much less likely to ignore evidence that conflicted with their beliefs and to exhibit a stronger belief in a just society tradition. Study One concluded that there appeared to be a stronger belief in the ability of concerned citizens to make a difference on the part of the debate study group as compared to their *non-debate* peers.

[...]

All four comparisons were statistically significant. Whereas *Study One* reported no significant differences between *debate* and *non-debate* subject pools in the assessments *propensity to distort the truth* or *belief in situational ethics, Study Two* reflects dramatic changes for both groups. *Non-debate* respondents were more likely to distort the truth and to believe in situational ethics. Modest changes occurred for the *debate* group reflected through a slight rise in the propensity to ignore conflicting evidence and a slight decrease in the belief in a just society tradition.

In summary, *Study Two* demonstrates that during the four-year, post-graduation period the *debate* respondents continued to report statistically significant differences between their behaviors and belief systems and their *non-debate* peers. During the post-graduation period, the positive outcomes reported for undergraduate *debate* participants in *Study One* held somewhat steady or increased. Undergraduate *debate* participants continued to be far less likely to *ignore evidence that conflicted with their beliefs* than their *non-debate* peers as they moved through the post-graduation, graduate programs and professional world. The *debate* group continued to be much more likely to believe in a *just society tradition.* Finally, though *Study One* reported no statistically significant differences between the two groups, in this follow-up study, the *debate* group was much less likely to *distort the truth* or to *believe in situational ethics.*

Critical Outcome 5—*Psychological Multipliers*

Study One reported statistically positive behavioral outcomes for those who participated in *debate* in all five areas as compared to their *non-debate* peers. *Debaters* reported significantly less feelings of depression, anxiety or feelings of being overwhelmed under pressure and significantly higher feelings of confidence and a positive outlook on life. *Debaters* also reported significantly higher levels of confidence in their ability to communicate their feelings and positions through oral and written communication and were significantly more flexible in their outlook on life. The only area where the study groups exhibited no significant differences was in their ability to maintain successful long-term relationships. Again, *Study Two* sought to confirm the continued relationship between these positive outcomes and debate participation beyond graduation.

[...]

During the four-year follow-up period of *Study Two*, debate respondents continued to demonstrate stronger relationships than their *non-debate* peers to positive mental health outcomes. *Debate* participants were significantly less likely to report feelings of *depression or anxiety* or feelings of being *overwhelmed under pressure* than their *non-debate* peers. They reported even stronger *feelings of self-confidence* and a *positive outlook* postgraduation, widening the gap between themselves and the *non-debate* group reporting lower levels of confidence and a more negative outlook. The correlated relationship between groups in the assessments *confidence in communication skills* and *flexibility* remained fairly constant, with the *non-debate* group reporting a slight decrease in confidence and a slight increase in *flexibility*. Both measures remained statistically significant in terms of differences in positive outcomes. The assessment measuring the ability of the groups to *maintain long-term relationships* changed dramatically during *Study Two*. At the close of *Study Two* the *debate* group was much more successful at *maintaining long-term relationships* than their *non-debate* peers.

In summary of the examination of critical outcome 5) *Psycho-logical Multipliers*, in each of the six critical assessments, the *debate* group demonstrated much higher positive outcomes. In the four years after graduation, the *debate* group was much more likely than their *non-debate* peers to continue to benefit from a much healthier mental outlook through higher overall confidence in themselves and their communication skills, lower levels of depression, anxiety and feelings of being overwhelmed under pressure, a more positive mental outlook, and an ability to more successfully maintain long-term relationships.

One final area of analysis is advanced. In addition to the 84-item survey instrument measuring the five critical outcomes, the subjects were asked to provide responses to a number of questions designed to solicit information pertaining to their professional career experiences. No statistical interpretation of the responses is advanced; thus, some degree of caution regarding any conclusions made from the data is suggested.

[...]

In pursuit of an answer to RQ2: *Are there differences in performance between debate and non-debate groups in their career paths post-graduation(?)* some differences in performance are reported. The *debate* group had considerably more job offers in their field of study upon graduation than their *non-debate* peers. They report more often being able to change jobs voluntarily, are forced to change jobs much less, and have experienced a slight edge in terms of receiving an increase in pay. They also experienced proportionately more positive evaluations from their supervisors. When asked to identify key factor(s) that contributed to negative evaluations, both groups reported some difficulty in getting along with a co-worker or supervisor. In addition the *debate* group had some difficulty meeting work product deadlines. The *non-debate* group reported inferior work product and a lack of communication skills. Conversely, when asked to identify key factor(s) that contributed to positive evaluations, the *debate* group cited good communication skills and an ability to think and analyze problems. The *non-debate* group reported that when evaluations were positive, they were most often cited for good work product and their ability to be a team player and/or to get along with co-workers. Therefore, there are at least some differences in performance between groups in their career paths post graduation. Interestingly enough, the *debate* group reports being happier in their various career choices than the *non-debate* group.

Conclusion

Of course, some care should be exercised when making generalized claims from this study sample to the larger *debate* and *non-debate* populations across the United States. The participants who remained in the study for the entire eight-year period displayed above-average commitment levels to the research and, therefore, may not be indicative of larger, less motivated subject pools. Further research with larger study populations is absolutely critical to the proper evaluation of the claims explored through this study. It would also be interesting to follow the respondent group as they continue through life. Initial choices in career paths and overall performance levels are almost always modified with the passage of time. Additional, more sophisticated research should be undertaken to look for statistical differences in the performances of the groups as they matriculate through life. Again, does undergraduate participation in forensics lead to life-long positive outcomes? Finally, threats to casual conclusions should be explicitly considered before making more generalized conclusions. This difficulty in interpreting the direction of the casual relationships is somewhat mitigated by the longitudinal nature of the study. However, generalized conclusions regarding the casual relationship between debate participation and positive outcomes should be advanced with caution.

In conclusion, the intent of *Study Two* was to provide valid, empirical data to answer the research question: Will significant positive differences in the five critical areas of: academic success; social responsibility; psychological multipliers; cultural tolerance and understanding; and moral/ethical issues as reported in *Study One* continue for the *debate* study population in their post-graduation experiences? The data suggests that, as was concluded in *Study One*, participation in forensics during the study population's undergraduate experience is strongly correlated with increased positive outcomes, in this specific case, beyond graduation. During the additional four years of study, the *debate* group maintained every positive academic, social and behavioral edge reported during the initial study period. In addition, the *debate* group increased the positive outcome gap between themselves and their *non-debate* peers in the assessment areas of: increased propensity to vote; maintaining a GPA above 3.5; being less likely to ignore evidence that conflicts with what they already believe; having greater self-confidence; and demonstrating an increased propensity to engage in social volunteerism and political and social advocacy. Finally, whereas *Study One* reported no statistical differences between groups in several key areas, *Study Two* found that four years later, there were statistically significant differences in the *debate* group's post-graduation experiences, specifically in increased propensity to engage in cross-cultural relationships and to hold membership in cross-cultural organizations, to matriculate on time through graduate and professional programs, and to maintain long-term relationships. *Debate* respondents were also less likely to distort the truth or to believe in situational ethics. Therefore, *Study Two* concludes that the answer to the research question is that again, in almost every case, in almost every area, forensic participation during the subject population's undergraduate experiences has led to sustained, significant positive life outcomes beyond graduation.

Additionally, there does seem to be at least some evidence that participation in forensics during a student's undergraduate experience does lead to some differences in performance on the job; and therefore, positive options in terms of positive evaluations by superiors, slight increases in the rate of pay raises and promotions, and the ability to move voluntarily from one job to another. Also, those with *debate* experience tend to be involuntarily separated from a job less than their *non-debate* peers. While these findings need further research and support, it would seem safe to conclude that at least for this study's subjects, undergraduate debate participation led to increased professional benefits during the four-year period following graduation.

REFERENCES

Anderson, K. (1974). A critical review of the behavioral research in argumentation and forensics. *Journal of the American Forensic Association, 10,* 147–155.

Bartanen, K. M. (1998). The place of the forensics program in the liberal arts college of the twenty-first century: An essay in honor of Larry E. Norton. *The Forensic of Pi Kappa Delta, 84*(1), 1–15.

Bartanen, M., & Frank, D. A. (1994). *Nonpolicy debate* (2nd ed.). Scottsdale, AZ: Gorsuch Scarisbrick.

Beckman, V. (1957). *An investigation of the contributions to critical thinking made by courses in argumentation and discussion in selected colleges.* Unpublished doctoral dissertation, University of Minnesota, Minneapolis, MN.

Brand, J. (2000). Advancing the discipline: The role of forensics in the communication field. *The Forensic of Pi Kappa Delta, 86*(1), 1–14.

Brembeck, W. (1949). The effects of a course in argumentation on critical thinking ability. *Speech Monographs, 16,* 172–189.

Brownlee, D. R. (1978). The educational value of forensics. *The Forensic of Pi Kappa Delta, 64*(2), 18–20.

Carleton, W.G. (1949). Benefits of debate. *The Forensic of Pi Kappa Delta, 35*(1), 7–10.

Colbert, K. (1987). The effects of CEDA and NDT debate on critical thinking. *Journal of the American Forensic Association, 23,* 194–201.

Colbert, K., & Biggers, T. (1985). Why should we support debate? *Journal of the American Forensics Association, 21,* 237–240.

Cross, G. (1961). *The effects of belief systems and the amount of debate experience on the acquisition of critical thinking.* Unpublished doctoral dissertation, University of Utah, Salt Lake City, UT.

Derryberry, B. R. (1998). Forensics as a cooperative agent: Building a tradition within an academic community. *The Forensic of Pi Kappa Delta, 83*(3), 33–41.

Freeley, A. J. (1996). *Argumentation and debate: Critical thinking for reasoned decision-making* (9th ed.). Belmont, CA: Wadsworth.

Gruner, C., Huseman, R., & Luck, J. (1971). Debating ability, critical thinking and authoritarianism. *Speaker & Gavel, 8*, 63–64.

Hill, B. (1983). Intercollegiate debate: Why do students bother? *The Southern Speech Communication Journal, 48*, 77–88.

Hill, B. (1993). The value of competitive debate as a vehicle for promoting development of critical thinking ability. *CEDA Yearbook, 14*, 1–23.

Hollihan T.A., & Baaske, K.T. (1994). *Arguments and arguing: The products and process of human decision-making.* Prospect Heights, IL: Waveland.

Howell, W. (1943). The effects of high school debate on critical thinking. *Speech Monographs, 10*, 96–103.

Horn, G., & Underberg, L. (1993). Educational debate: An unfulfilled promise? In D. A. Thomas & S. C. Wood (Eds.), *CEDA 20th anniversary assessment conference proceedings* (pp. 37–74). Dubuque, IA: Kendall/Hunt.

Hunt, S. K., Garard, D., & Simerly, G. (1997). Reasoning and risk: Debaters as an academically at-risk population. *Contemporary Argumentation and Debate, 18*, 48–56.

[…]

Huseman, R., Ware, G., & Gruner, C. (1972). Critical thinking, reflective thinking, and the ability to organize ideas: A multivariate approach. *Journal of the American Forensic Association, 9*, 261–265.

Jackson, T. R. (1961). The effects of intercollegiate debating on critical thinking ability. Unpublished doctoral dissertation, University of Wisconsin. *Dissertation Abstracts International, 21*, 3556.

Jones, K. T. (1994). Cerebral gymnastics 101: Why do debaters debate? *CEDA Yearbook, 15*, 65–75.

Level, D. (1957). Objectives and effects of debate. *The Forensic of Pi Kappa Delta, 42*(2), 42–44.

Millsap, S. (1998). The benefits of forensics across the curriculum: An opportunity to expand the visibility of college forensics. *The Forensic of Pi Kappa Delta, 84*(1), 17–26.

Pratt, J. (1990). Business leaders' perceptions of forensics. *The Forensic of Pi Kappa Delta, 75*(2), 7–17.

[…]

Rogers, J. E. (2002). Longitudinal outcome for forensics: Does participation in intercollegiate, competitive forensics contribute to measurable differences in positive student outcomes? *Contemporary Argumentation and Debate, 23*, 1–27.

Rowland, R. C. (1995). The practical pedagogical function of academic debate. *Contemporary Argumentation and Debate, 16*, 98–108.

Schneider, V. (1984). Debate experience aids professional success. *The Forensic of Pi Kappa Delta, 70*(1), 9–11.

Spangle, M., & Knapp D. D. (1996). The effectiveness of debate as a corporate decision-making tool. *The Southern Journal of Forensics, 1,* 138–157.

Stenger, K. (1999). Forensics as preparation for participation in the academic world. *The Forensic of Pi Kappa Delta, 84*(4), 13–23.

[...]

Walker, D. (1971). Is contemporary debate educational? *The Forensic of Pi Kappa Delta, 56*(2), 9–10, 14.

Williams, D. (1951). *The effects of training in college debating on critical thinking ability.* Unpublished Master's Thesis, Purdue University, Lafayette, IN.

Williams, D. E., McGee, B. R., & Worth, D. S. (2001). University student perceptions of the efficacy of debate participation: An empirical investigation. *Argumentation & Advocacy, 37,* 198–209

Wood, S., & Rowland-Morin, P. (1989). Motivational tension: Winning vs. pedagogy in academic debate. *National Forensics Journal, 7,* 81–98.

*****Jack E. Rogers** is a professor and director of forensics at the Department of Communication, University of Central Missouri.

Rogers, Jack E. "Graduate School, Professional, and Life Choices: An Outcome Assessment Confirmation Study Measuring Positive Student Outcomes beyond Student Experiences for Participants in Competitive Intercollegiate Forensics." *Contemporary Argumentation and Debate* 26 (2005): 13–40.

Used by Permission.

The Impact of Prior Experience in Intercollegiate Debate upon a Postsecondary Educator's Skill-set

by Doyle Srader*

[…]

The assumption that successful debaters belong in law school is widespread, but Matlon & Keele's (1984) survey of NDT alumni indicates that teaching rivals law practice as a post-debate career. Two major motivators that drive excellent students to become educators are prior experience with intensive research and public recognition for their academic accomplishments (Lindholm, 2004). For those who teach K–12, there is training in the mechanics of instruction, and student teaching hones their debate-developed communication abilities into the necessary skill-set for classroom teaching. But those who pursue an advanced degree to teach postsecondary students, often enter their first classroom with nothing more than content knowledge, a few tips from a colleague, a class roster, and whatever talents they possessed before they entered graduate school (Reybold, 2003; Feldhusen et al., 1998; Wolverton, 1998).

Little has been written about debate experience as preparation for a career in postsecondary education; yet, the foundations of such research have been laid in broader inquiry into postsecondary teaching. University teachers should help students recognize complete, cogent arguments (Bain, 2004), should have excellent organization and oral communication skills (Chesebro, 2003), and should speak bluntly when students produce sub-standard work (Fram & Pearse, 2000). Cros (2001) asserts that most classroom communication events are best understood as argument. Colbert (2003) finds that participation in policy debate increases argumentativeness, while Schrodt (2003) finds at least a modest link between argumentativeness and credibility with students.

The relationship between debate experience and success as a university educator merits further study. Reybold (2003) argues that the preexisting academic culture from which professors emerge is the key to understanding the variance in teaching quality from classroom to classroom. And debate program directors clearly would benefit from an understanding of what elements of debate experience might be emphasized, downplayed, or altered for students who show promise as future educators. Such efforts could become a potent argument in justifying the continued existence of their programs, an argument that would hit very close to home for university administrators faced with tight resource constraints.

Because virtually no research exists on the effect of past debate experience on educators' classroom behaviors, this is a pilot study whose purpose is to lay groundwork for future studies by identifying particular topics of interest, both positive and negative, to educators who once debated. The items were written to elicit from the educators themselves the variables to be examined in later research.

Method

Participants

Calls for participants were posted to the eDebate and CRTNET listservs in February and March of 2005. The calls specified that subjects should have competed in intercollegiate policy debate at a time when it was evidence-intensive and involved rapid delivery, that they should have reached a level of minimum competence, operationalized as a normal performance of no worse than three wins out of eight preliminary debates, or two out of six preliminary debates, in an open-division tournament. It finally specified that they should currently be working as college educators, but not as debate coaches. Those who responded to the call were emailed a

URL which led to the informed consent briefing, and then to the survey. Participants were further screened with an introductory question which asked them to describe their three most significant accomplishments in intercollegiate debate.

One hundred and twenty-six people responded, and one hundred and eight unspoiled responses were collected. Thirty participants were female and seventy-eight male. Seventy taught in the field of Communication, seventeen in Law, and the remaining twenty-one in other fields.[1] Number of academic terms' experience as an educator varied, with the bottom quartile ranging from one to eleven terms taught, and the top from 35 to 74 terms taught.

[...]

RESULTS

Open-ended Question Responses

The overwhelming answer to the first question on benefits of debate experience for teacher preparation was research. Sixty-four participants cited it as a benefit, with thirty-one mentioning it first. Some comments linked this to teaching: "The ability to go to the library (or online) and get up-to-date information on virtually any subject has made keeping my course current a much easier job. Also, when I have been 'asked' to teach outside my specific areas of interest/expertise, I have been able to read-up much more rapidly than my colleagues." Others tied it to publication for professional advancement: "While the process of getting books, articles, and conference papers published is rigorous, those reviewers are not nearly as tough as my debate opponents were." A second freestanding response that was striking in its frequency was the introduction to the subject matter participants now teach: 21 responses indicated that the participant chose their academic field, or their particular area of study, after first encountering it through debate. One reported, "As a history major, debate was my entry into the field of

Communication and helped prepare me for a[n] MA and PhD in Speech Communication." Another commented, "High-school and college debate taught me academic research skills; it also introduced me to writings in the academic study of IR, social theory, and other disciplines I draw upon in my current scholarly activities."

The other responses can be grouped into three broad categories: effective teaching behaviors, generating and structuring knowledge, and cultivating personal traits. *Teaching behaviors* included delivery skills (mentioned in 45 responses), managing time effectively (25 responses), being fast on one's feet (17 responses), being prepared to teach students how to argue (9 responses), using language effectively (8 responses), having a wealth of examples from past debate research (7 responses), fielding questions (6 responses), anticipating student questions (5 responses), and handling discipline problems (2 responses). "As a teacher, I am well organized, well informed, well spoken, and quick in the classroom. My students enjoy my classes and are often awed with my quick analysis or answer to their questions." Four participants reported that summer clinics or peer coaching experiences were their first opportunities to teach.

Generating and structuring knowledge chiefly includes organizational skills (39 responses) and making arguments to students, to administrators, to colleagues (37 responses), but also includes analyzing others' arguments (25 responses), thinking critically (21 responses), being a problem-solver (9 responses), writing clearly (8 responses), thinking conceptually and seeing relationships between ideas (6 responses), and taking notes (5 responses). "I learned to think about writing, teaching, speaking as making arguments. I learned analytic skills that are useful in my teaching and research—how to break down or see problems in someone else's argument or my own, how to substantiate claims, how to identify what's missing."

Personal traits that former debaters reported they had cultivated included being more confident (44 responses), being open-minded enough to see and understand two or more opposing sides in a controversy (21 responses), being self-disciplined (7 responses), teamwork (8 responses), making durable friendships (5 responses), having competitive fire (4 responses), handling conflict (3 responses), and being passionate about current events (3 responses). One participant began her response,

> I started out as a high school debater. I was very shy, quiet, and reserved. I had very few friends. Joining the debate team in high school and participating in competition allowed me to realize that I was smart, and that I could be rewarded for being smart. Many girls that I went to high school with masked their intelligence so that they could date guys, or appear cool. For me, debate opened up an avenue for self-expression. After a year on the team, I became much more out-spoken and was able to excel in school. So, after years of debating and several years of coaching, I feel confident in my ideas, or at least know how to appear confident.

Another summed up, very simply, "It changed my life. Organized me in amazing ways."

Responses to the second prompt, which elicited commentary on the negative residue of debate experience, produced many more challenges and fewer topical clusters. One response dwarfed all others: participants reported that they speak too rapidly. Thirty-four participants admitted to this flaw, and twenty-three listed it first. Twenty-one participants reported that they were too argumentative, and twelve said they had unreasonable expectations of their students' abilities. No other response came from more than ten subjects, but the following appeared on more than five responses: impatient (with narrow-minded people, with slow talkers, with bad arguments, with slow thinkers, with slow-moving committee meetings), can't let things go, expect a winner in every conversation, rely too much on debate time management and wind up procrastinating, stop listening halfway through someone's statement once the point appears complete, criticize too much, missed college opportunities such as math and language classes, and overly analytical.

Seven participants responded that debate experience had in no way hindered their work as educators. Two responses gather together many threads found in other contributions. One participant synthesized the problems debate can breed in educators' handling of the *substantive* end of their work:

> Debate has a number of negative implications for the way participants evaluate scholarly arguments. First, it puts a premium on extreme claims because those claims make for stronger impacts (whether in the causal or discursive sense). Second, it encourages an assumption that if "someone makes an argument" that provides a sufficient warrant for a claim. In both cases, debate can undermine effective evaluation of the strength and weaknesses of the internal arguments of scholarly work. Third, it can encourage superficial working knowledge of theories, approaches, and claims. Witness debate's engagement with post-structural argumentation in the middle 1990s. I think all of these deleterious impulses were things I had to overcome as I matured as a scholar.

Another wrote at length about interpersonal dynamics which are already found in academic communities, and cannot be laid entirely at the feet of debate, but clearly are fueled by some of debate's competitive excesses:

> I think competition is, generally, a good thing. Nonetheless competitive atmospheres can occlude, perhaps sour, opportunities for collegiality and cooperation in an academic setting. For example, academic conferences need not be as "competitive" as they can occasionally be for me. Now, debate itself is not directly to blame for my framing of certain academic experiences. Nonetheless, there is (and has long been) a level of schadenfreude that obtains in the debate tournament experience, particularly at the national level, that has seeped from time to time in my digestion of conference experiences. Debate coaches through the years have a pretty poor record of fostering feelings of respect for others on the circuit. Their debaters, of course, emulate this manner of speech and, given the zero-sum nature of tournament competition and the natural neurosis attendant to the prospect

of "loss" in this context, often find themselves saying sadistic things among their competitive allies about their opponents from other schools. In this context, competitors get arguments "shoved," "rammed," and "smothered." Students are described as being "face-crushed" or "smacked-down." Now, all of this had been said many times before, and it is not my aim, simply, to echo this refrain. But I do often think that I could get more out of intellectual exchanges and public academic discussion if I had not spent 21 years on the circuit (6 as a competitor and 15 as a coach) thinking about how to dismantle other people's arguments and strategies. I think what I am really saying is that academia itself has more than a trace of sadism in the manner it conducts itself. The problem, essentially, is one of ego and anxiety. Debate is not to blame for any of it. Nonetheless, an extended immersion in debate tournament competition certainly has the potential to reinforce some of the nastier elements in academic life. I know it has in my case.

Likert Item Responses

On all seven proffered positive teaching behaviors, the mean response for the entire pool of participants was over 4, representing "Slightly Agree." The most popular answer was "I am good at thinking on my feet" ($M=4.85$, $SD=0.51$), and the least was "When I consider a major change in approach such as changing a course policy or adopting a new assignment, I am able to think of and prepare for all, or nearly all, likely student responses" ($M=4.19$, $SD=0.78$). The behavior most strongly tied to experience in debate, based on the follow-up prompt "If so, this is due entirely or in large part to my debate experience," was thinking on one's feet ($M=4.46$, $SD=0.66$), and the weakest was "I am confident dealing with disruptive behavior by students" ($M=3.34$, $SD=1.08$).

On the Likert items measuring negative teaching behaviors, the reported association was weaker, and the responses were more scattered. The strongest reported association was with the behavior, "I am impatient" ($M=3.56$, $SD=1.24$), and the weakest was "I frequently hurt a student's feelings by being excessively abrasive or confrontational" (M=2.02, SD=1.21). Interestingly, when the numbers were broken out by academic field, people who taught political science and international relations pulled the mean up to 3.18, with six of eleven selecting "Slightly Agree" or "Strongly Agree." The follow-up prompt, tying negative classroom behaviors to previous debate experience, found the strongest linkage with "I speak so rapidly, my students struggle to keep up or to understand me all or a lot of the time" (M=3.38, SD=1.13), and the weakest with "I struggle at letting students participate in class because I enjoy doing most of the talking" (M=2.64, SD=0.91).

DISCUSSION

Former debaters report that they have held on to the lessons of thinking rapidly and with rigor, and putting those thoughts into words, and doing so with extreme confidence. They are less unanimous on the leftover *bad* habits trained in by their experience in debate; very many of the responses to the open-ended question about negative behavior phrased it as "I *used* to" or "Debate is by no means bad, *but* . . ." One participant confessed that he occasionally talks too fast, overstates conclusions in his research ("but heck, we all do that"), and is forceful in faculty meetings perhaps to excess, but concluded, "I really don't 'blame' debate for anything 'bad' that I do. In other words, the disadvantages are small and unimportant in my mind." The value of durable skills, the transformative experience of having grown into intellectual (and, in many cases, emotional) maturity through debate may move its alumni to defend it even against unspoken charges.

Few of the self-reported strengths and weaknesses are truly surprising. All of the Likert-scale items, even the ones with which few participants agreed, turned up as boasts or concerns spontaneously in a number of the responses to the open-ended items. A few were mildly unexpected, such as the positive effect of debate that it teaches one the acceptability (and inevitability) of defeat, and how to handle it gracefully. Three participants cited that lesson. On the negative side, one participant mentioned that his time spent coaching forensics postponed the start of his more serious academic career, and several other participants spoke of other opportunity costs, including time-consuming coursework and other social and civic activities on campus. Several participants reported, in varying but related complaints, that their heightened efficiency, or research ability, or rapport with students, had actually bred tension with their colleagues, and that to have a truly collegial relationship they might be forced to hamstring themselves, or otherwise conceal the lessons they learned from debate.

The response from political science faculty is puzzling. It is unclear whether debaters who move into political science have more difficulty shedding the confrontational behaviors they pick up in debate, or whether political science students expect more relaxed interaction with their professors, or whether the sample size is so small that the finding is meaningless. For whatever reason, among this segment of political science professors who were once debaters, an ongoing problem of interpersonal tension and hurt feelings exists.

The dominant strengths of debate, according to educators who are former debaters, are the training in research, repeated exposure to speaking situations, and the building of confidence. The dominant problems are a struggle to slow down one's delivery, and a struggle not to be argumentative in all situations. Other strengths and weaknesses seem to be offshoots of this core. Debaters are highly efficient at producing knowledge and imposing order on information, but may be straitjacketed by a limited repertoire of thinking approaches. Debaters are thoughtful, disciplined and passionate, but in many cases struggle with empathy and fail again and again to listen to others complete a thought. Debaters have a wealth of illustrations, answer questions well, and make their classrooms into interactive, participatory encounters, but they also love their own voices, overlook nonlinear perspectives, and squash poorly conceived ideas so powerfully that they take a good deal of student self-esteem with them.

To say these observations are preliminary is an extreme understatement. The sample is heavily skewed toward men, and toward educators in the Communication field. Future research should attempt to even out those imbalances, and might also address the effects of high school debate on subsequent careers in education, as well as soliciting input from educators of younger students. But this study has identified some of the directions in which future work might proceed, some of the issues, both positive and negative, that might direct survey construction or matching of debate-instilled behaviors with recognized educator competencies.

CONCLUSION

With classrooms desperately in need of energetic, confident, efficient educators who are comfortable processing enormous volumes of information, who see through slogans and demagoguery, and who thrive on give-and-take and active learning, it can definitely be said that champion debaters are *not* destined for law school. Whatever the imperfections of debate, and there are many, its strengths as teaching preparation are too potent to be ignored any longer. The teaching profession beckons.

NOTE

1. 9 in Political Science, 3 in Philosophy, 2 in International Relations, and 1 each in Community College Education, Economics, History, Cognitive Science, Management, Math, and Sociology.

REFERENCES

Bain, K. (2004). *What the best college teachers do.* Cambridge, MA: Harvard University Press.

Chesebro, J.L. (2003). Effects of teacher clarity and nonverbal immediacy on student learning, receiver apprehension, and affect. *Communication Education, 52*, 135–147.

Colbert, K.R. (1993). The effects of debate participation on argumentativeness and verbal aggression. *Communication Education, 42*, 206–214.

Cros, A. (2001). Teaching by convincing: Strategies of argumentation in lectures. *Argumentation, 15*, 191–206.

Feldhusen, J.F., Ball, D., Wood, B., Dixon, F.A., & Larkin, L. (1998). A university course on college teaching. *College Teaching, 46*, 72–75.

Fram, E.H., & Pearse, R. (2000). 'Tough love' teaching generates student hostility. *College Teaching, 48*, 42.

Lindholm, J.A. (2004). Pathways to the professoriate: The role of self, others, and environment in shaping academic career aspirations. *Journal of Higher Education, 75*, 603–635.

Matlon, R.J., & Keele, L.M. (1984). A survey of participants in the National Debate Tournament, 1947–1980. *Journal of the American Forensic Association, 20*, 194–205.

Reybold, L.E. (2003). Pathways to the professorate: The development of faculty identity in education. *Innovative Higher Education, 27*, 235–252.

Schrodt, P. (2003). Students' appraisals of instructors as a function of students' perceptions of instructors' aggressive communication. *Communication Education, 52*, 106–121.

Wolverton, M. (1998). Treading the tenure-track tightrope: Finding balance between research excellence and quality teaching. *Innovative Higher Education, 23*, 61–79.

***Doyle Srader** is an associate professor of speech and communication at Northwest Christian University.

Srader, Doyle. "The Impact of Prior Experience in Intercollegiate Debate upon a Postsecondary Educator's Skill-set." Paper presented at the annual meeting of the National Communication Association, San Antonio, TX, November 16–19, 2006, http://northwestchristian.academia.edu/documents/0011/5331/Paper.pdf (accessed March 7, 2011).

Used by Permission.